George Alfred Henty: The Story of an Active Life

PORTRAIT OF GEORGE ALFRED HENTY

GEORGE ALFRED HENTY

THE STORY
OF AN ACTIVE LIFE

BY

GEORGE MANVILLE FENN

Yours Truly
G A Henty

Salem Ridge Press
Emmaus, Pennsylvania

Originally Published
1907
Blackie & Son, Limited

While the main text of this book is public domain, the added content,
including maps, notes and definitions, is © 2010 Salem Ridge Press.

Republished 2010
Salem Ridge Press LLC
4263 Salem Drive
Emmaus, Pennsylvania 18049

www.salemridgepress.com

Hardcover ISBN: 978-1-934671-40-5
Softcover   ISBN: 978-1-934671-41-2

Publisher's Note

In *George Alfred Henty: The Story of an Active Life* author George Manville Fenn has given us a fascinating look at the life of one of the most famous and popular boys' authors of the 1800's. Fenn himself was a famous boys' author and one might almost have expected him to view Henty as a competitor but there is never any trace of such feelings in his writing. In fact, Fenn's writing is filled with commendations of Henty, both his character and his writing. In the end, this is not just a biography, it is the record of a man's life written by a friend who had known him for almost thirty years.

Fenn does not cover every area of Henty's life, but what he includes seems specially chosen to appeal to boys who have read and loved Henty's books. From his early life as a sickly child, to dodging bullets in the streets of Paris as a fearless war correspondent or tramping through the jungles of the African Gold Coast, Henty's life reads like one of his stories. Although few boys will live a life as filled with thrilling adventures, I hope that this story will inspire boys to be men—men of courage, character and conviction, who take an active, rather than a passive, role in the world around them. I trust that this will be the case because this biography is indeed *The Story of an Active Life*.

Daniel Mills

September, 2010

PREFATORY NOTE TO THE 1907 EDITION

G. A. Henty occupied so large a place in the hearts of boys that, when his active life all too soon came to a close, it seemed desirable that those readers whom he had entertained for so many years should have an opportunity of knowing something more of the man himself than was contained in his books. Every writer, consciously or unconsciously, reveals himself in his work, but nevertheless it cannot fail to be interesting to boys to read of the actual experiences of the sturdy war correspondent—those experiences which furnished him with many a vivid background for his romances. It was at once the fascination and the value of his tales that, while nominally fiction, they were built up on a solid substratum of fact. When the present writer, however, was asked to undertake this memoir of his old and valued friend, he was confronted with a grave difficulty. Of few men of George Henty's eminence is less known about their private lives. A staunch and loyal friend, he yet strongly believed, to use the old Cockney phrase, in "keeping himself to himself." His letters were never autobiographical, and about himself he was never very communicative. Little more than his vivid letters from foreign countries exist to give an insight into the man and his character.

In his many absences from England during his career as a war correspondent, Henty contented himself with the briefest of home communications, and these told little more than where he was and what was the state of his health. He always said that those he loved could refer to the newspaper he represented for the rest.

Prefatory Note

To the courtesy of Mr. C. Arthur Pearson, the present proprietor of *The Standard*, who placed the whole of the files of that paper unreservedly at his disposal, the writer is very greatly indebted, while for much valuable information he would like to thank the editors of *The Captain*, *Chums*, *The Boy's Own Paper*, *Great Thoughts*, *Young England*, and *Table Talk*.

G. M. F.

HISTORICAL NOTES

As a correspondent for *The Standard*, Henty wrote about wars and events that may not be familiar to modern readers. The following are brief descriptions of the major events mentioned in this book and the chapters in which they are covered:

The Crimean War (Chapters 2-3): Begun in 1853, the Crimean War centered around the expansion of Russia southward toward the area surrounding the Black Sea and the efforts of Britain, France and the Turkish Ottoman Empire to prevent that expansion. Russia was eventually defeated and a peace treaty was signed in 1856.

The Austro-Prussian War (Chapters 5-8): A short war fought during the summer of 1866, the Austro-Prussian War pitted the Austrian Empire against the Kingdom of Prussia. The recently formed Kingdom of Italy also declared war on Austria in exchange for the promise of the return of the province of Venetia, in northeastern Italy, in the event of victory. Prussia defeated Austria and Venetia returned to Italian rule.

The Abyssinian Campaign (Chapters 14-19): During the 1860's King Theodore II of Abyssinia (Ethiopia) imprisoned several foreign missionaries and their families. He then imprisoned a British ambassador sent to negotiate their release. In 1868 a British army arrived in Abyssinia with orders to free the prisoners. The British marched to Theodore's stronghold at Magdala and quickly and completely destroyed Theodore's army.

The Suez Canal (Chapter 20): Completed in 1869, the Suez Canal connected the Mediterranean Sea with the Red Sea, shortening the trade route to India by thousands of miles.

Historical Notes

The Franco-German War (Chapter 21): Concerned over the growing power of Prussia, France declared war in 1870. Prussia quickly defeated the French troops led by Emperor Napoleon III and proceeded to capture Paris, the French capital. A peace treaty ending the war was signed in the spring of 1871.

The Paris Commune (Chapters 22-25): Taking advantage of the uncertainty caused by France's recent defeat in the Franco-German War, French Communist revolutionaries seized control of Paris for two months during the spring of 1871. The revolution was quickly put down by the French army.

The Ashanti Campaign (Chapters 26-31): In 1871 the British purchased the Dutch Gold Coast in western Africa from the Netherlands. Two years later the African Ashanti Empire invaded from the north, claiming the territory. British troops began to arrive at the end of 1873 and by the summer of 1874, the Ashantis were defeated and their capital city of Coomassie (Kumasi, Ghana) had been destroyed.

The Third Carlist War (Chapter 32): Beginning in 1872, the Third Carlist War was the third attempt in about forty years to overthrow the Spanish government and place Don Carlos (1788-1855) or one of his descendants on the Spanish throne. After four years of fighting, the Carlists were again defeated in early 1876.

The Turco-Servian War (Chapters 34-36): In the summer of 1876 Servia (Serbia) declared its independence from the Ottoman Empire. The Servians were aided in their struggle by the Russians and in 1877 Russia negotiated a temporary peace between the two countries. Shortly thereafter, negotiations failed and Russia declared war on the Ottomans. The following year Servia was acknowledged as an independent country in the peace treaty signed by the Russians and the Ottomans.

CONTENTS

CONTENTS

ILLUSTRATIONS AND MAPS

George Alfred Henty: The Story of an Active Life

HENTY'S EARLY DAYS

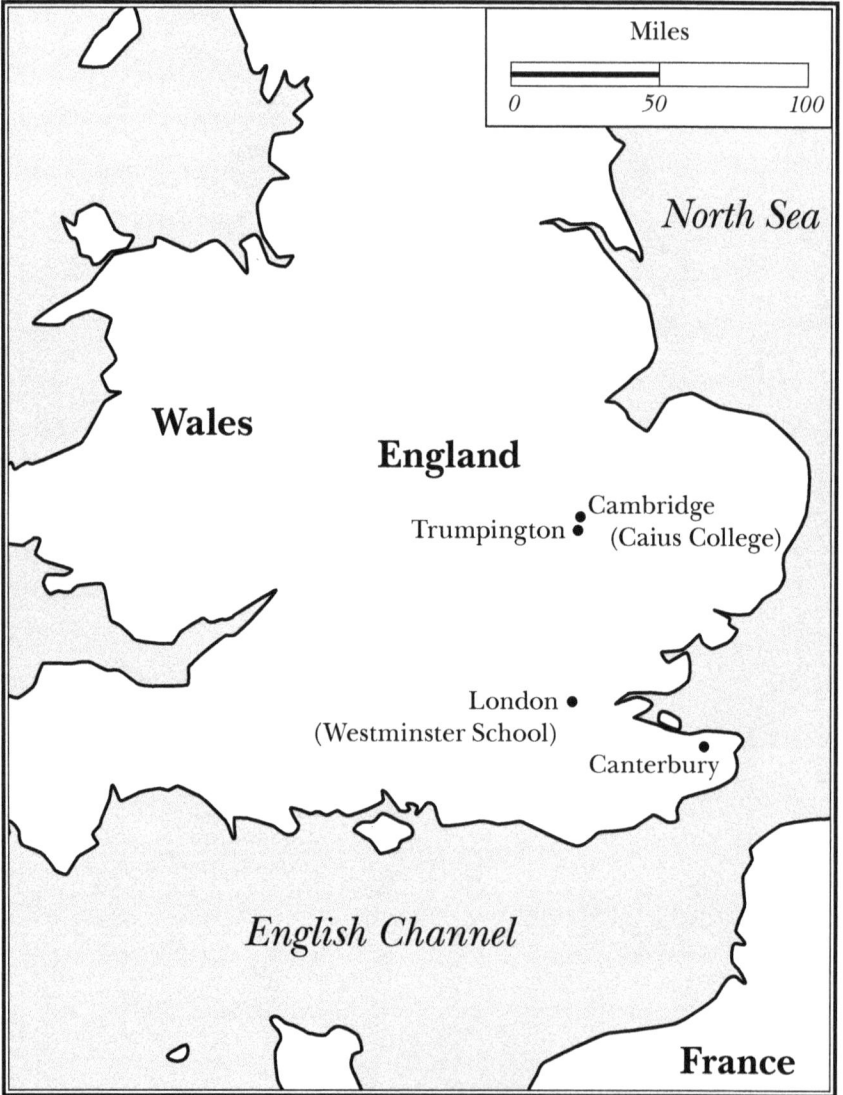

GEORGE ALFRED HENTY
THE STORY OF AN ACTIVE LIFE

CHAPTER I

EARLY DAYS

W̲E might know very little of the life of the late George Alfred Henty—writer for and teacher of boys, novelist, and one of the most virile of our war correspondents—but for one fortunate fact. His busy pen soon made him popular, and in course of time this popularity was sufficient to make editors of journals for the young realize that their readers would gladly learn something of the early life of the man whose vivid tales of adventure were being read with avidity wherever the English language had spread. In these days few are content to know a man only by his work, and even boys like to know something about the personality and experiences of the writers who have given them keen pleasure. As a result the inevitable came to pass, and the modern chronicler of personal details sought out the author. To his interviewers Henty told fragments of his past life, and these reminiscences were taken down in short or long hand, and built up into articles, and have remained, to bring before us vividly what would otherwise never have been known save perhaps by tradition.

It is strange now to reflect that the big, robust, heavy, manly-looking Englishman of whom these lines are written, was once a puny, sickly boy who was looked upon by his relatives as one who could never by any possibility attain to man's estate; but so

VIRILE: *vigorous, manly*
AVIDITY: *enthusiasm*
ATTAIN TO MAN'S ESTATE: *live to grow up*

it was. Here are his own words: "I spent my boyhood, to the best of my recollection, in bed."

Descended from an old Sussex family, George Alfred Henty was born at Trumpington, near Cambridge, on December 8, 1832, and it would appear that he was a confirmed invalid. This ill-health was the more unfortunate because it was in the days when doctors were inclined to be narrow-minded, and parents and guardians in almost every household had intense belief in the virtues of physic. Most mothers then were given to doctoring, and at springtime and fall considered it to be their duty to administer filthy infusions, decoctions, and very often concoctions, to unhappy boyhood; and a powder at night, to be followed by a nightmare of the draught that was to be taken in the morning, is a painful recollection to some of us.

Happy boys of the present generation! Why, who among them now know the meaning of words which must almost seem like cabalistic characters? Jalap, rhubarb, magnesia, salts and senna, gamboge, James's powder—these were all in constant request, without taking into consideration the secrets promulgated by the wicked writers of books on domestic medicine.

It was in those days that George Henty was born. He tells of an early removal at the age of five to Canterbury, to a fine old house whose garden ran down to the River Stour. Here for the next five years his mind became stored with those most wholesome of recollections connected with boy life. It was the bird, bee, and butterfly time, brightened by the presence of a grand trout stream, to whose banks he would creep, so as not to send the spotted beauties darting off in a flash of ruddy gold to seek some hiding-place from the gigantic shadow that had suddenly been cast athwart the stream. He tells, too, in many a page of his later life, how the influences of this good old garden were a solace and delight to him during

PHYSIC: *laxatives*
INFUSIONS, DECOCTIONS, CONCOCTIONS: *various homemade remedies*
DRAUGHT: *drink*
CABALISTIC: *mystical*
PROMULGATED: *put forward*

many a weary tramp or journey in the saddle far away; in the course of his journeys through Europe, the wilds of Asia, and the savage mountains and dense tropic forests and swamps of Africa.

The boy was fortunate, too, in his leanings towards natural history, for he speaks of a grandfather who was always ready to play the part of instructor to the young inquiring mind in regard to scientific matters, and explain the why and the wherefore of such objects as he collected.

When not confined to his bed, Henty attended a Dame school, where the love of reading was started, and grew and grew so that the sick boy's lot was softened to the extent that the weariness and suffering of confinement to his bed became almost pleasant in the forgetfulness begotten by books. That which was wanting in the way of education was made up in these long hours by reading. To use his own words, he "read ravenously"—romance, adventure, everything—perfectly unconscious, of course, of the fact that he was laying in a mighty store for the future, preparing himself, in fact, for the great work of his life, the broad and wide education of the boys of a generation to come.

In those days, though the classics hardly had place (there was little of Latin or Greek), he was piling up general knowledge such as comes to the lot of few lads now, in spite of the boasted advance in educational matters and all the elaborate apparatus and routine. And yet it must not be supposed that the boy's regular education was neglected. When ten years old there was an end to his simple country life, for though far from well he was sent to London to begin life in a private boarding-school, a life sadly interfered with by sickness and relapses into ailments more or less severe, among them being that terrible disease whose sequelæ have shattered many lives—rheumatic

ATHWART: *across*
SOLACE: *comfort*
DAME SCHOOL: *a school for young children run by a woman in her home*
WANTING: *lacking*
SEQUELÆ: *aftereffects*

fever. One of his ailments seems to have been near akin to that of the late Prince Leopold, namely, a tendency to profuse bleeding. For this he was attended by a well-known specialist of the time, whose great remedy for the boy's complaint was camphine, this being the popular term in those days for one of the refinements of the so-called rock oils, nowadays known as petrol or paraffin.

Henty recorded to one of his interviewers that he was so thoroughly dosed with this peculiar medicine that the specialist warned the nurse in these words: "I don't say that if you put a light to the boy he will catch fire, but I advise you not to risk it." This was accompanied with further counsel that the future chronicler of boys' adventures should not be allowed to handle sharp instruments, lest a cut or puncture should result in his bleeding to death.

Much reading in these early days had so influenced the boy that he had already become a story-teller, and, as is often the case with first attempts at writing, pleased with the jingle and flow of words, he had dropped into poetry. Now a young poet, as soon as he has satisfied himself with his lines and has carefully copied them in his best penmanship, burns to see himself in print. He then imagines, or is flattered into the belief, that numbers of people are as anxious as he to see his work become public; and it appears to have been so here, for owing to the well-meant kindness of a friend, certain of his early verse was printed, and it would appear to have been extremely sentimental and remarkably mild.

It was soon after this, when Henty was fourteen, that he went to Westminster School. Liddell was headmaster then, and the boy became a half-boarder, and in a very little while, in his boyish and very natural vanity, he let his tongue run a little too fast. He had written verse, and consequently esteemed himself

HALF-BOARDER: *a student who only has one meal per day provided by the boarding school*
ROASTING: *merciless ridicule*
ENSUED: *followed*
COVERT ALLUSIONS: *veiled references*

something of a poet, so it was not long before he mentioned the fact of his having his work in print. He quickly began to wish he had held his tongue. He had not counted upon the mischievous delight a pack of schoolboys would take in their special poet. If he had written Latin verses it would have been a different thing; but a love-tale with threatened difficulties to a lady was too much for them, and a long and continuous "roasting" ensued. Chaff flew, indirect and covert allusions were made, and then came bullying. Henty says: "It seemed as if the whole school bore a personal animosity towards poets, and as if they looked upon my publishing the unlucky book as a bit of 'side' unworthy of a Westminster scholar."

This particular poem was unfortunately lost, and the same fate befell another attempt written later, for the school banter did not crush out the rhyming faculties. The later work was written upon a more serious occasion, and, devoted to his future wife, it was cared for and preserved for long years as a valued treasure; indeed, only about ten years before his death, Henty was taking it up to town and accidentally left it in the railway carriage. Attempts to recover it proved vain, and though he offered a large sum of money as a reward, he never heard of it again.

As the lad's education progressed at Westminster it was not long before he began to realize that the curriculum was not complete, and that no boy's studies were perfect without a thorough knowledge of the noble science of self-defence. Indeed, he had not been long at the great school before he came in contact with one of the regular school bullies, who began to tyrannize until young Henty awoke to the fact that he possessed a high spirit and an absence of that weak pusillanimity which makes men slaves. He was no "mute inglorious Milton,"[1] though he aimed at being a poet.

---

[1] From "Elegy Written in a Country Churchyard" by Thomas Gray

SIDE: *arrogant pride*

FACULTIES: *abilities*

PUSILLANIMITY: *cowardice*

NO MUTE INGLORIOUS MILTON: *not a poet willing to keep silent*

The boy was father to the man he became, and he bore little before he turned in defiance and challenged his tyrant. The natural result was that he was thrashed out of hand and sent smarting with pain and mortification to where he could ponder over his defeat. But he was not of the mettle to sit down painfully under humiliation, and, to use his own words, "I soon changed all that."

It was something to learn, something to study; how to acquire the power, the science, which makes a comparatively weak man the equal of one far stronger, and, judging the boy by what he was as a man, it was from no desire to become bully in his turn that he took lessons in boxing, but from a genuine ambition to hold his own in the matter of self-defence and to be able to protect those who looked to him for help. It was with this desire that, later, when he left Westminster for Cambridge, at a time when the so-called noble art was at its highest tide, and when professors of the science had quite a standing at the universities, he continued its study, and one of the first professors to whom he applied for lessons (out of college) was the once celebrated Nat Langham, who, by the way, was the only man who ever vanquished Tom Sayers. Not contented with this, but being then in the full burst of his growing youth and strength—a sort of young athlete thirsting for power like a boyish Hercules—he took to wrestling, perfectly unconscious then of the good stead in which it might stand him in the future. In this sport he chose as his instructor a Newcastle man, one Jamieson, famed in his way as being champion of the Cumberland style as opposed to the Cornish. It must be borne in mind that all this was prior to the days of the Great Exhibition,[1] when pugilism was considered no disgrace, and before young men had begun to foster athleticism in other forms.

It was a strange reaction in the youth who had passed the greater part of his early life upon a sickbed, and it seemed as if

[1] The first World's Fair, held in London in 1851

OUT OF HAND: *at once*
METTLE: *disposition*
PUGILISM: *boxing*

the brave nature within him was exerting itself to throw off his natural weakness.

That thrashing he received in his early days at Westminster seemed to have roused him, spurred him on to gain strength, and he was encouraged too by the stirring times in which he found himself. Boating and cricket were all-important at Westminster. The studies were hard, but the masters, wisely enough, encouraged all sports; for the Westminster boys, as our chronicles have shown us, learned there to hold their own the wide world round. One need not here point to the long roll of famous names. These pages are devoted to one alone.

Henty takes a very modest view of his own prowess, and says of his life at Westminster: "Boating or cricket—you had your choice; but once made, you had to be perfect in one or the other. Fellows rowed then and played cricket then. They had to."

The Thames was their course. There was no St. Thomas's Hospital then, and the boat-houses were on the banks. The river was pretty handy to the great school, and at the sight of the Westminster crews the boatmen used to come across to fetch the boys. These were the days before the Thames Embankment, when the river sprawled, so to speak, at low water over long acres of deep mud, swarming with blood-worms, and though the river tides ran swirling to and fro the current was greatly quickened. Later the number of steamers increased and cut up the Westminster rowing, so that it went all to pieces. It was so greatly affected that the Old Westminsters' Club tried to move the sport to Putney; but it never regained its old standing. Westminster, however, though known best as a boating school, was a great cricketing one as well. At one time five Westminster men played in the All England Eleven; but Henty was not a cricketer. As a young athlete, he selected rowing. Both sports could not be managed; the standard was too high.

CRICKET: *a popular British sport, somewhat similar to baseball*
PROWESS: *exceptional skill*

Henty describes himself in his growing days and at Cambridge as a sort of walking skeleton; but he was big-boned, and the life he led as manhood approached made him fill out and grow fast into the big, muscular, burly man that he was to the end of his life. In fact, he has said that in later days, when he went down to the Caius College Annual Dinners, while he knew most of the men of his own standing, not one recognized him. And this can easily be grasped when it is understood that in his college days at nineteen he weighed nine and a half stone, while as a man in vigorous health he was as much as seventeen.[1]

He does not forget to credit his school with the education his *Alma Mater* afforded him. He says: "She did give me a good drilling in Latin. Perhaps not elegant classical Latin, but good, everyday, useful, colloquial stuff." In his time the masters were great upon the old dramatic author whom so many of our modern dramatists have tapped right through Elizabethan, Restoration, and more modern times, down to the present. In Henty's early days, just as is annually the custom now, one or other of Terence's comedies[2] was chosen for a performance by the Queen's Scholars, while every other boy as a matter of course had to get up one play as the lesson of the year as well, and doubtless, as has been the case with many a schoolboy in turn, would fall a-wondering how it was that the great Latin poet possessed an Irish name.

Latin verses and Latin colloquial phrases were hard enough to pile up, while parents and guardians, ready enough to complain, found fault at so much time being devoted to the dead languages to the exclusion of those which are spoken now. Hear, ye grumblers, what George Henty says thereon to an interviewer:

"When I went out to the Crimea, and later, to Italy, I found that everyday Latin invaluable. It was the key to modern

---

[1] A "stone" is a British unit of weight equal to fourteen pounds; Henty weighed 133 lbs. and 238 lbs. respectively.

[2] Roman playwright Terence (195-159 B.C.) wrote six comedies.

ALMA MATER: *school or college; literally "nourishing mother" in Latin*
COLLOQUIAL: *informal*

Italian, and a very good key too. But more than that, it meant that wherever I could come across a priest I had a friend and an interpreter. Without my recollections of Terence I don't know where I should have been when I first tackled life as a war correspondent."

He speaks of Westminster as giving him his first introduction to boating, not merely rowing, but boating with the use of the sail. There was a man on the Surrey side in those days, named Roberts, from whom the boys used to hire their four-oared and eight-oared cutters, wager boats, and the occasional randan for three, two oars and sculls. This man had a small half-decked boat which Henty first learned to handle. In it he learned also the stern necessity of always being on the alert after hoisting sail—a necessity which doubtless gave rise to the good old proverbial warning, "Look out for squalls." Yet, in spite of everyone knowing and often using this warning phrase, it is too often neglected by careless boating people, who will not realize what a duty it is never to make fast the sheet.

Here at Westminster and in the little half-decked boat commenced the healthy passion of Henty's life, and he acquired something of the skill which enabled him through manhood to go to sea and feel no fear even in rough weather, strengthened as he was by the calm confidence that accompanied, in the broad sense of the term, "knowing the ropes."

The days of a public-school boy came to an end, and with their conclusion arrived the feeling that he was a man. But after all it was the schoolboy feeling of manhood, though it was very manly in one thing, for it brought with it the knowledge that he had spent too much time in play, and with it too the feeling that he must make up for the past.

Hence it was that he went in for what he termed a burst of hard reading as soon as he reached Cambridge and entered at

CUTTERS: *rowboats*
WAGER BOATS: *tiny boats holding only one person*
RANDAN FOR THREE: *a rowboat rowed by three people*
SCULLS: *small, narrow boats*
MAKE FAST THE SHEET: *fasten the rope controlling the sail*

Caius College. In the full realization of his failings he proved that he was still a boy, for he set to and began reading night and day for about three weeks, so as to acquire as much as should have taken him about six months' work.

As a result nature said nay, and gave him a severe lesson in the shape of an illness which knocked him over, so that he had to go down for a year's rest, as it was termed, but it was in reality a good spell of health-giving instructive work which greatly influenced his future career. In fact, he now began to pick up the information which he so largely utilized afterwards in his books. Here was his first study for *Facing Death*, one of his most widely read boys' stories—boys', though it was as much read by men. For he went down into Wales, where his father possessed a coal mine and iron works, and at the latter he acquired such knowledge and insight into engineering as to enable him at a critical time in his career as a war correspondent to call himself an engineer. Reporting himself as an English engineer desirous of studying the practical effect of great gun fire, he had no difficulty in getting permission to accompany the Italian Fleet in what was virtually the first battle between ironclad men-of-war.

Henty's subsequent military training, together with his physique and stern decision of manner, made him naturally an excellent leader of men. In ordinary civilized life he was one who, at a gathering, would be pretty well sure to be selected as chairman, for upon occasion he could abandon his quiet soft-spoken manner, fill out his chest, and, if slightly roused by opposition, speak out with a decision and a firmness that would lay antagonism low; while, if it happened to be in a lower stratum of not to say savage but uncivilized life, his training had made him a picked disciplinarian, one who had his own particular way of maintaining order and gaining the

PHYSIQUE: *physical size and development*
STRATUM: *layer of society*
OBSTREPEROUS: *unruly*

affections as well as the obedience of those whom he had to command.

This was simple enough in the army with disciplined men, but there were occasions when his services were selected to guide and govern the undisciplined and those of the roughest and most obstreperous nature.

Upon one occasion he, the cultivated scholar and Westminster boy, was placed as foreman, or as it was termed amongst the men, "ganger," over a strong body of men engaged upon the construction of some small military railway. His men were a very lively party, extremely insubordinate at first, and ready if matters did not go exactly as they pleased—if the work seemed too rough, or the supply of available strong drink too handy— to throw down their tools, or reply with insolence to their foreman, whose calm, quiet ways and speech seemed to invite resistance. It was in ignorance that the fellow who offended did this thing, and he did not offend a second time, for Henty was leader with plenary powers, and he had but one way of dealing with a rough. It was to order him at once to the place which he used as his business office, and with quiet firmness and decision, and in the presence of his following, to pay the man off there and then, to the great delight of the rest of the gang, who knew what was to follow. The offender was paid in full and told to be off from the line. He, of course, retaliated with an outburst of flowery language, noting the while the gathering together of his mates. Henty meantime was quietly taking off his coat and rolling up his sleeves preparatory to showing the unbelieving ruffian how a muscular athletic English gentleman, a late pupil of a great professor of boxing, could scientifically handle his fists and give the scoundrel, to the intense delight of the lookers on, a thoroughly solid and manly thrashing. This invariably ended in the offender crying, "Hold! Enough!" and accepting

INSUBORDINATE: *defiant*
INSOLENCE: *extreme rudeness*
PLENARY POWERS: *unlimited powers*
PAY THE MAN OFF: *give the man the money owed him*
PREPARATORY: *in preparation*

his punishment without bearing malice; and in almost every case the gang was not only not weakened by the loss of a man, but it maintained a more willing worker than it had possessed before.

As may be readily supposed, the gentleman ganger lost no prestige amongst his men by such an exhibition of his prowess, for he knew most accurately with whom he had to deal, that is to say, so many big stalwart men of thews and muscle, such as our contractors have utilized for linking land to land with road and bridge, men of untiring energy and endurance, but with the mental ability of children. These formed Henty's gang, and to his credit be it recorded that his treatment proved as efficacious as it was firm, the punishment being given calmly and in cold blood, to the astonishment of the man who received it.

STALWART: *strong, sturdy*
THEWS: *strength*
EFFICACIOUS: *effective*

THE CRIMEAN WAR

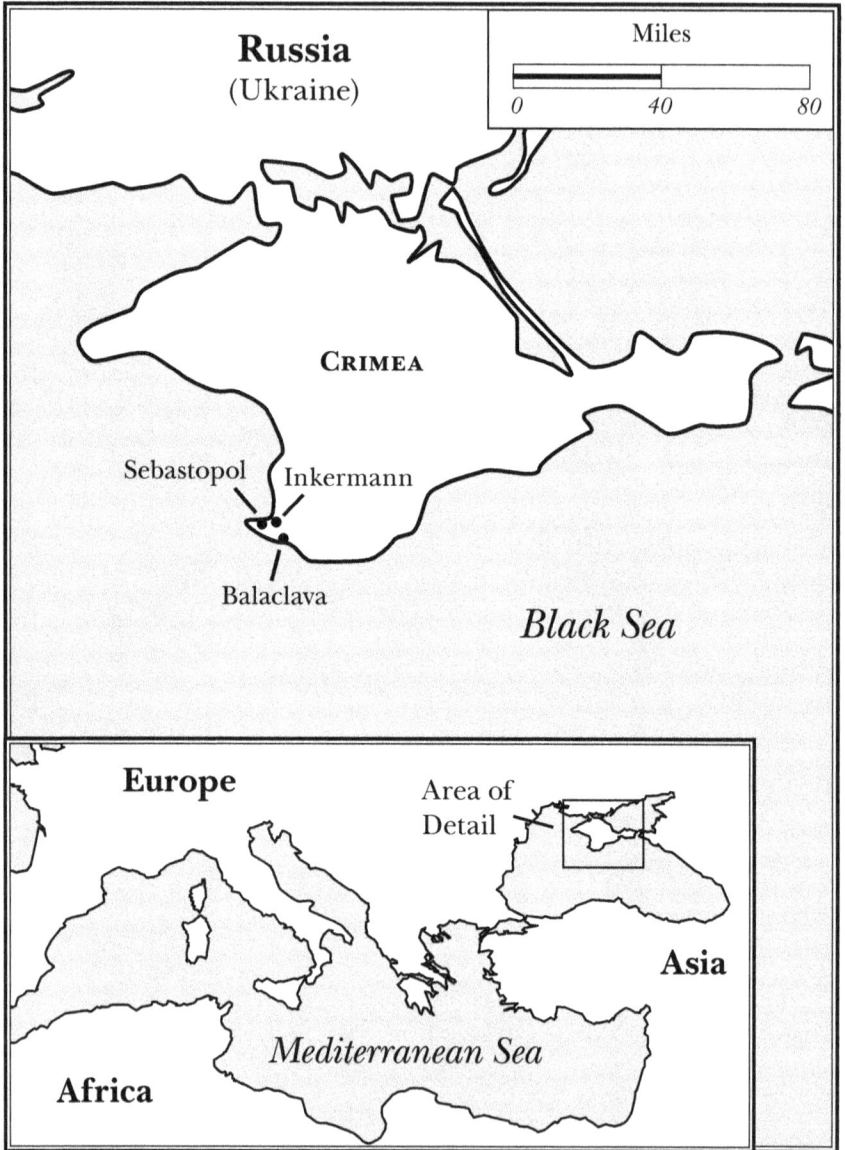

CHAPTER II

FROM CAMBRIDGE TO THE CRIMEA

SOON after his return to Cambridge troubles with Russia were "on the tapis," and as if to show the preparedness for war which did not exist, *Punch*,[1] as is usually the case, began to take notice of our army and navy. It signalized the latter by referring to an event of the day, to wit, the sham-fight at Spithead, and represented a theatrical combat of the melodramatic Surrey or Victoria Theatre type between two British sailors, one being down and his comrade resting over him, hands on knees and cutlass in suspense, with the lines beneath: "Ah, it's all werry well, Bill, but my, if you'd been a Rooshian!"

Then sham-fights and assumed preparation for war died into thin air. Matters came to a head, and our unpreparedness was awfully written in disease, starvation, and death for those who studied the columns of news from the Crimea.

All young England was in a state of excitement. The Crimean War was upon every lip, and every hot-blooded young man burned to get to the front. Among these was George Henty. The quiet student life at the university became painful; the days passed in Caius College seemed to be prison-like. He too, strung up by that natural instinct that has made "Englishman" a name famous in the world's history, grew more and more restless. In the nick of time he was offered an appointment in the

[1] A satirical weekly magazine
ON THE TAPIS: *under discussion*
SIGNALIZED: *noted*
SHAM-FIGHT: *pretend fight*
IN SUSPENSE: *held back*

Commissariat Department of the army, and the first steps were taken which enabled him to claim the rank of lieutenant in the British army, though it was to be in the utility more than in the fighting ranks.

One of our distributors of Attic salt once wrote, in the plain and pungent witticism of his time, that an army crawled upon its stomach in its progress to conquest; and by a strange irony of circumstances the young lieutenant—for, as said above, that was the rank Henty bore during the few years he served in the British army—found himself providing and superintending the supplies of that army in order to enable it to progress on that portion of its anatomy which keeps it alive, that is to say, when he was not busily engaged in superintending hospital wards and organizing arrangements, sanitary and otherwise, in those depressing asylums for the wounded and the sick. The work was arduous enough, but Henty was the man to do it, in spite of the fragile promise of his youth, and the head-shaking as to his future of those who knew him. He must have been a very disappointing man to his social prophets, seeing that he grew above the ordinary height, and came to be big-boned and stalwart, his powerful frame well-clothed with sinew and muscle. He was endowed with everything in fact suited to the making of what would be called a good all-round man, while his education, fostered by his natural pluck and determination, rendered him one who in his early manhood was a thorough athlete. Enough indeed has been said to show that in addition to being a powerful and skilful wrestler, and a formidable competitor in a friendly contest with the gloves, he was a dangerous adversary when necessity compelled him to make full use of what was veritably the noble art of self-defence against the brutal scum of European life with which he was brought into contact.

COMMISSARIAT DEPARTMENT: *the department in charge of supplies*
PUNGENT WITTICISM: *sharp criticism*
ASYLUMS: *institutions*
ARDUOUS: *difficult*
VERITABLY: *truly*

In the full vigour of his manly youth he was a splendid walker, thinking nothing of doing fifty miles in a day, and this not at the expense of exhaustion, for after a brief period of rest he could repeat the walk with comparative ease. Muscular to a degree, he was a steady and dependable comrade in a boat. In addition, aided by the possession and the capacity of a broad deep chest, whose buoyancy was a tremendous asset, he could swim with ease and untiring skill.

Then, too, he made himself a good wielder of the foils, and the usual training of a military man enabled him to handle the service sword with as much ability as he displayed in pistol practice or with the rifle. Following up the ordinary education of a youth and young man with the acquiring and strengthening of such accomplishments as these, his appearance was such as would render him in competition one who would be chosen on any emergency as a leader of men, one who would be obeyed, and whose word would be law to those over whom he was placed.

Excitement was raging in England after the failures and disappointments that were being canvassed during the Crimean War; all England was wroth as William Howard Russell's letters were read, telling the terrible tales of disease, starvation, and neglect suffered by our brave soldiers. Accusations against the authorities were rife, accusations which stirred the Government to action and to making more systematic provision for our troops. It will be readily understood, therefore, that the offer made by a man, so full of energy as Henty, to become a recruit in the Purveyors' Department in the Crimea, that is to say, the Hospital Commissariat, was accepted at once, though his place would more naturally have been in the fighting line.

However, it was ordained that he was to do good work in connection with the provisioning of the unfortunate soldiers who

---

FOILS: *blunt practice swords*
CANVASSED: *investigated or discussed*
WROTH: *full of anger*
RIFE: *widespread*
PURVEYORS' DEPARTMENT: *the department in charge of supplying food*

had suffered so cruelly during the previous winter.

Attacking his task with his customary energy, as soon as he reached Balaclava in the early spring of 1855 he was found busy among the stores which were to be distributed, or arranging the contents of the huts which were filled with wine and the more medicinal stimulants which were to be reserved for the sick or the wounded that were brought into the temporary hospital.

Here he was brought into touch with the officers of the medical and surgical department, and in connection with the transport service, for order was now springing up fast where chaos and despair had reigned so long.

Henty writes home about the preparation of food and comforts for the sick, and the provision of mules and their drivers for the transport of the sick and wounded. And now his fighting times commence—not with the sword and revolver with which he was armed; his encounters were with the shadow of death, as an adjunct to the strong body of surgical and medical men who were struggling so hard to make up for the want of preparation in the past.

With regard to the mule service there is a grim touch in one of Henty's letters home concerning the duties of these useful, hardworking but stubborn brutes. Where he found himself, this portion of the transport service was kept in readiness, some fifty strong, to take ammunition down to the trenches, and on their return journey to bring the wounded back.

A strange life this, superintending and aiding in such matters, for a young man fresh from Cambridge University. It must have been a curious disillusionizing to be hurried out to the Crimea, nerve and brain throbbing with warlike aspirations connected with the honour and glory of war, and then to find himself in the sordid atmosphere of the wet tents and rough

ADJUNCT: *assistant*
SORDID: *miserable*
MAGAZINES: *storage sites for ammunition*

huts, where the winter was still holding its own, while the constant booming of the great guns added to the general misery and wretchedness. The possibility of an explosion was another cause of anxiety, for there was ever the prospect of a shell falling in one or other of the magazines which supplied the batteries, and a resulting disaster unless the fire could be extinguished in time. These alarms generally occurred in the night, when, following upon the lurid display of flames from some hut or workshop set on fire by Russian shot, there would be the roar of orders, the shouting of men, and the dread of the fire being communicated to the crowd of shipping in the little sheltered harbour.

It was a wondrous change from the calm and quiet of the university city to the roar and turmoil of the besieging camp with the thunder of our batteries, the return fire from Sebastopol, and the constant shells dropping in from the enemy's forts.

Very shortly after he reached Balaclava he seized an opportunity to ride over the field of Inkermann, the scene of the surprise attack made by the Russians nearly six months before, and he says that at the top of the hill where the principal struggle took place, the ground was still covered with the remains of the contest—ammunition pouches, Russian caps, broken weapons and other grim relics—while, rather ironically, in allusion to the way in which the allies were surprised, he says that this spot is now commanded by heavy batteries recently erected, and alludes to the old adage about locking the stable door after the horse is stolen. Even then, so many months after the fight, many bodies of the Russians were still unburied, and lay there as though to demonstrate the horrors of war, while the hill slope and a valley were so exquisite that the writer fell into raptures about the beauty of the place. The steep cliffs were honeycombed with caverns, a ruined castle stood on an

BATTERIES: *cannons*
LURID: *horribly glowing*
WONDROUS: *remarkable*
ALLUSION: *reference*
ADAGE: *saying*

eminence, and the place was beautifully wooded, a stream that trickled through the valley amidst the exquisitely fresh and green grass adding to the wonder and the beauty of the scene. But his daydream was given a rude awakening by a hint thrown out, of the risks to which a war correspondent is exposed in the pursuit of his duty, for there was the sharp crack of a rifle and the dull thud of a bullet burying itself in a tree, having missed him narrowly, for luckily the Russian who had fired at him had not been quite correct in his aim.

Hurrying back, he forgets the danger that he has escaped, and to his mind it is April once more, and he begins to describe the beauty of the wild flowers with which the slopes are clothed—irises varying in tint from pale yellow to orange, others alternating from light blue to purple, the early spring crocus of pure white, and wild hyacinths in abundance.

On his way, as everything is fraternal among the besiegers, he and his companions pass through the French camp and taste the hospitality of their allies, receiving proof that in this camp, too, matters have been mended after the horrors of the past winter, for the English visitors are welcomed with what Henty declares to be first-rate provisions. But he is dreadfully matter-of-fact and businesslike directly after, as behoves an officer of the Purveyors' Department, for he falls a-wondering why it is that the French bread is far superior to that made by the bakers in Balaclava, the latter having a sour taste that is unpleasant and, he thinks, unwholesome. For his part he prefers the biscuit, but feels that on their return to England he and his comrades will be entitled to a handsome compensation for wear and tear of teeth in the service of their country. Then, as if by way of comparison with the alarms that had suggested a fresh attack, he states that the night was less noisy than usual. "In the early part our sharpshooters and the Russians

EMINENCE: *hill*
FRATERNAL: *brotherly*
SUBALTERN: *a low ranking British officer*

were cracking away, but about eleven the Russian works opened upon the parties engaged in the new parallel." The next night he announces that a colonel of a French regiment of infantry was struck down while talking in the trenches to a subaltern— "a sixty-eight pound shot shattered him frightfully."

At this time England was in the throes of expectation. The long-delayed assault upon Sebastopol was expected at any moment, and the main subject of conversation out in the camp was what day would be appointed. But Henty says, "What day that will be no one but Lord Raglan[1] knows—even if he does himself." However, at last the long-expected bombardment did begin. From a complete circle of batteries round the town, jets of smoke were bursting, while a perfect shower of shot and shell was poured into the town and was as incessantly answered. The wonder was that buildings did not crumble into dust before such a tremendous fire, for from our great crescent of mortars a shell was sent every ten minutes during the night, and the mules that bore the ammunition to the trenches came back sadly laden with wounded.

Day after day the assault went on, and Henty devoted his spare moments to recording the various proceedings of the historic siege—the continuous fire of the English and their French allies, which, in spite of their vigour, only silenced the Russian batteries for fresh ones to be opened again after a few hours' hard work; the occasional skirmishes where attack was made by the Russians to carry a battery and be repelled; the destruction of rifle pits; the surprises caused by the Cossacks beginning to show themselves out upon the plain; attacks when prisoners were taken; replies and rescues. Then his interest was taken by the allies who now appeared upon the field in the shape of the Turks commanded by Omar Pasha in person. He describes them as a fine body of men who spend most of their

[1] Commander of the British troops during the Crimean War
PARALLEL: *defensive trench*
THE THROES: *an agony*
INCESSANTLY: *ceaselessly*
CARRY A BATTERY: *capture a unit of artillery*

time in drilling; for they display a great want of military discipline, and their movements are little better than a shuffle. But Henty compliments them with the remark that they are getting into order. Then he describes their arms and the excellence of their French rifles, and goes on to display the keenness of his observation as he seems to bring to bear old recollections of the *Arabian Nights* and the peculiarity of the immense number of hunchbacks among the Turks, nearly all of whom have high round shoulders, which in a great many amounts to actual deformity. It is hard to understand, though, why this should be attributed to their sitting cross-legged. However, he says the Turkish cavalry and artillery are good, the horses small but strongly made and in good condition. Altogether he thinks the Turkish army a most welcome reinforcement. All the time the siege goes on vigorously, with the English men-of-war and gunboats rendering all the help they can by checking the fire of the forts.

Something of the weird state of affairs around the young Commissariat officer and correspondent is seen in his description of a leisurely walk he took to one of our marine batteries. "The air," he says, "was so still that I could hear not only the explosion but the whiz of every shell most distinctly, though distant seven miles as the crow flies."

The delicious spring weather that lasted for a time was followed by a gale with sleet, and then by forty hours of rain. The change was mournfully depressing, the streets of Balaclava were a perfect sea of mud, everything was forlorn, miserable, and deserted, the officers in their waterproofs were dejected, and everyone was despondent. However, the purveyor officer remarked that the Guards were by this time all provided with waterproof coats, which kept them dry as they stood at their posts. But a thick mist hung over everything; the rain was

ARMS: *weapons*
CHECKING: *holding back*
FETLOCKS: *the joint above their hooves*

soaking through all the tents; the ground had become so soft that the horses sank in over their fetlocks, while their heads were drooping, and they appeared the picture of discomfort. The soldiers going down into the trenches carried a perfect load of clay upon their shoes, while those returning came back wet, exhausted, and soaked to the skin.

In another letter, written just after this dreary time, Henty writes that the night closed in dark and lowering with every promise of wet, a horror for those dwelling in tents; just the sort of night, he says, which the Russians delight in for making a sortie from the besieged city, besides which, he says, they had been unusually quiet, a sign that mischief was afloat; but as the attacking force was growing pretty well-accustomed to the habits of the enemy, a very strong body of men was sent down into the trenches. In proof that this was wise, about ten o'clock there came somewhere out of the darkness in front the sound of men using picks and shovels, as if the Russians were raising a breastwork prior to an attack. Then an order rang out, and from our own trenches a sharp fire was opened upon the attacking party; but owing to the darkness and want of aim it was probable that little damage was done, and the defenders crowded together in utter silence, listening and waiting for the attack that all felt was bound to come.

At last, about one o'clock, there was a dull, heavy roar from out of the foggy night. It was the signal gun, and instantly the enemy made a rush at the advanced trenches, to be met with a tremendous volley and stagger back, but only to come on again bravely out of the darkness, thousands strong, while the musketry firing was fiercer than anything that had taken place since the commencement of the siege. This went on for two hours, during which time the whole of the Russians, according to custom, supplemented their fire with the most demoniacal

LOWERING: *threatening*
A SORTIE: *an attack*
BREASTWORK: *chest-high wall, usually quickly constructed of dirt*
COMMENCEMENT: *beginning*
DEMONIACAL: *demon-like*

yells, which were responded to by their friends in the town and answered in defiance by the cheers of our men in the other batteries at each repulse which the Russians sustained, for never once, in spite of the bravery of the attack, did they succeed in entering our advanced trenches. The next morning, after they had retired, in spite of the number of wounded and the dead, whom it was their practice to carry off with them, the ground was covered with the fallen.

What an experience for the young war correspondent who was making his first essay in that which was to become his profession for years, and who in this instance proved how thoroughly adequate he was for his task!

Undaunted by their failure and their immense losses, but a short time elapsed before the besieged made another sortie, which proved as unsuccessful as the last; and though the Russian losses must have been immense, in our bayonet-bristling trenches but few men suffered. Henty goes on to say it is quite impossible to describe these night sorties accurately, for those engaged in them know next to nothing in the darkness and confusion. If asked in the morning, they would reply that the Russians came out strong, and that our men loaded and fired in their direction as fast as they could, that the Russians yelled awfully, and the shot whizzed about like hail! This was the invariable account of a sortie by those engaged in repelling it, unless there was a surprise and the Russians got inside our trenches, when in the darkness and confusion all were so mixed up that it was hard to know enemy from friend. "Can anything wilder be conceived?" Henty asks in a description of an attempt made by the Russians to seize one of our batteries and spike the guns. The confusion was tremendous. Imagine an attack on a dark night, the rain pouring, the men up to their knees in mud, fighting away all mixed up together, the constant flashes and

ESSAY: *attempt*
SPIKE THE GUNS: *disable the cannons by driving a spike into their touchholes*

reports of guns and pistols—the revolver being a most useful weapon on these occasions—the cheers of our men and the yells of the Russians. At the commencement of one of these attacks one of our men saw someone crouching over one of the guns. He asked him what he was doing. The only answer was a cut of the sword, which took off luckily only the tip of his nose. He immediately pinned the man to the gun with his bayonet. He turned out to be a Russian artilleryman who had managed to get in to spike the gun.

These were strange surroundings for a young literary man, for a rough hut was often the study of one who was to grow by degrees one of the widest known of English writers. Not only the pen, but the pencil had become familiar to his fingers, and, possibly to fill up dull moments, he began to make sketches of such objects as took his attention; and the idea striking him that such subjects might prove attractive to one of the editors of an illustrated paper at home, he from time to time tried his hand at some little scene or some quaint-looking character which had caught his eye.

These supplemented his long letters to a relative, and the idea growing upon him, he elaborated his writing, making these letters, evidently with latent hopes for the future, the germs of those which later grew to be so familiar to the British public. Everything is said to have a beginning. Certainly this was the commencement of George Henty's life as a war correspondent, but these efforts were not entirely successful. The sketches were duly taken by their recipient to the different London illustrated papers, but whether from not being up to the editorial artistic mark, or from the fact that each paper was already fully represented, no success attended their presentation. The letters, however, fared better in one case, for upon their being offered to the editor of the *Morning Advertiser*, with a statement as to

LATENT: *hidden*

who and what the writer was, and where he was engaged, the editor promised to read them. He kept his word, and proved his acumen by writing out to the young lieutenant with an invitation to him to represent the paper and send him from time to time a series of letters containing the most interesting occurrences of the campaign that came under his notice.

The opening was eagerly seized upon, and proved highly advantageous to both parties. The young officer was a privileged person at headquarters, and his letters show that he had a keen power of observation and a great faculty for selecting subjects that were of interest to English readers. As a consequence, he continued to represent the *Morning Advertiser* until he was invalided home.

ACUMEN: *good judgment*
INVALIDED HOME: *released from duty and sent home due to sickness*

CHAPTER III

INVALIDED HOME

HENTY'S Crimean experiences were to be but short, but they enabled him to give us many admirable and vivid pictures of those stirring days. Although a non-combatant, he was in the thick of the fight before Sebastopol, and he seems to have missed nothing, from the most sordid features to the brightest and best. He paints the horrors, and takes note of the pathetic, the good, and true.

He gives us straightforward, telling lines regarding the Turks, and he records how our comparatively pitiful strength for the gigantic task upon which we had embarked, and in which our meager forces had to be supplemented by the gallant sailors landed from the fleet, now grew into immense strength, the last ally being Sardinia with her little army of eighteen thousand men.

He has something to say about Soyer and his culinary campaign and model kitchen, so urgently needed for the sick and suffering, and of the great aid it was to the doctors, whose hands were more than full of the sick and wounded when their battle began with the dire cholera. He has sympathetic words, too, for the heroine of Scutari,[1] where she seems to have led a charmed life, saving the sinking and suffering by her calm sweet presence, and encouraging in their continuous struggle the nurses

---

[1] Florence Nightingale (1820-1910), who served as a nurse at the Scutari military hospital located near the southern shore of the Black Sea

PATHETIC: *sympathetic*

who would have given up in despair. No wonder that the name of Florence Nightingale was at the time on every lip, and that even now, from the far West and the antipodean South, the English-speaking race pay a pilgrim-like visit to the peaceful home in Derwent Dale where the illustrious lady is spending the evening of her life.

Henty paints, too, his own existence in camp during those spring days when the rain was upon them. He says to his readers: "Let them plant a small tent in the centre of an Irish bog, for to nothing else can I compare this place [before Sebastopol] when it is wet; the mud is everywhere knee-deep, while the wet weather has had another bad effect, in that it has accelerated the attacks of cholera, which is of a most malignant type, and a very large proportion of cases are fatal." He begins one paragraph, too, with a short sentence which is terribly suggestive of a peril that had passed: "Miss Nightingale is better."

But all through his narrative, so full of the observations of a young, clear-minded, energetic man, there stands out plainly the fact that he was there upon a particular duty—that connected with the department of which he was an officer. At one time he is writing about the water, the excellency and purity of the supply; then he is condemning the arrangements, and no doubt pointing out the need of a better system, so that this bounteous supply should not be wasted by allowing the horses and mules to trample it into a swamp of mud. And the need for these precautions was soon shown, even during his stay, for as the weeks passed, even where the produce of the springs was plentiful, the men had to go farther and farther afield for a fresh supply.

At another time he is falling foul of the bread which is served out to the officers and men. He denounces it as quite unfit for human food. It was by no means first-rate at the time of its

ANTIPODEAN SOUTH: *far south of the globe*
EVENING: *last days*
MALIGNANT: *dangerous*
FALLING FOUL OF: *attacking*

leaving the ovens at Constantinople, but by the time it arrived it was "one mass of blue mould;" yet it was served out regardless of its condition and at a very great risk to the health of the soldiers. In fact, he notes that it was so bad that even animals refused it. No wonder he made comparisons between this and the admirable supply served out to the French army.

Thoughtful and wise too in these early days, Henty has much to say regarding sanitary matters, the necessity for care, and above all—no doubt this was forced upon him by their propinquity—he is eloquent about the hospitals; again, and this would scarcely have been expected from one so young, he points out the way in which the air is tainted by the dead animals which are allowed to lie unburied.

He began his duties at Balaclava in April, and at the beginning of June he writes, as might have been expected, that he is sorry that his letter this time will have to be a short one, as he has for the last two days suffered from a severe attack of the prevailing epidemic, which has prevented him from going out at all. Three days later he sends word that the great bombardment of Sebastopol has recommenced. He too is better—well enough to show his interest in the great general hospital kept especially for the reception of the wounded, and to record that it is filling fast. He has sympathetic words for the sufferers and their ghastly wounds from shot and shell splinter. He talks from personal observation of the firmness and patience of the poor fellows over their wounds, and of the extraordinary coolness and *sang-froid* with which they suffer the dressing, even to the amputation of an arm above the elbow, both bones below being broken by a Minié ball.[1] The conduct of these humble heroes brings to mind the old naval story of the past, of the Jack whose leg had been taken off in action, and who resented the idea of being tied up while amputation was performed. "No,"

[1] A type of rifle bullet designed by Frenchman Claude Minié

PROPINQUITY: *nearness*
SANG-FROID: *calmness*
JACK: *sailor*

he said; "only give me my pipe;" and he sat up and smoked till the surgeon had operated. This in the days, too, when anesthetics were not in use, and hemorrhage was checked by means of a bucket of tar. Poor Jack sat up consciously and looked on!

Henty's record is that when one soldier's operation was performed and he was about to be carried into the hospital ward, he exclaimed, "I'm all right," rose up and walked to his ward, lighted his pipe, and got into bed. This is given as a single instance taken at random from among numbers of cases.

In his last letter from the Crimea, dated June 18, 1855, he records that there had been a serious reverse to the allied armies. He had by this time somewhat recovered from his severe fit of illness, but he had long been over-exerting himself. The doctors delivered their ultimatum, and he became one of the many who, weakened by the terrible exposure, were invalided home.

Unfortunately a harder fate attended his only brother, Fred, who left England with him when he obtained his appointment to the Purveyors' Department, for he was seized by the prevailing epidemic, cholera, and died at Scutari.

ULTIMATUM: *final command*

G. A. Henty After the Crimea, Aged 23

CHAPTER IV

THE FIRST GLIMPSE OF ITALY

THE department which invalided George Henty and sent him home to recoup did not lose sight of the man who had earned such a good name in the Crimea, and as soon as he was reported convalescent it began to look about for a position in which his services would prove valuable.

Here was a man who, in connection with his duties in the Purveying Department during the late war, had more or less distinguished himself by the acumen he had displayed and the reports he had sent in concerning the state of the temporary hospitals and the treatment of the sick and wounded. There is not much favour shown over such work as his. The fact was patent that in Henty the authorities had a man of keen observation who grasped at once what was wanted in time of war in connection with the movements of an army, one whose mission it was not to direct movements and utilize the forces who were, so to speak, being used in warfare, but who knew how to make himself a valuable aid to supplement doctor and surgeon, and to carry on their work of saving life—in short, the right man in the right place.

So he was selected and sent out to Italy charged with the task of organizing the hospitals of the Italian Legion. The very wording of such an appointment as this is enough to take an

RECOUP: *recover*
CONVALESCENT: *to be recovering*
PATENT: *obvious*

ordinary person's breath away. It might have been supposed that the department would have selected as organizer some mature professional man and M.D., with the greatest experience in such matters, ripened in the work and well-known as a great authority; but to their credit they grasped the fact that Henty's experience was proved and real. Book-lore and the passing of examinations were as nothing in comparison with what this young man of twenty-seven had learned in roughly extemporized hospital, tent, and hut amidst the inclemency of a foreign clime, in the face of the horrible scourge of an Eastern epidemic, where the wounded died off like flies, not from the wounds, which under healthy environment would rapidly have healed, but from that deadly enemy, pyæmia, or hospital gangrene. It was this which proved so fatal after the otherwise healing touch of the skilful surgeon's knife—for these were the days prior to the discoveries made by Lister,[1] which completely revolutionized the surgical art.

While in Italy in 1859 in connection with the hospital work, Henty stored his mind with the results of his observations. They were stirring times. War was on the way; Sardinia's army, fresh from fleshing its sword in the Crimea, was eager for the fight that was partially to free Italy, and the name of Garibaldi[2] was on every lip, for he and his Red Shirts were burning to attack the hated Austrian. While finding an opportunity to be present at some of the engagements, Henty was busy preparing himself for writing history, and his brain was actively acquiring the language and habits of the people in a way that was an unconscious preparation for a future visit to the country in connection with the duties of a war correspondent.

It was during this visit to Italy in 1859, and while performing his duties of inspector and organizer of the Italian hospitals,

[1] Joseph Lister (1827-1912), an English surgeon who pioneered the use of antiseptics to prevent infection during surgery

[2] Giuseppe Garibaldi (1807-1882), an Italian national hero who fought for Italy's unification and independence from Austria

EXTEMPORIZED: *improvised*

INCLEMENCY: *harshness*

that Henty made his first acquaintance with Garibaldi and his enthusiastic army so bent upon freeing Italy from the yoke of Austria. In a number of most interesting letters, picturesque and full of the observation and training that he was gathering for the construction of the series of adventurous stories now standing to his name, he details his meetings with the Red Shirts. Bright, high-spirited boys they were in many cases, ever with the cry of liberty upon their lips, and only too ready to welcome and to fraternize with the daring, manly young fellow who thought as little as they of the personal risks which had to be faced, and who was subsequently to chronicle this portion of their history and the warlike deeds of their chief.

After his return from the organizing expedition with the Italian Legion, Henty was placed in charge of the Commissariat Departments at Belfast and Portsmouth, and now held the rank of captain. A plodding life this for a military man with all the making in him of a strong, thoughtful soldier, one who would have become the strongest link in the vertebræ of a regiment, so to speak, the one nearest the brain.

Circumstances, however did not guide him in that direction, but, as we know now, led him towards becoming the critic of armies instead of an actor in their ranks.

Judging from Henty's nature and the steadiness and constancy of his life in the pursuit of the career which he chose, it could not have been lightly that he came to the decision that from the way in which he had entered the army there did not seem to be any future for him worthy of his attention, for the British army has always been marked by the way in which birth and money have been the stepping-stones to promotion. Of course there have been exceptions, but the British soldier has never been famed for carrying a field-marshal's baton in his

CLIME: *climate*
FRATERNIZE: *associate*
VERTEBRÆ: *backbone*

knapsack, and it is only of comparatively late years that the famous old anomaly of promotion by purchase has died out.

Certainly Henty entered the army as a university man and a gentleman, but he must have begun to feel, taught by experience, that he had gone in by the wrong door, the one which led in an administrative direction and not to the executive with a future of command.

During Henty's stay in Ireland he had a very unpleasant experience with a rough in Dublin, or rather, to be accurate, a rough in Dublin had a very unpleasant experience with Henty. Somehow or other, while out walking with his young wife, for he was now married, a brutal fellow offered some insult to Mrs. Henty, in the purest ignorance of the kind of man whose anger he had roused. One says roused, for in ordinary life Henty was one of the calmest and quietest of men; but he had plenty of chivalry in his composition, and moreover, as has been shown, he had had the education and training of an athlete, leavened with the instructions of the north country trainer who taught him the jiu-jitsu of his day as practised by a Newcastle man. What followed was very brief, for there was a quick, short struggle, and the Dublin Pat—a city blackguard, and no carrier of a stick—was sent flying over Henty's head, *hors de combat*, much surprised at the strength and skill of such a man as he had possibly never encountered before in his life.

ANOMALY: *oddity*

PROMOTION BY PURCHASE: *soldiers purchasing positions of higher rank*

JIU-JITSU: *weaponless self-defense*

BLACKGUARD: *scoundrel*

HORS DE COMBAT: *"out of action" in French; disabled*

HENTY IN ITALY

Switzerland

Austria

CARNIOLA

Como
Brescia
Peschiera
Venice
Trieste

Ravenna
DALMATIA

Rimini
Sinigaglia
SAN
MARINO
Ancona
LISSA

Italy

Adriatic
Sea

Naples

Sardinia

Tunisia

Sicily

Mediterranean
Sea

Miles
0   100   200

CHAPTER V

THE ITALIAN WAR

HENTY proved early the excellence of his capabilities, and that he was a man who would be all that was required for the preservation of men's lives; but such as he meet with scant encouragement, and at last, as said above, he made up his mind to try in a fresh direction, and resigned his commission.

Led no doubt by his leanings, and taught by old experience in connection with his father's enterprises in coal-mining, he made a fresh start in life in mining engineering, and was for some time in Wales, where his knowledge of mining, and natural firmness and aptitude as a leader and trained controller of bodies of men, made him a valuable agent for the adventurous companies who are ready to open up new ground. His operations were so successful that after a time he entered into engagements which resulted in his proceeding to the Island of Sardinia. Here there was much untried ground to invite the speculation of the enterprising and adventurous; for it is a country rich in minerals, several of them being so-called precious stones, and there seemed excellent promise of profit. A good deal of speculative research was at one time on the way, and here, following his work in Wales, Henty spent some busy years, not, though, without finding the value of his early athletic education, for the lower classes were not too well disposed to the young English manager under whom they worked.

COMMISSION: *position as an officer*

Returning to England early in the sixties,[1] he once more turned his attention to his pen, having proved, while in the Crimea, his ability for writing quick and observant descriptive copy, specimens of which were extant in the columns of the *Morning Advertiser*, and of which he had examples pasted up and preserved. Moreover, when he began to make application for work, he had the satisfaction of finding that his articles had already excited notice in the literary world. This helped him to obtain an engagement, somewhere in 1865, as special correspondent of the *Standard*, and he carried out his duties so successfully that he became a standard of the *Standard*, and was sent out in 1866 as one of the special correspondents of that paper to Italy, to report upon the proceedings of the Italian armies which had then united in the operations against the Austrian forces.

Italy was to some extent familiar hunting-ground for Henty, inasmuch as at the time when he went to undertake the task of reorganizing the hospitals of the Italian Legion he had seen a good deal of the country, picked up much of the language, and had become acquainted with Garibaldi and his followers when, as said before, they were engaged in the encounters which resulted in partially freeing Italy from the Austrian yoke.

It was now that his early experience of the country and the mastery he had obtained over the Italian language stood him in good stead, while, as a matter of course, his experience and general knowledge of the country made him an ideal chronicler of the movements of the campaign.

Plunged, as it were, right in the midst of the troubles, he seems to have been here, there, and everywhere, and by some means or another he was always on the spot whenever anything exciting was on the way. Now he was at sea, now with the Garibaldians scouting on the flanks of the Austrian army, now

[1] 1860's

EXTANT: *preserved*

G. A. Henty at 28

making journeys by *Vetturinos* across the mountains, to turn up somewhere along with the forces of the king, and always ready to bring a critical eye to bear—the eye of a soldier—in comparing the three forces, the volunteer Garibaldians, the Italian regulars, and the Austrians. The last mentioned seemed to him to be, in their drill, unquestionably superior to the Italians, displaying a strong *esprit de corps*, rigid obedience to their officers, and an amount of German impassibility far more adapted to make them bear unmoved the hardships and discouragements of long struggles and reverses than the enthusiasm of the Italians—an enthusiasm which was manifested in a perfect furore of delight throughout Italy on the news of the declaration of war, tidings reaching Henty from every city, of illuminations, of draping with flags, and other celebrations.

"Even Naples," he says, "which has been far behind the rest of Italy in her ardour for the cause, began to rejoice at the termination of the long delay;" but he declares there was no doubt that the reactionary party had been very hard at work there, with the result that a number of turbulent spirits had been sent away from among the volunteers, the excesses which they had committed threatening to bring the Garibaldians into disrepute.

He now fully proved his ability for the task he had undertaken. Writing home as soon as he had crossed Switzerland early in June a long series of most interesting letters, he commenced with his first meeting with Garibaldi and his followers at Como, and continued throughout the war until victory crowned the efforts of the united armies of Italy and the patriots, and ended (as in a culminating outburst of pyrotechnic display) with the triumphant spectacles at Venice after the Austrians were finally expelled.

VETTURINOS: *Italian carriages*
ESPRIT DE CORPS: *common bond*
IMPASSIBILITY: *lack of emotion*
FURORE: *outburst*
ARDOUR: *enthusiasm*
PYROTECHNIC DISPLAY: *fireworks*

Later, Henty gave permanency to his ephemeral contributions to the journal upon which he was engaged; but in these early days he was a comparatively unknown man, with nothing to commend him to the notice of an enterprising publisher, and the makings of a most interesting descriptive work sparkled for a few hours in the pages of the big contemporary newspaper and then died out, with the ashes only left, hidden, save to searchers in the files preserved at the newspaper office and in the British Museum. For Henty, wanting time and opportunity, never reproduced these letters in their entirety, though they remained in the journalistic print and *in petto*, ready for use, as in a kind of brain mine when, as time rolled on, his adventures in story-land began to achieve success and excite demand. Then they doubtless supplied pabulum for such tales as *Jack Archer*, *The Cat of Bubastes*, and *The Lion of St. Mark*, stories quite remarkable for the truth of their local colour. The last named so influenced a young American lad on a visit to England, that he prevailed upon his father to take him to see Henty, while afterwards, on being taken to Venice, he wrote a clever, naïve letter, which is quoted elsewhere, to the author of his choice, telling him of his delight in coming to Europe and seeing for himself the Venice of today, where he recognized the very places that Henty had so truthfully described.

It is a pity that these letters were not reprinted in book form; but long before an opportunity could have served, the brave struggles of the Italians to free themselves from the Austrian yoke, and the fame of Garibaldi, had grown stale as popular subjects for the general reader, and the question with the publisher, "would a book upon this subject sell?" being only answerable in the negative, nothing was done. In fact, in those days, save in one instance, there was no demand for the reprinting of a journalist's contributions to a daily paper. This particular

EPHEMERAL: *short-lived*
IN PETTO: *in reserve; literally "in secret" in Italian*
PABULUM: *the basis*
NAÏVE: *simple*

instance seemed to stand out at once as the prerogative of one man alone,[1] he who has only just gone to his well-earned and honoured rest, and whose contributions to the *Times*, *My Diary in India*, that vivid narrative of the suppression of the Indian Mutiny, became a classic.

It was like old times to Henty, after crossing Switzerland, to find himself at Como awaiting the arrival of Garibaldi, who was reported to be on his way. A portion of the Garibaldian army was already there, and in a short time, to his great satisfaction, Henty found that their chief was hourly expected to take command of the volunteers.

His information proved to be true, and in the midst of tremendous enthusiasm he found the volunteers drawn up in double line reaching through the town, flags waving, the people shouting, and everyone working himself into a fever of heat.

As the chief approached, the people seemed to have gone out of their minds. Caps were thrown up recklessly, at the risk of never being recovered, and the people literally roared as the general, looking in good health, though older and greyer than when Henty last saw him in 1859, rode along the ranks of the seven thousand or so of volunteers that he was about to review and passed on, waving his hand in reply to the cheering, as if thoroughly appreciating the greeting, much as he did during his reception in London.

The town seemed afterwards to be swarming with his soldiers. It appeared as if two out of every three persons in the streets upon close examination proved to be Garibaldians— close examination was necessary, for it needed research to make sure that they were volunteers, consequent upon the fact that in many cases anything in the shape of uniforms was wanting.

As a rule their uniform, he points out, should have been the familiar red shirt, belt, and dark-grey trousers with red stripe,

[1] Sir William Howard Russell (1820-1907)

PREROGATIVE: *exclusive right*
REVIEW: *formally inspect*

surmounted by red caps, with green bands and straight peaks. In one of his early letters at this stage Henty describes the incongruous nature of the men's dress. Perhaps one-fourth would have the caps; another fourth would look like the ancient Phrygians or the French fishermen. Perhaps one-third would have the red shirts; possibly nearly half, the regulation trousers; and where uniform was wanting they made up their dress with articles of their usual wear—wide-awakes, hats, caps of every shape, jackets, coats black and coloured. Some were dressed like gentlemen, some like members of the extreme lower order, altogether looking such an unsatisfactory motley group as that which old Sir John Falstaff[1] declared he would not march with through Coventry.

But in spite of this there seemed to be the material for a dashing army amongst these men. They promised to make the finest of recruits, though certainly the observant eyes of Henty told him that many of them were far too young to stand the fatigue that they would be called upon to suffer during the war, a number of them being mere boys, not looking above fifteen. But Garibaldi was said to be partial to youngsters, and he liked the activity of the boys, who, he declared, fought as well as men.

On the whole, according to Henty's showing, Garibaldi's volunteer troops were very much the same as flocked to our best volunteer regiments in London during the early days. In short, the enthusiasm of the Garibaldians was contagious, and Henty wrote of them with a running pen; but his enthusiasm was leavened with the common sense and coolness of the well-drilled organizing young soldier, who made no scruple while admiring the Garibaldians' pluck, self-denial, and determination to oust the hated Austrian, to point out their shortcomings as an army and their inability to prove themselves much more than a guerrilla band.

---

[1] A comic character in three of William Shakespeare's plays
SURMOUNTED BY: *topped with*
INCONGRUOUS: *out of place*
WIDE-AWAKES: *wide-brimmed hats*
MADE NO SCRUPLE: *did not restrain himself*

They were an army of irregulars, of course, but with a strong adhesion based upon enthusiastic patriotism. With such an army as this it may be supposed that the followers of their camp sent order and discipline to the winds, and the war correspondent had to thank once more that portion of his athletic education that had made him what he was. To use his own words, out there in Italy he "thanked his stars" that his youthful experience had made him a pretty good man with his hands. He found himself in his avocations amongst a scum of Italian roughs ready to play the European Ishmaelite, with their hands against every man—hands that in any encounter grasped the knife-like stiletto, ready, the moment there was any resistance to their marauding, to stab mercilessly Italian patriot or believer in the Austrian yoke, friend or foe, or merely an English spectator if he stood in their way. But to their cost in different encounters these gentry learned that the young correspondent was no common man, for Henty, in recording his experience with the pugnacious Garibaldian camp-followers, says calmly and in the most naïve manner, and moreover so simply that there is not even a suggestion of boastfulness or brag: "I learned from experiment that if necessary I could deal with about four of them at once; and they were the sort of gentry who would make no bones about getting one down and stabbing one if they got the chance." It was no Falstaff who spoke these words, for they were the utterances of a perfectly sincere, modest Englishman, albeit rather proud, after such a childhood, of his robust physique and of the way in which he could use his fists or prove how skilfully he could deal with an attacking foe and hurl him headlong, much in the same sort of way as a North-country wrestler might dispose of some malicious monkey or any wasp-like enemy of pitiful physique—comparatively helpless unless he could use his sting.

OUST: *force out*
AVOCATIONS: *callings*
STILETTO: *a long, slender dagger used for stabbing*
PUGNACIOUS: *quarrelsome*
UTTERANCES: *words*

Henty took all such matters as these quite as a matter of course. He felt, as he wrote, that a war correspondent to do his duty must accept all kinds of risks in his search for interesting material to form the basis of his letters to his journal. But incidentally we learn about semi-starvation, the scarcity of shelter, the rumours of the old dire enemy, cholera, whose name was so strongly associated with past adventures in the Crimea, risks from shell and shot, and ugly dangers too from those who should have been friends.

For there is one word—spy—that always stands out as a terror, and it was during this campaign that in his eagerness to obtain information he approached so closely to the lines that he was arrested as such by one of the sentries and passed on from pillar to post among the ignorant soldiery.

In this case he had started with a friend for an investigating drive in the neighbourhood of Peschiera, at a time when encounters had been taking place between the Italian army and the Austrians. Upon reaching a spot where a good view of the frowning earth-works with their tiers of cannon could be obtained, they left the carriage, and climbed a hill or two, when they were attracted by the sound of firing, and hurrying on they came to a spot where some of the peasants were watching what was going on across a river. Upon reaching the little group they found out that it was not a skirmish, but that the Austrians were engaged in a sort of review on the ground where there had been a battle a few days before.

Henty felt that he was in luck, for he found that the peasants had been witnesses of the battle from that very position and were eager to point out what had taken place, the men giving a vivid description of the horrors they had witnessed and the slaughter that had taken place.

BUT INCIDENTALLY: *only as an aside*
FROM PILLAR TO POST: *from place to place*

Having obtained sufficient from one of the speakers to form an interesting letter, he and his friend returned to their carriage and told the driver to go back. Henty had picked up a good deal of Italian, but not sufficient to make himself thoroughly understood by the driver, and, as is often the case, a foreigner of the lower orders failed to grasp that which a cultivated person would comprehend at once. The consequence was that the man drove on instead of returning, and his fares did not find out the mistake till they caught sight of a couple of pickets belonging to the Guides, the finest body of cavalry in the Italian service. Seeing that they were on the wrong track, Henty stopped the driver, questioned him, and then, fully understanding the mistake, told him to drive back at once. But the pickets had seen them, and came cantering up. Explanations were made, but the Guides were not satisfied. They had noticed the coming of the carriage, and had become aware of what to them was a very suspicious act. The occupants were strangers, and had been making use of a telescope, which from their point of view was a spyglass—that is to say, an instrument that was used by a spy—while they might have come from the Austrian side before ascending the hill. This was exceedingly condemnatory in the eyes of a couple of fairly intelligent men, but they treated them politely enough when they explained matters and produced their passports.

A very unpleasant *contretemps*, however, began to develop when the pickets said the passports might be quite correct, but they did not feel justified in releasing the two foreign strangers, who might be, as they said, Englishmen, but who were in all probability Austrians. So they must be taken to their officer, who was about a mile farther on.

It was a case of only two to two, and Henty's blood began to grow hot at the opposition. He was on the point of showing his

FARES: *passengers*
PICKETS: *guards*
CONTRETEMPS: *awkward situation*

resentment, but wiser counsels prevailed; after all, it was two well-mounted and well-armed soldiers of the flower of the Italian cavalry against a couple of civilians, and, feeling that this was one of the occasions when discretion is the better part of valour, especially as a seat in a carriage was a post of disadvantage when opposed to a swordsman in a saddle, he swallowed his wrath and told the driver to go in the direction indicated by his captors. For the first time in his life he realized what it was to be a prisoner with a mounted guard.

The officer, who proved to be a sergeant, received them with Italian politeness, listened to their explanations, and at the end pointed out that the movements of the carriage, which might have come from an entirely different direction from that which they asserted, and the use of the telescope, looked so suspicious in the face of the nearness of the enemy, that he must make them accompany him to his captain about a couple of miles away.

Matters were beginning to grow dramatic, and the feeling of uneasiness increased, for as a war correspondent no one could have realized more readily than Henty that he was undoubtedly looked upon as a spy, and one whom the sergeant felt he must in no wise suffer to escape, for he and his companion were now being escorted by a guard of four of the Guides.

There was nothing for it, however, but to put a good face upon the matter and keep perfectly cool, though, to say the least of it, affairs were growing very unpleasant. It was an accident the consequences of which might be very ugly indeed, and this appealed very strongly to his active imagination. When he set off from the offices of the *Standard* upon his letter-writing mission, no thought of ever being arrested and possibly sentenced as a spy had ever entered into his calculations.

Henty gives the merest skeleton of his adventure, but as a man who was in the habit of writing adventures and who possessed

SKELETON: *outline*

the active imaginative brain previously alluded to, it stands to reason that in the circumstances he must have thought out what he would have set down if he had been writing an account of the treatment likely to be meted out to an enemy's spy, especially to a hated Austrian, by the hot-blooded patriotic Italians.

Some distance farther on in the warlike district, Henty and his companion were escorted to a small village occupied by about a hundred of the Guides and about twice as many Bersaglieri. Here they were in the presence of superior officers, before whom they were brought, and to whom they again explained and produced their passports, and in addition Henty brought out a letter of recommendation to the officers of the Italian army, with which he had been furnished before starting on his journey by the kindness of the Italian ambassador in London.

Here there was another example of the refined Italian politeness, and Henty must have felt a strange resentment against this extreme civility, so suggestive of the treatment that was being meted out to a man who was being adjudged before an ultimate condemnation, for the officers declared that the explanations were no doubt perfectly correct, but that in the circumstances it was their duty to forward the two prisoners to their general. The general was about half a dozen miles away, while, as unfortunately one of their men had been wounded, they must ask the strangers to put their carriage at the service of the poor fellow, who was suffering terribly from the jolting of the bullock-cart in which he lay with five other wounded men, lesser sufferers.

Accordingly Henty and his friend had to take their places on the bullock-cart with five wounded Austrian prisoners, and the procession started. A circumstance that was extremely ominous was that they were preceded by another cart in which was

BERSAGLIERI: *Italian sharpshooters*
METED OUT: *given*

another prisoner. This man was a spy about whom there was not the slightest doubt, for he had been caught in the reprehensible act, and his fate would most probably be to have an extremely short shrift and be shot in the morning. These were facts that impressed themselves very painfully upon the imagination of the young war correspondent, who must have felt that going before the general in such extremely bad company was almost enough to seal his fate, and he felt the more bitter from the simple and natural fact that it would be most likely impossible for him to send a final letter to the *Standard* to record that his unfortunate engagement was at an end.

The decision having been made as well as the change, matters looked worse and worse, for the procession was now guarded by a line of about thirty cavalry. In front and rear marched a company of the Italian foot, while the officers proceeded cautiously, as the road on their side ran close to the Mincio,[1] across which the Austrians might at any moment make a sortie.

Then the proceedings grew still more dramatic and depressing, for several military camps were passed, out of which the men came running to look at the prisoners, and on hearing from the escort that one of the party was a spy, they began to make remarks that were the reverse of pleasant. All the same the young captain in command of the Guides was particularly civil to Henty, and did all he could to make his position as little unpleasant as possible, chatting freely about the last engagement and the part his squadron had taken in the fight. But he was much taken up in looking after his troops, and his English prisoners had plenty of time for meditation as to their future prospects, and the outlook was not reassuring.

At last headquarters were reached, and after a short detention the prisoners were taken before the General, Henty

[1] A river in northern Italy

REPREHENSIBLE: *shameful*
SHORT SHRIFT: *a hurried time for the confession of sins to a priest*

preserving all the time the calm, firm appearance that he had maintained from the first; and in all probability it was his quiet confidence that saved his life.

The General examined the passports and the Italian ambassador's letter of recommendation, and at length in the most polite way set them at liberty, but in a manner that suggested that Henty must grasp the fact that in a state of war, if he went too close to the scene of action, such incidents were bound to occur.

Their carriage was brought round, and in better spirits they started back. At the first town they reached they found the place was full of troops. Hungry and hopeful of a pleasant meal, they tried, but in vain, at the different hostelries to get something to eat, though finally, as a favour, they obtained a piece of bread, the last in the house, and some wine. They again started, but when they reached another town their tired horses gave in, and they had to get out and walk.

It was now nearly eleven o'clock at night, and one may imagine the weary tramp they had before they reached the Garibaldian pickets. There they were again stopped and were told that without the password they could not enter the town, but must spend the night in their carriage.

More arguments, more explanations, but all proved in vain, and there was a wretched prospect of the rest of the night being passed in misery; but nature seemed at last to have ceased to persecute them, for by good fortune the officer of the night approached making his rounds, and after some parley allowed them to accompany him back to the town. Here, however, more trouble awaited them, for on reaching their hotel at midnight, utterly famished, and calling for supper, it was to find that the Garibaldians had consumed everything. All they could obtain was a cup of coffee, without milk, and they retired to rest,

HOSTELRIES: *inns*
PARLEY: *discussion*

Henty with the feeling upon him that he had had a very narrow escape from being either shot or hanged.

A culminating disaster, by the way, connected with the miserable march to the presence of the general, who was to decide whether or not the war correspondent and his companion were to be treated as spies, was the disappearance of the valuable telescope with which Henty had come provided for making observations in connection with the various engagements between the Italian and the Austrian forces. It was in the carriage when it had to be given up for the use of the wounded, and, as the owner very mildly puts it, "someone took a fancy" to his glass, and he never saw it again, though he met with plenty of occasions when he had bitter cause to regret its loss.

GLASS: *telescope*

CHAPTER VI

THE SEARCH FOR AN ARMY AND A MEAL

IN his early days as war correspondent everything was fresh and bright, and his letters display the keenness of his observation, especially in the way in which he compares, with a soldier's eye, the uniforms and accoutrements of the Italian soldier with those of the troops at home. The special war dress, adapted to the season (June), was of coarse brown holland or canvas, with a loose blue-grey greatcoat, and belt at the waist outside; the cavalry, it being summertime, wore red caps with tassels in place of helmets; the artillery had short jackets and canvas trousers. Everything seemed useful and serviceable. But now the critic comes in, for he writes: "I do not so much like the appearance of the army when on the march." The rate of march was about one-fourth quicker than that of our own soldiers, and to keep up this swift pace the men seemed to be too heavily laden, the greatcoats too hot and cumbrous, and the knapsacks of calfskin too heavy. He begins to calculate what a slaughter there must have been of calves to furnish skins of exactly the same shade of brown for the four hundred thousand infantry of the Italian army.

Then, to add to their load, the men's water-bottles, which were barrel-shaped, were rather larger than those of the British soldier, and each man also carried a canteen about the same

ACCOUTREMENTS: *equipment*
HOLLAND: *a cotton cloth*
CUMBROUS: *bulky*

size. They had a blue haversack well-filled, and to crown all, at the top of the knapsack each man bore the canvas and sticks which form a little tent under which the Sardinian soldier sleeps during a campaign.

Of course he bore also his rifle, bayonet or sword, and ammunition, which increased the weight he had to carry; but the tent added immensely to his comfort, for whereas the British soldier has to pass the night as best he can, perhaps in heavy rain on wet ground, to wake cold, wet through, and unrefreshed, with the seeds of rheumatism in his limbs, the Italian pitches his *tente d'abri* and sleeps in comparative comfort. During the campaign in the Crimea Henty often had occasion to note the magical way in which the Sardinian camp sprang up. The little tents were pitched, the cooking-places established, arbours were made of boughs of trees for the officers' mess-tents, and everything assumed a general air of cheerfulness which contrasted favourably with the camps of the English and of the French.

In these early days in Italy difficulties were many, and he laughingly commences one letter by stating that his doings ought to be headed "The Adventures of a War Correspondent in Search of an Army," for though battalions, regiments, brigades, and even small armies were on the move, the difficulty of getting upon their track was supreme. He writes on one occasion: "We drove through the village" (he was with a companion) "down to the water-side." Here lay the Po,[1] a wide, deep river, as broad as the Thames. There was no bridge of boats. How, then, had the Italians crossed? There was a sentry who looked at them peculiarly, and who when asked if they could pass over to the other side shook his head. They explained that they wished to join the camp, where they had friends, but they could obtain no information. Meanwhile their presence had been attracting attention, and it was evident that they took

[1] A large river flowing across northern Italy

HAVERSACK: *a sack carried over one shoulder*
TENTE D'ABRI: *a tent made of cotton cloth waterproofed with rubber*
MESS-TENTS: *dining tents*

Henty's companion, who was wearing a red shirt, for one of Garibaldi's lieutenants in disguise. The people were appealed to for information as to whether the Italian army had crossed there, and at last they managed to gain the information that fifty thousand soldiers had crossed in the night. But that was all the news to be gleaned.

At last, however, they got upon the track of the army and well amidst the fighting that was going on, and he writes to his paper that he proposes during the next few days to give full accounts of the desperate encounters between the Sardinian army, aided by the Garibaldians, and the Austrians, "unless a bullet should put a period to my writing."

But, as stated in another place, where Henty deals with the effect produced upon an observer by shells and the amount of mischief they do in the open, a man who has his business to think of in connection with reporting the movements of an army has not time to think of the risks he runs, and Henty troubled himself but little concerning the destiny of a stray bullet. The old proverb says that every bullet has its billet, the falsity of which statement has been often enough proved in modern warfare by statisticians comparing the numbers of killed and wounded with those of the ball cartridges expended during some fight, unless, indeed, the word billet is taken to include the place where every missile falls. In fact, when dealing with the firing at Magdala,[1] where the British infantry made use of the breech-loading rifle for the first time, Henty criticized severely the waste of cartridges by the men, who, armed with the new easily-loaded weapon, scattered the bullets, without stopping to aim, at a rate calculated to leave them without cartridges in a very short space of time.

Speaking as a practised officer of the Commissariat Department, his attention was much more drawn to the difficulties

---

[1] The capital city of Abyssinia (Ethiopia), destroyed by the British during the Abyssinian Campaign of 1868

BILLET: *lodging*

BREECH-LOADING RIFLES: *rifles loaded at the "breech" or base of the barrel rather than at the muzzle*

in connection with the task of obtaining enough to eat. As regards shelter and sleep, he was ready enough to make shift with anything that offered of the former, and many a time the open sky was his cover, and a blanket or waterproof sheet his only protection from the rain.

He fared worst, save in the way of sociability, when following in the track of those gallant, thoughtless Sons of Freedom, the Garibaldians. On one occasion he and a companion made their way to one of the many battlefields by the side of one of the Italian lakes, where the ground that had been defended by the Garibaldians was covered with scattered trees. Beyond these the hillside was bare, but dotted with huge boulders of stone, which had been taken advantage of by the Austrian Tyrolese riflemen, and where they sheltered themselves to pick off the young patriots.

Down below, the road ran by the shore of the lake, and here the Austrian column had done their best to cut off the Garibaldians. On passing through this debatable ground the road rose considerably, and it became necessary for the two correspondents to practise care lest they should be mistaken for enemies, for by the side of the road were numbers of the shelter arbours run up by the Garibaldians, and these were occupied, for the sake of the shelter they afforded from the burning sun.

Here Henty describes the beauty of the scene across the valley at the head of the beautiful lake. Full in view were two villages, occupied, the one by the followers of the great Italian patriot, the other by the Austrians. The mountain road had been guarded on one side by a low parapet wall to save it from the rushing storm waters that swept down from above after heavy rains, and here in two places ominous preparations had been made in readiness to check any advance on the part of the Austrians, the parapet being cleared away to form embrasures, out

EMBRASURES: *narrow windows or openings*

of which grinned the muzzles of the field-pieces, ready to belch forth their deadly shower of grape and round shot. Here, too, was a deep ravine coming down at right angles to the road, offering excellent ground for a tactician to place his forces to advantage and deal out destruction upon advancing troops.

Along the side of the ravine ran the road to the Italian village, for which the two correspondents were making, in the hopes of obtaining food and shelter. As they passed on they found parties of Garibaldians encamped along the whole length of the road, and their sentries were ready to stop farther advance and demand their business and their passes. These, however, were found to be *en règle*, and they were allowed to continue their journey to the village, which they soon found was occupied by portions of a couple of regiments and a battalion of Bersaglieri, by far the finest and most reliable portion of Garibaldi's forces.

Henty and his friend, warned by previous experience, had taken the precaution to carry supplies with them, the said supplies being of the simplest description, a substance, in fact, which is always welcome to a hungry man, made delicious by the addition of the proverbial sauce. In other words, they carried in their satchels portions of the homely cake-bread of the country, upon which they depended, feeling no anxiety about obtaining their share of the abundant spring water of the district.

Thus provided, they had but one trouble, and that was as regarded lodgings. They went at once to the only inn of the village, to find it closed. This was discouraging, and they passed on, to find that almost all the shops of the little place were also closed. Checked by this, they made for a group of the Bersaglieri, who seemed to be well-supplied with their little thin cigars, the pale-blue threads of smoke from which curled lightly out in the evening sunshine.

GRAPE: *grapeshot, small metal balls fired from a cannon*
TACTICIAN: *someone who is skilled in military tactics*
EN RÈGLE: *"in order" in French*
HOMELY: *simple*

The deeply-bronzed soldiery politely exchanged salutes as the travellers questioned them about the prospect of finding a resting-place for the night, the answer to which was: "Have you any bread?" "Yes," replied Henty. "Well, then," said a Garibaldian, with a smile which showed his white teeth, "you may think yourselves very lucky, signori, for we have had none today, and though we have had notice that some will come in this afternoon, it is more likely that it will not."

This was disconcerting; but feeling that they could travel no farther they determined to persevere, in the hope that something might turn up; and if matters did prove to be at the worst they still had their open carriage, which would, at all events, with its cushions make sleep more easy, and keep them off the ground.

They had given a lift to one of the Garibaldians, and though amused by their predicament, he laughingly tried to assist them by suggesting that they should go on, and stop and knock at every door until they found someone who would give them a lodging. The notion seemed to be good, and to carry out the Italian's suggestion they drew up at the best-looking house they could see, and knocked boldly at the door.

This was opened by an elderly priest, who raised his eyebrows in wonder, and glanced at the carriage and its occupants, and then at the Garibaldian who was acting as their guide, when an eager conversation ensued in the soft fluent Italian tongue. The guide, speaking with energy, explained with enthusiasm that those whom he had brought to claim the priest's hospitality were two English gentlemen, whose hearts were in the Italian cause, and who, much interested, had come out on purpose to see the war; they were weary with their long journey and sought a refuge for the night—a lodging for which they were perfectly ready to pay with the customary generosity of their nation.

DISCONCERTING: *unsettling*
FLUENT: *flowing*

It was all very flowery, but most effective, for the priest smiled and bowed and bade them enter, declaring his readiness to place a room at their service, but shrugging his shoulders as he told with much gesticulation how he lamented that owing to the exactions of the Austrians, who had been there only the week before, and many of whom had been quartered in the house, he had nothing in the way of food to offer them; however, anything they could procure his servants would cook.

Perhaps it was due to perseverance having been rewarded and to having gained a lodging that, hungry though they were, they began to contemn their supply of bread. Surely, they thought, in a village like this it should not be impossible to find something more tasty, now that they were provided with a cook. So they sallied out, and leaving the more frequented streets, which swarmed with the hungry volunteers, they turned down first one lane and then another with no result. At length Henty, tired by his journey, was beginning to feel a return of the despondency which attacks a hungry man, when he stopped short, catching his companion by the arm and holding up his hand, for from a small house on one side of the lane he heard a familiar suggestive sound, which is precisely the same in the boot of Italy as it is in some rustic English county. It was the welcome cluck of fowls, shut up somewhere behind bars for safety. This promised a prize if negotiation were carried to a successful issue, and hands involuntarily plunged into pockets, to be followed by the faint and smothered chink of coin. Money should be able to purchase poultry at some price or other, even in times of war; if not, as it *was* a time of war, and as the two young Englishmen were upon a foraging expedition in a foreign country, why should they not—

Dark thoughts suggested themselves, and visions of a bright fire and a browning chicken began to dawn and sharpen the

GESTICULATION: *gesturing*
EXACTIONS: *demands*
QUARTERED: *housed*
CONTEMN: *regard with contempt*
SALLIED OUT: *set out*

rising appetite, but they were dissipated at once by the opening of the door, at which they had loudly knocked. An animated parley commenced with the occupant of the cottage, the said parley ending at last in the correspondents becoming the masters of a couple of fowls, whose united ages, by the way, they found, when they came to eat them, must have been a long way on towards the age of one of themselves.

But all the same they felt satisfied in their ravenous condition at having obtained even these world-worn birds at only about five times their proper price, especially as on returning towards the priest's house they again encountered the friendly Garibaldians, who had been less fortunate than themselves.

There was still another drawback, that which comes to a hungry man even though he has obtained a whole fowl to himself, and this was the waiting while it was cooked. While this was in process Henty had to try and curb his impatience by examining the beauty of the scenery. But at last the repast was ready, and their friend the priest made them up beds, on which they passed the night in a far more luxurious manner than they had anticipated.

DISSIPATED: *dispelled*
REPAST: *meal*

CHAPTER VII

THE BATTLE OF LISSA

THERE were times when Henty had to take shelter from the Austrian fire, and others when he found himself exposed to that of the friendly army, whose skirmishers, made plainly visible by their scarlet shirts, began to send up little puffs of smoke from behind hedges and amongst trees, while crack! crack! the reports of the rifles rang out and echoed down the ravines, to die away amongst the distant hills.

Then, too, one of his narrow escapes happened when he was on his way to Brescia. He had some difficulty in getting there, for every vehicle was requisitioned for the public service, and he thought himself extremely lucky in being able to get his luggage sent on, leaving him free to undertake the walk of some five-and-twenty miles. This was no serious undertaking to a well-shod athlete, being only one-fifth more than a tramp across our own Dartmoor, but with this difference, that the home walk would be through the crisp bracing air some fif-teen hundred feet above the sea, while here the labour was very heavy, the heat of the Italian July sun being tremendous.

However, just when he had proceeded halfway on his jour-ney, and was suffering severely from the torrid air, which felt too hot to breathe, he, little anticipating what was to prove the outcome, congratulated himself upon what he looked upon as

REQUISITIONED: *taken by the government*
TORRID: *scorching*

a stroke of luck, for, hearing wheels behind, he drew up by the side of the road, to stand panting and wiping his streaming brow, signing to the military driver of a government cart. This man willingly agreed to give him a lift as his destination was the same, and explained that he was going to fetch a load of ice for the benefit of the wounded.

It was rough travelling, but the change from the labour of tramping the road, which seemed to return the heat of the sun with fivefold power, was delightful, and the rattle and bumping of the clumsy cart by contrast became almost an exquisite pleasure.

In this way five more miles were added to those which he had walked, and in describing the adventure which followed, Henty naïvely remarks that doubtless he should have ridden happily the whole distance into Brescia had not the ill-groomed, blind mare which drew the cart, suddenly conceived that she was being ill-treated by the addition of this stranger to her load. She accordingly stopped short and began lashing out most viciously, nearly breaking the arm of the soldier who was driving, and then dashed off at full speed. Seeing that she was blind, her course was not a very long one, and before they had gone far down the mountain road which gradually grew more and more shelf-like, the mare's flight became wildly erratic, until she checked herself most painfully by running her head against the rocks which rose up on their right. After holding his breath for some time Henty relieved his overburdened chest in a deep sigh, for he had been debating in those brief minutes whether he should not risk everything and trust to his agility to spring out. He now, however, began to breathe freely, and, dropping down from the cart into the road, he stared about him at his position, and realized how very near he had been to bringing his correspondent's task to a sudden end. Had the mare in her

ERRATIC: *unpredictable*

blindness turned to the left instead of the right, horse, cart, and its occupants would have gone headlong over the low protecting parapet at the side, deep down a stony precipice, with only one result.

In his matter-of-fact way Henty goes on to say: "This was not a thing to be tried twice, and I once more set off to walk, and in a mile came to a village, where by great luck I found a vehicle which brought me into Brescia in safety."

In his eagerness to obtain the fullest information about the military proceedings between the opposing armies, Henty never spared himself. Wherever there was an engagement pending, or taking place, if it were in the slightest degree possible he would be there, running all risks, and at any cost; so that when the news came of the possibility of there being a naval engagement between the Italian and Austrian fleets, it was only natural that with his sailor-like proclivities Henty should wish to be present.

As we have seen, he was well-provided with introductions and credentials which facilitated his being with the army; but these hardly seemed likely to benefit him much with the navy. However, he was not the man to be daunted by difficulties. If a naval fight did take place, it was bound to be one of special interest, for though for years past the old-fashioned wooden walls and two- and three-deckers of this and other countries had been gradually changing into armour-clads, this was to be the first occasion when an encounter would take place between the ponderous monsters. It was an event which would prove, not only to scientists but to their captains and crews, how they would behave.

The question that arose, therefore, was how the representative of the *Standard* could get on board one of the vessels. Doubting what reception would be given to one who announced

PROCLIVITIES: *tendencies*
PONDEROUS: *massive*

himself as a war correspondent, Henty proceeded, sailor-like, upon another tack. After the training he had gone through and the work he had done, he considered himself justified in posing as an engineer eager to grasp exactly what would take place under fire, and in this character, as a scientific man, the difficulty was solved, for he was allowed to be present at the naval battle which took place in the Mediterranean off Lissa, the principal island of Dalmatia, some forty miles from the mainland, on the 20th of July, 1866.

It was no trivial affair, but one as worthy of notice as any of the great battles of history, for the Italian fleet which set sail consisted of twelve iron-clads and eight wooden frigates, with their attendant gun and dispatch boats.

The island was strongly fortified by the Austrians, and the battle began with an attack upon the forts, which responded fiercely, and the grim reality of the encounter was soon learned by those on the iron-clads when shells began to burst on board. But this attack was only in anticipation of the coming of the Austrian fleet, which was soon after signalled as being in sight, and its formidable nature was evident directly it approached. Its three lines were composed of seven iron-clads, one wooden ship of the line, five wooden frigates, two corvettes, and twelve gunboats, the last mentioned carrying six guns each.

The two fleets were not long in coming to close quarters, and it was soon proved that sailors could fight as well in iron-clads as in the towering old wooden craft of yore.

The thunder was deeper from the much heavier modern guns, the impact of the modern missiles (elongated bolts, not balls) and the crash of the bursting explosive with which they were charged far more awful; but amidst the noise, confusion, and deafening explosions the spectator could grasp but little of what was taking place outside the vessel he was on.

TACK: *course of action*
CORVETTES: *small, fast warships*
YORE: *olden days*
NOVELTY: *uniqueness*

There was a certain grim novelty about being rammed, and the shock sent everyone who was not holding on prostrate, convinced, or at least quite ready to imagine, that the vessel struck must be sent to the bottom. But this portion of the encounter did not prove to be so damaging as was anticipated, probably owing to the close quarters into which the two fleets were brought, and to the want of impetus of the striking ship. In fact, as the broadsides were exchanged, and the vessels were passing and repassing each other, they were in such close neighbourhood that at times the muzzles of the guns almost touched each other, and the effect was terrific. Numbers of men were killed on board the vessel upon which Henty made his mental notes. Shells crashed upon the iron armour, and were in some cases thrown off, but others passed in through the portholes and burst inside, committing terrible havoc, while at one time a broadside was received which glanced off. A vast amount of damage was done, though, when they ran stem on to the nearest opponent with an awful crash and then backed off, to see dimly through the smoke that the Austrian adversary was evidently sinking.

The result was that the Battle of Lissa supplied ample proof of the consequences following an encounter between two ironclad fleets; but it was days after the noise and turmoil of the battle were at an end that Henty found an opportunity to pay a visit to the Italian fleet with the object of ascertaining how the various systems of iron-plating had borne the hammering of the shot and shell during this novel sea-fight.

His first visit was to a vessel of nearly six thousand tons burden, and before going on board he was pulled slowly round her, stopping from time to time to examine the shot marks in her side. And now it was surprising to see how little damage had been done. The shot had made round dents of four to

PROSTRATE: *flat on the deck*
IMPETUS: *motion or force*
TERRIFIC: *frightful*
HAVOC: *destruction*
ASCERTAINING: *seeing for himself*

five inches in diameter, and from one to two and a half inches deep, but the marks made by the shells in the armour-plate were more ragged, some of the dents being from eight to twelve inches in diameter, rough and uneven, while, when a shell had struck where the plates joined, pieces were broken completely off. Altogether, as far as her iron armour was concerned, this vessel, which had been engaged for more than an hour with two or three Austrian iron-clads, came out of the ordeal remarkably well. Not one of her plates was penetrated, cracked, or seriously loosened; but on getting round to her stern her weak point was at once noticeable, and that was the rudder, which was quite unprotected. Some six or seven feet of the unarmoured stern also was quite exposed, a fact which resulted in the loss of a sister ship, whose rudder was disabled almost at the beginning of the contest, so that she soon became an easy prey to her adversaries.

In the case of the *Re de Porto Gallo*, the vessel Henty visited, her iron-plating was covered with a casing of wood, some nine inches thick, to a height of two feet above the water-line, and upon this her copper sheathing was fastened. The whole of her port bulwark, with the exception of some fifty feet at the stern, was carried away by a collision with the adversary, the two vessels grinding together along their whole length.

On mounting to the deck, Henty goes on to say, he first began to see to what a terrible fire she had been exposed. Her rigging had been cut to pieces; black ragged holes where shells had struck and burst were to be seen; her boats were completely smashed to pieces.

In the case of another vessel, the shot and shell marks were rather deeper, and the dents and ragged marks of the shells indicated that she had had to encounter heavier metal, while Henty's keen scrutiny showed him that the iron-plating which

STERN: *the back of the ship*
PORT: *the left side of the ship*
BULWARK: *a wall running along the main deck*

protected her must have been of a much more brittle nature; but even here it was quite plain to him that the protection afforded by the ponderous iron plates was most effective, and it was remarkable, considering how close the adversaries had been together, that more serious damage had not been done.

In noticing Henty's account of the iron clothing of the Italian fleet, and the effect upon the ships of the enemy's guns, it must be borne in mind that some forty years have wrought vast changes in naval warfare, and it can easily be conceived how different would have been the havoc wrought if the encounter had been with the armament of such a vessel as, say our own unfortunate *Montagu*,[1] or the *Sutlej*, with the twin occupants of its revolving turrets and the ponderous bolt-shaped shells they could hurl.

These investigations appear to have been of the greatest interest to the young correspondent, but he was not satisfied; the sailor within him made itself heard. He was satisfied with the value of armour-plates in protecting a man-of-war, but he wanted to know how, plated with these ponderous pieces of iron, such vessels would behave in a heavy sea.

He had not long to wait, for he wrote directly afterwards that there had been a heavy squall, and one of the iron-clad fleet had had to run for the harbour, rolling so much from her weight, and shipping so much water, that she went down; but, fortunately, all hands were saved.

There had been a day of intense heat. The next morning it was hot and close without a breath of wind, and Henty states that he had been rowed across the harbour for his morning dip. At that time there was not a ripple upon the water, but on his return at nine o'clock the sky was becoming a good deal overcast, while about half-past ten he was a witness of one of the squalls peculiar to the Mediterranean, and made familiar

---

[1] The battleship *HMS Montagu* ran aground during a fog in 1906.

MAN-OF-WAR: *warship*
SHIPPING: *taking in*

to old-fashioned people in the words and music of "The White Squall."[1] Sheets of water, without the least preliminary warning, dropped suddenly from the clouds; the furious wind tore along, driving before it every light object; outdoor chairs and tables were swept away, and the wind was master of everything for about twenty minutes. When the fierce storm had passed on, and the rain had ceased, he, knowing what the consequences of such a raging tempest must be, hurried down to the landing-place to note what the sea had done.

He was astounded. His first looks were directed at the ironclads. They were lying at anchor, and rolling bulwark-deep in so alarming a manner that it was fully proved to him that, had necessity forced them to go into action, they could not have opened their portholes to work their guns, for had they done so they would certainly have been swamped.

Nature seemed to be mocking at the ponderous vessels, and green seas were rushing completely along the decks of the ironclad which afterwards foundered.

He could see at the time by means of a telescope that the crew were engaged in dragging tarpaulins over her hatchways, while from the funnels of the whole fleet dense clouds of black smoke were rolling up, as the engineers were evidently working hard to get up steam, so as to relieve the strain upon their anchors, or to enable their captains to shift their berths. Later he could see that several of the vessels had taken shelter in the harbour, but the *Affondatore* was still in her berth, with her engines hard at work going ahead to relieve the strain upon her anchor.

Speaking as one accustomed to the sea, he was under the impression that the captain was afraid to make for the harbour, outside which the vessel lay, for to have done so would have necessitated his exposing her broadside to the tremendous waves, which, though the sea had somewhat subsided, still swept right

---

[1] A poem written by William Makepeace Thackeray (1811-1863)

FOUNDERED: *filled with water and sank*
BERTHS: *the places where the ships were anchored*

over her bows. These were now apparently two or three feet lower than the stern, so that at the utmost the ponderous vessel was only six feet out of the water altogether, and she looked as if she had taken a great deal of water on board.

At length, as Henty watched, he began to see that she was changing her position. Her head turned slowly towards the harbour, her main-sail was set to steady her, and she began to steam slowly in. But in spite of the sail that had been hoisted she rolled heavily, and by degrees seemed to have lost all power of riding over the waves, which now made a clean sweep over her, until at times he lost sight of her bow for some seconds together.

At last, after expecting from time to time to see her founder, he saw that she had reached the harbour in safety, to anchor just inside the end of the mole, some three hundred yards from shore, and, growing excited as he felt in doubt about her position, he jumped into a boat and pulled out to her, to find that her bow was not above two feet out of water, while her stern was a foot higher than it had been on the previous day. In spite of man-of-war order, a good deal of excitement evidently prevailed. The crew were busily engaged in relieving her bows by carrying all weight as far aft as possible, and evidence of the peril of her position was plainly shown by the engines being hard at work pumping.

So he began to feel hopeful that as the vessel was now in still water she would be safe, but the hope was vain. Either recent repairs over the shot holes received in action had given way, or some of her upper plating, weakened by a shot, had opened with the strain. Whatever was wrong, as Henty watched he could see that she was getting lower in the water, which in little more than another half-hour was level with her bow.

Then it was that, feeling that it was impossible to do more, orders were given which resulted in the boats being lowered,

BOWS: *the front of the ship*
MOLE: *a breakwater used to protect the harbor*
AFT: *toward the rear of the ship*

and with discipline well-preserved they were manned, while launches came out to her assistance and took off the crew to the last man.

It was a painful scene which soon followed. The grand vessel's bow was now some distance below the surface, while the stern still maintained its buoyancy; but all at once, as if the iron-clad monster were making a desperate struggle for life, she gave a sudden heavy roll before steadying herself, and remained in her proper position with only a slight list to starboard. Then she sank slowly and calmly, and all was over with the gallant ship.

Henty described at length the Battle of Lissa, of which no better account could have been given than that of this unbiased spectator; but upon the appearance of a lengthy official report, he did not hesitate to turn stern critic and fall foul of the brag and bombast which disfigured its columns. No doubt to flatter Italian pride this was so full of inflation, that the English correspondent flatly compared it with the never-to-be-forgotten narrative delivered by the stout knight to Prince Hal and his companions.[1]

---

[1] *Henry IV, Act 2, Scene 4* by William Shakespeare (1564-1616)
LIST: *lean*
STARBOARD: *the right side of the ship*
BRAG AND BOMBAST: *pompous boasting*
INFLATION: *an exaggerated view of the events*

Chapter VIII

The End of the War

HENTY writes of Brescia as a Garibaldian town, that is to say, a town garrisoned by volunteers, and after being there for some days gaining knowledge of these patriots, he takes advantage of the occasion to attempt some description of their state.

At one time he found the station crowded as if the whole population had assembled, and he explains the reason of the unusual scene. A train of enormous length had just entered the station crammed with red-shirted volunteers, who were being received with tremendous cheers, which they responded to as lustily. Then ensued an affecting scene, for numbers of the regiment had friends and relations in the town who were searching eagerly from carriage to carriage inquiring if they were safe.

The train was only to stop for ten minutes, and the men were not supposed to alight; but no orders could keep them in, and a scene of wild embracing, handshaking, and kissing ensued, mingled with eager inquiries after relatives in other regiments, good wishes, and farewells. Then the station bell rang and the train moved on, the soldiers waiting till the last moment and then jumping on as it was in motion, so that as it moved out of the station it presented an extraordinary aspect, men in scarlet

GARRISONED: *defended*
LUSTILY: *enthusiastically*
ALIGHT: *leave the train*
ASPECT: *appearance*

shirts leaning out of every window and standing on the footboard the whole length as closely as they could, while others were even on the roofs, and all waving their hands and cheering. He heard afterwards that some of the men in their enthusiasm and excitement rode the whole of their journey upon the steps, while three or four in the various trains were killed from leaning too far out and striking their heads against the abutments of bridges.

The commissariat arrangements, into which as a matter of course he would be prone to inquire, were, he declares, vile. In fact, he says the arrangements for feeding these poor fellows were, like all other matters connected with the volunteers, shamefully bad. Some of them, in a three days' journey, had no food but bread and cheese and a little wine.

At another town he found the place crowded with Garibaldians, who had taken possession bodily of the inn he reached. Tables were spread out in the courtyard, at which parties were sitting; upstairs and down the inn was thronged. The landlady and waiters received their English visitors with an air of languid indifference very different from their customary manner. At the first complaint Henty was assured that for three days and nights they had not rested, and that as fast as one regiment of the volunteers went off another took its place. The men were all famished by long fasting in the train, and only too glad to sit down to a regular meal again.

Here he found that although the Garibaldians were better clad than when he first encountered them, for they had all got red shirts, and caps of some shape or other, many of them were sadly neglected. Some were almost shoeless, others had only just previously received their arms. Moreover, with the exception of the Bersaglieri regiments, which had ten rounds of ball cartridge each, no ammunition whatever had been supplied.

ABUTMENTS: *the supports on either side of bridges*
LANGUID: *sluggish*

They were in a melancholy state for an active force just taking the field—no shelter tents, so that they had to sleep in the open air, and most of them had only one blanket to serve as a cloak in the daytime and a cover at night.

Some of them had not even this poor protection, and had to sleep on the ground, however wet the night, with no other protection than their red shirts and trousers. Fortunately for them, they had patriotic faith and enthusiasm; but there was no ambulance train or any accommodation whatever for the wounded, and, speaking generally, the commissariat arrangements were so bad that it was no unusual thing for a regiment to go all day without food.

The result was indignation on the part of the volunteers at the scandalous treatment they were receiving; but this only made them still more desirous to get at the enemy and show that, ill-used though they were, when it came to fighting they could do as well as the line. For it seemed that there was considerable jealousy and ill-feeling between the two services, the Garibaldians believing firmly that the treatment they were receiving was caused by those in authority, and when the news came of a disastrous defeat of the regular troops, it was received by the volunteers with something like satisfaction and a full belief that they would do better when their turn came.

"Indeed," says Henty, "it must be owned that they had very much more than a sufficiently good opinion of themselves, for they firmly believed that they could defeat anything like an equal number of Austrians, even though the latter were provided with artillery, as they would be."

Henty learned from the plucky fellows that they did not believe much in the value of ball cartridges, but pinned their faith entirely on the bayonet, against which weapon he did not believe that they would be able to stand for an instant.

THE LINE: *the regular troops*
OWNED: *acknowledged*

His opinion was that if the Garibaldians came upon a body of the well-drilled Austrians in a steep place, or where they were in confusion, the volunteers' impetuous onslaught would be irresistible; but on the other hand, he could not believe that out on the plain disorderly rushes could ever break the Austrians' steady steel lines.

At this time a battery of mountain artillery was attached to Garibaldi's command; but the guns were so clumsy and the carriages so primitive that Henty believed they were not likely to prove of much assistance, and, continuing his remarks about the uniformity and aspect of the Garibaldian troops, he grimly notes that consequent upon sleeping upon the wet ground, the red shirts were beginning to lose their original brilliancy of colour. He has, though, a few words of praise for the volunteer cavalry, the Guides, who were extremely useful as vedettes. Their grey-blue uniform with black cord braiding, natty scarlet caps and high boots, gave them a very soldier-like appearance, while for night duty they had very long cloaks of the same colour as the uniform, and lined with scarlet.

Henty had always words of praise for the unquenchable pluck of the Garibaldians, the indomitable determination that, in spite of bad drilling, clumsy discipline, and bad leading, finally led them to success. Garibaldi himself, however, came in for criticism, for he declares, after recording a wound that the general had received, that it was greatly to be regretted that he should expose himself to danger, and that his young officers should be so eager to do the fighting themselves instead of steadying their men and leading them.

Then again he attacks the commissariat in his customary, vigorous way, while reporting after one of the fights the wantonness which could send three thousand men from a town to

IMPETUOUS: *sudden*
VEDETTES: *mounted scouts*
NATTY: *neat, trim*
INDOMITABLE: *unconquerable*
WANTONNESS: *carelessness*

march twenty-five miles without breakfast to begin with or supper to finish with, this being only a common specimen of the commissariat arrangements. "Certainly," he seems to growl, in a quotation, "somebody ought to be hanged; I do not know who it is, nor do I care, but such mismanagement has, I believe, never been equalled. All the same," he says, "the volunteers take it with wonderful good temper."

Picturesque, he says, as was the appearance of the Garibaldian camp, so bright and gay with the scarlet shirts of the soldiery and the green arbours, that it looked like a gigantic military picnic, it was the abode of as badly a fed set of men as were to be found in Europe. A little bread or biscuit and soup, doled out at the most uncertain intervals, with occasionally meat and frequently nothing at all, was the food which the government of Italy bestowed upon her volunteers, many of whom had left luxurious homes to fight her battles; and in some cases the men were so reduced from weakness that at certain stations many of them had to be taken into hospital. The poor fellows were fed, when fed at all, with a mixture with bread swimming in it which was called soup, but which was utterly innocent of meat in its composition, and tasted simply of tepid water; a sort of raw sausage, flavoured strongly with garlic, and a mess of either rice or macaroni, with something called meat in it, but utterly untastable; and yet this same food was at one time, while Henty was with the volunteer army, all that he could depend upon for himself—that or nothing. Campaigning with the Garibaldians was sorry work, but, soldier-like, Henty tightened his belt and fought his way on with the volunteers in expectation until they won.

Still with the headquarters of Garibaldi, and in the midst of the heat of an Italian July, Henty writes again in the midst of

WONDERFUL: *surprising*
INNOCENT: *free*
TEPID: *lukewarm*

warfare, with all day long the boom of cannon and the sharp crack of musketry sounding in his ears. And as he writes, he says, the confusion outside, the talking of innumerable Garibaldians under the window of the humble room of which he thinks himself fortunate to call himself master for the time, the rumbling of carts, the shouting of the drivers, and the occasional call of the bugle, all remind him that he is in the midst of war on a large scale.

The heat has been terrible; not a breath of wind stirring, and the cicada in the vineyards which line the roads through which he has passed have been in the full tide of song. "The noise," he says, "that these insects make on a hot day is something astounding. It is a continued succession of sharp shrill sounds such as might be made by a child upon a little whistle." He asks his reader to imagine an army of children, thousands strong, lining the road and all blowing upon these whistles, "and you will have an idea of the prodigious thrill of sound produced by myriads of these creatures."

"Zeno," he says, "the old Greek philosopher who was mated to a shrew, is reported to have exclaimed: 'Happy the lives of the cicadæ, since they all have voiceless wives.' But I think that it is equally fortunate for humanity in general, for if the female cicadæ were in any way as voluble as the males, it would be impossible to exist in the neighbourhood of the vineyards at all without losing one's sense of hearing."

But insects, the boom of cannon, the rumble of tumbrels, and the crackle of musketry notwithstanding, the war correspondent's communications had to be written, and two of his most interesting pieces of news, which are rather ominous in sound, are that the general's son, Ricciotti Garibaldi, who is serving as a private in the Guides, is at present ill, though nothing serious is apprehended, while Garibaldi's wound still

PRODIGIOUS: *tremendous*
MYRIADS: *great numbers*
MATED: *married*
SHREW: *a violent, ill-tempered woman*
VOLUBLE: *talkative*

causes him great pain and inconvenience. He can do nothing for himself, but he is the enthusiastic general still, even though he has to be lifted from the sofa upon which he lies all day, and carried by four men to his carriage, the anxiety he feels at the state of affairs greatly retarding his recovery.

TUMBRELS: *two-wheeled carts used to carry ammunition*
RETARDING: *hindering*

CHAPTER IX

IMPRESSIONS OF ITALY

IN what had now become a sight-seeing perfect holiday time for Henty, prior to his being present to witness the entry of the Italian troops into Venice and the departure of the Austrians, Ravenna, with its antiquities, its museums and traditions, was too great an attraction to a literary man to be passed over. He appreciated to the full the ruins of the old Christian churches, the cathedrals, the traces of the Roman emperors, the glorious fir woods with their pleasant shades, and raked up memories of poet and student who had been attracted there in their time, such as Dante, Boccaccio, and Dryden. All three have written their recollections, while Byron worked there, finding other points of interest beyond its quiet charm. For it was in Venice that he wrote *Marino Faliero, The Two Foscari, Cain*, and other poems.

But every city of the Italian plains had its attractions for Henty, and his writings at this date are one long record of a country which teems with memories of the past.

Much as he was interested in the fairs and markets and antiquities, Henty was too much of the sailor and soldier not to be attracted by a little scene at Ancona on his last morning there, and that was in connection with the landing from the fleet of a body of sailors for certain evolutions upon the parade. They brought ashore twelve light guns, apparently about

TEEMS: *overflows*
EVOLUTIONS: *maneuvers*
PARADE: *public square*

five-pounders, each manned by six Italian Jacks. These guns were promptly taken to pieces, and a couple of the men caught up the gun, the rest the wheels, ammunition boxes and carriages, and bore them down to the boats. Then, at the word of command, they carried them up again to the drill-ground, and in a little over a minute the guns were put together, mounted, loaded, and ready to open fire, the limber, in charge of two of the six men, standing a little in the rear. The whole evolution was remarkably good, and the rapidity most striking. At the word of command the guns were fired; they limbered up directly, and the men attached a sort of harness which went across their chests, and dashed off as fast as they could run till a halt was called, fresh position taken up, the guns unlimbered, loaded, and discharged again in an incredibly short space of time.

As Henty watched them the sailors seemed to be taking their task as if it afforded them the greatest amusement, and to one who had never witnessed any such drill before it appeared to be an exercise that ought to be introduced to our own navy, which, as far as he knew, had not been furnished with these light portable guns for landing operations, "for there is no question," he says, "that they would be of immense service if two or three of these little guns were added to every vessel of our fleet."

This was, of course, prior to Henty's experience in connection with Magdala and Ashanti, where he found our sailors on landing expeditions in no wise behind those of the Italian fleet. Later it came to his lot, after his own war-corespondent campaigns were at an end, to deal with correspondence, letters, and telegrams connected with the Boer War,[1] in which our Jacks performed wonders, not with toy guns, but with the monsters on their specially-contrived carriages, under the manipulation of Captain Hedworth Lambton and Captain Percy Scott, which startled our enemies.

[1] The Boer War was fought from 1880 to 1881 in South Africa.
LIMBER: *the cart used to tow the gun*
LIMBERED: *attached the guns to the limbers*
MANIPULATION: *skillful management*

With ears relieved from the incessant roar of cannon to listen instead to the ringing of joy-bells and the cheers which welcomed the declaration of an armistice, Henty gladly availed himself of an opportunity to visit the old Italian cities, so as to see what life was like in these old-world places. Much of the quaint and antiquated still lingers round these towns, not only in the buildings, but in the habits of the people, suggestive of the days when Shakespeare and his contemporaries constructed their dramas, laying their scenes in Verona, Venice, Padua, Mantua, and other places, the very names of which suggest slashed doublets, rapiers, family enmities, relentless vendettas, keen-bladed swords, stilettoes, bravoes, feathered caps, poisoned cups, and all the rest.

Starting from Ancona, he went over to Sinigaglia, now upon the railway, but formerly a Roman station, and later of considerable importance in the Middle Ages, when war used often to rage between the states of the Pope and the family of Malatesta at Rimini. Here, too, Cæsar Borgia made his name infamous by causing the Condottieri, his allies, to be strangled, an act of treachery suggestive of the massacre of the Janissaries at Constantinople.

These names suggest old-world celebrity, but Henty had come over for a change, sick for the time being of war and its rumours. The bow-string had been tight for some time, sending literary arrows speeding west, and the fact that a rather famous fair was being celebrated attracted him, in expectation of seeing what Italy would be like when its people were *en fête* at a function similar to our own old Bartlemy or Greenwich.

In visiting Sinigaglia, a place associated with such names as the above, he fully expected to revel in the picturesque; but he found that the Italians, troubled as they are with such terrible

---

ARMISTICE: *truce*
SLASHED DOUBLETS: *tight-fitting jackets, slit to reveal the fabric underneath*
VENDETTAS: *bitter rivalries*
BRAVOES: *hired assassins*
EN FÊTE: *celebrating*

epidemic visitations, have grown to pay greater respect to sanitary measures than did their ancestors, and in consequence ancient ruins with their echoes of the past do not receive the respect we pay to them in England. He found one grand old citadel, but the Italians had been behaving to it like Vandals,[1] or, to be more familiar of speech, like our honest old British churchwardens when they distribute whitewash. Other ruins, such as nowadays we place under the care of some learned society, he found had been patched up and turned to some useful purpose.

The fair was in full force, but by no means English-looking. There were no roundabouts, either steam or worked by expectant boys in return for an occasional ride; no swings, no dramatic shows, no giants, no fat or spotted ladies, no freaks such as our American friends accustomed to St. Barnum of show fame rejoice to see, no music, no noise. It did not seem at all like a fair; but he found other attractions in the large town of about twenty-three thousand inhabitants, which was built as a fort about a third of a mile from the almost tideless sea, which, after the fashion of Venice, was connected therewith by a wide and deep canal. This canal offered passage for good-sized vessels, and ran up right through the town, all of which was very interesting from a commercial point of view; but it was the middle of hot August, and the place had a greater attraction for our traveller because it happened to be one of the most fashionable watering-places of eastern Italy. Henty here draws attention to the great advantage the Italians possess in living on a sea like the Mediterranean, where bathing-places can be erected, and where at all times there is a sufficient depth of water to enable one so desirous, to have a plunge without having to go lumbering out in one of the miserable rickety boxes on wheels which we call bathing-machines.[2]

---

[1] A Germanic tribe who sacked Rome in the 5th century A.D.
[2] Small bathhouses for wheeling swimmers into the water

CITADEL: *fortress*
ROUNDABOUTS: *merry-go-rounds*
WATERING-PLACES: *seaside resorts*

The same advantages are offered in the harbour of Ancona, at which town, at this period, Henty was making his headquarters. Here he found floating baths represented by a chamber of about fifteen feet square, into which the sea had free ingress, and also a larger bath big enough for a swim, while if one were so disposed there was egress to the sea.

To return to Sinigaglia: seeing that it was fair time the streets were furnished with awnings to keep off the sun, and the place was after all very attractive, with its streets filled with women displaying their baskets of goods for sale. Being a fête day the peasantry had flocked in from the surrounding country in their best and most picturesque costumes of bright colours and snowy white, with their hair carefully dressed in a peculiar fashion, and a plentiful display of gold necklaces or earrings. Their dark hair, warm complexions, and large dark eyes all tended to form a very attractive scene.

Henty however always displayed a mind receptive of anything connected with utility. As a rule he looked out for matters concerning sanitation, and while he condemned the vandalism, he had a word to say here respecting the purifying effect of whitewash. But in a place like this, so intimately associated with the old and historical, it is amusing to find that he takes a walk round the outskirts of the ancient city, and very unpoetically notes that the hills about Sinigaglia would gladden the heart of a London brickmaker if they could be dropped down in the neighbourhood of the metropolis. It stands to reason that he must have had Southall in his eye, for he says that the Sinigaglia hills are entirely composed of fine brick clay of apparently unlimited depth and extent.

As far as the fair was concerned, Henty writes soon after from Rimini—most poetic of names!—that he was glad that he went back to Ancona for the fair in that town, for it differed

INGRESS: *entrance*
EGRESS: *an exit*

entirely from that at Sinigaglia, in that it was especially lively, amusing, and attractive.

"The fair," he says, "begins where Ancona ceases." The attractions were almost entirely devoted to the young, so that for the time being the place was turned into an attractive toy-land. The Grand Promenade of Ancona, in the neighbourhood of the sea, and planted with rows of trees, was the centre of interest. The fair stalls, which were most abundant, were small, but were made most attractive. Each had its speciality, and was, of course, thronged with eager, bright-eyed children. One contained drums only; the next military toys, small swords, guns and pistols; the next would be all small carts; then came one with dolls' furniture, most neatly made in japanned tin or iron. A little farther on the stalls were filled with the noisy playthings so dear to children's hearts—whistles, trumpets, accordions, and rattles of the most ingenious construction and maddening power. Then, again, there were stalls displaying the ingenuity and delicacy of Italian taste, where they sold only dolls' head-dresses, the most jaunty little caps, hats, and veils conceivable, quite an equipment, in fact, for the heads of a whole troop of little fairies.

Then, again, there were many stalls with dolls dressed in the extreme of fashion; but in a fatherly manner, suggestive of thoughts of home, he goes on to say that, "the dolls themselves would not at all come up to an English child's idea of what such a toy ought to be, being all cheap wooden dolls. I did not see one made of wax in the fair."

Many of the toys exhibited were unquestionably German, similar to those seen in our own bazaars, but some, particularly the drums, he noticed were Italian. It was easy to detect the difference in the colouring, the paints used being of less clear and bright shades; and they were unvarnished,

JAPANNED TIN OR IRON: *tin or iron covered in a black varnish or lacquer, originally from Japan*

which is seldom or never the case with German toys. Round these stalls the crowd of little people and their friends was constant.

Observant of the country again, Henty goes on to say, with thoughts of home: "Children here have few amusements, few toys, and still fewer of those charming story-books with which so many of our booksellers' shop windows are full, especially about Christmas time." It is worthy of notice that this was in 1866, about two years previous to the production of Henty's first boys' story, and over thirty years before the time when, with scrupulous regularity, the booksellers' shop windows were annually displaying two or more of his own productions specially written for the young.

The parents and the friends seemed disposed to indulge the children to the utmost upon this occasion, for all had their hands full of toys. Boys drummed and blew trumpets and whistles till he was nearly deafened; little girls clung tightly to the skirts of their mothers' dresses with one hand, and with the other held out their new dolls admiringly before them; and appeared to be continually questioning their friends as to whether they were quite sure that sundry other purchases carried in paper bags were safe.

It was a charming scene, for the stalls were lit up by candles, which burned steadily in the serene summer air. Nothing could have been more attractive—the crowds, the pleasure of the children, the number of well-dressed people in their varied refinements of fashion, and the peasant women in their bright-coloured handkerchiefs, but many with no other decoration to their heads save their abundant smooth and neatly-braided hair.

Other picturesque features in the crowd were afforded by the soldiers, sailors, and marines, with their round hats and

SCRUPULOUS: *strict*
SUNDRY: *various*

drooping plumes of black cocks' feathers, and the uniforms of the National Guards and officers of all these services.

Passing onward, he came upon stalls significant of his being in a hot country, for at these only fans were sold—fans of every size and colour. In Italy, it must be remembered, as in Japan, nearly everyone carries a fan, and uses it instead of a parasol to shade the face when walking and to cool the bearer when sitting down.

And now began the stalls of the vendors of more useful articles. First were the basket-makers and turners, trades which seemed to be generally united, as if the women of the family pursued the one branch, the men the other. There were baskets of every size and form, from those which might hold a lady's fancy-work, right up to the enormous holder in which Falstaff himself might have been borne.

The turners' display of the works of their lathes was wonderful in variety, and included wooden bowls, platters, distaffs, and spindles, strings of buttons, bowls, and articles that were more the work of the carving tool, in the shape of spoons, taps, and pegs.

Then there were stalls with articles made from horn instead of wood, followed by displays of articles in iron and tin, notably small charcoal stoves, coffee-roasting apparatus, and ladles, while last in utility there were sieves of cane, wire, and horsehair. The variety was wonderful. Now the stalls were covered with hats—from the coarsest straw or chip, to those once fashionable in England and worn by our grandmothers under the name of Tuscan and Leghorn—while a brisk sale of cutlery was being carried on, men selling wooden-handled knives of the cheapest kind, such as the peasants always have at hand.

Elsewhere there were copper cooking utensils in plenty. Cooking in Italy is almost always done in copper pans and pots,

HOLDER: *container*
LATHES: *machines used to rotate pieces of wood while carving*
CHIP: *thin strips of wood*

and there is no cottage so poor that it has not its half-dozen, at least, of these brightly kept vessels.

And now, where the crowd was thickest, Henty found that he had been too hurried in his judgment of Italian fairs, for he found the old English fair equalled, if not excelled. Here were the shows and menageries, with the outside pictures of terrific combats with impossible animals, conspicuous among them being a snake, by the side of which the sea serpent would sink into insignificance, engaged in the operation of devouring a boat-load of Hindus, or so they seemed to be by their complexion and costume. This show boasted a band, while its neighbour contained our old friends the wax figures, representing heroes of modern times, among which he noted that, in remembrance of the Crimea, the showman had done England the honour of placing Lord Raglan. By way of extra attraction the little exhibition was furnished with an organ and cymbals.

If he had shut his eyes now, he says, he could almost have imagined himself in England—the music, the shouting of the touters at the booths, the blowing of trumpets and whistles, the beating of small drums, all recalling home. But there was one difference that was unmistakable. There was no pushing, no foul language; there were no drunken people, no roughs, all of which appear to be the inseparable elements of an English fair.

There were a great number of fruit stalls, which seemed to be doing a good business among the lower orders, especially at the counters devoted to the sale of slices of watermelon, which the people of Italy seem never tired of eating. Henty ventures to say they were very nice to one who got used to them, but for his part, he declares he would just as soon have eaten the same weight of grass.

When he left the place that night the proceedings were still in full swing, and when he returned to it at six o'clock the next

MENAGERIES: *collections of wild animals*
TOUTERS: *merchants "touting" or praising their wares*

morning, there was the same crowd as late the night before, and a brisk trade was still going on. Noticing again the vast number of fruit stalls, the thought occurred to him that it was fortunate that there was no cholera in the town, for if all the fruit that he saw in Ancona were consumed by the people before it got bad, it would produce an increase of that epidemic which was terrible to contemplate. There were hundreds of cart-loads of melons, watermelons, and peaches, which were poor tasteless things and always picked too soon; he declares he never tasted a ripe peach while he was in Italy. Pears too, figs, and grapes were plentiful; but he gives them no praise.

To his surprise and amusement, perhaps consequent upon Ancona being so old-world a city, he came upon one relic of the past, and that was a stall for supplying the matches such as our grandmothers used, such, in fact, as used to be sold by every pitiful vendor in the streets, in the shape of long thin strips of wood cut into a sharp point at each end, dipped in melted sulphur, and then tied up in bunches like fans. These were, of course, the predecessors of the lucifer matches,[1] as they were called, which were sold in neat little boxes, with an oblong piece of sanded card laid on the top. This folded across, and between its folds the match was drawn sharply, when it burst into flame. These were soon succeeded by a somewhat similar match, with the sandpaper a fixture on the bottom of the box, and the priming of the match so increased in inflammability that the ignition took place as at the present time, and the name Congreve Light came in, the "light" soon dying out, and giving way to Congreve or matches only. Of course, those which Henty saw on sale were for use in connection with the old-world flint and steel and tinder-box.

Passing on that morning, he went through the Custom House, to find beyond it the regular food market at its height.

[1] A type of early match patented by Englishman Samuel Jones

PITIFUL VENDORS: *vendors deserving of pity*
PREDECESSORS OF: *the ones that came before*
SUCCEEDED BY: *replaced with*

Hundreds of neatly dressed peasant women and girls were standing with their baskets before them, ready to supply eggs, butter, cheeses, fowls, turkeys, ducks, pigeons, and larks, for the most part alive, but doomed. There were one or two baskets which contained puppies, probably, however, not doomed, at least, to be cooked. But there were baskets in plenty containing delicacies in the nature of molluscs! He was within reach of the sea, but they were neither oysters, scallops, mussels, cockles, nor winkles, but the fine pale-shelled, spiral, Roman snails, that doubtless had been captured in the moist eve or early morn when ascending the poles of some vineyard. Delicate, but not tempting to the English taste.

To do the fair thoroughly, Henty, before leaving, visited the cattle, to find that the supply of horses was just then very small; but there was the prospect that, directly peace was signed and the enormous transport train paid off, horses would become as cheap in Italy as they then were dear.

There was a large show, though, of the beautiful patient, docile, draught oxen, which were fetching from twenty to thirty pounds a pair; and with these he concluded his inspection of the two fairs. He then suffered a most Inquisition-like examination of his baggage, and started for a visit to one of the smallest republics in the world, a country close to the Adriatic shore, which had been for some time attracting his attention. This he hoped to see and report upon before the festivities of peace should commence consequent upon the complete freedom of Italy, or troubles should arise once more and make busy in other ways the war correspondent's pen.

WINKLES: *small sea-snails*
DEAR: *expensive*
DRAUGHT OXEN: *oxen for pulling loads*

CHAPTER X

THE VISIT TO SAN MARINO

ON his way to San Marino Henty found himself at Rimini. This place is the Ariminium of the Romans. It was enlarged and beautified by Julius and Augustus Cæsar. Here, too, in A.D. 359 the Aryan doctrine was denounced.[1] As the centuries rolled by, the town fell into the hands of the Lombards, and was given by the Emperor Otho to Malatesta, whose family ceded it to the Venetians, from whom it was afterwards wrested by the Popes, and it remained part of the Papal dominions till 1860.

It has its antiquities, the principal one being an arch erected in honour of Augustus, and bearing still in perfect preservation the old Roman carvings, representing on one side Jupiter and Minerva, on the other, Neptune and Venus.

Another antiquity that took Henty's attention as being well worthy of notice, from the way in which it brought back to his memory Westminster School and his studies of the classics, was a short pillar in the market-place with an inscription stating that Cæsar stood upon it to harangue his soldiers before passing the Rubicon.[2] Cæsar, history informs us, was a short stout man, and Henty's old studies led him to believe that he could not have looked well upon that short column, upon which he would probably have been lifted by the officers of his staff; and

---

[1] The Arian (Aryan) heresy was first condemned at the Council of Nicæa in A.D. 325. Arius, a Christian priest, taught that Jesus Christ was created by God the Father, rather than being eternal.

[2] A small river in northern Italy

HARANGUE HIS SOLDIERS: *give a long, passionate speech to his soldiers*

somehow or other—perhaps the weather was not very genial—
the column did not impress him with any particular feeling of
veneration. His ideas ought to have been classic and stern; but
it is strange, as he says, what inopportune ideas strike one. He
approached the stone with a thorough belief in it, prepared to
picture Cæsar aloft, and the heavy-armed legionaries of the
Roman cohorts standing armed, leaning upon their spears,
with the eagles they had carried triumphantly through so many
campaigns erect in their midst. But as he came fully into sight
of the stone, the thought of the difficulty of getting upon it and
of Cæsar's ungraceful figure brought to his mind the remembrance of H. K. Browne's etching representing the immortal
Pickwick standing upon a chair, with one hand under his coat-
tails and the other outstretched, as he harangued the members
of his club. And all belief in the legend of the stone faded away
at once. In fact, Henty was not an imaginative man. Neither
was he a great humorist; but when he was in humorous vein his
humour was dry and good.

By the way, legend says that it was at Rimini that St. Anthony
preached to the fishes when the people refused to hear him,
and that San Marino,[1] who was a native of Dalmatia, across the
Adriatic Sea, came over and settled here. He gave his name
afterwards to the little republic and to the mountain which
Henty's driver pointed out to him—rising far above all the hills
in its neighbourhood, nearly fifteen miles away—at the beginning of a very charming drive in an open carriage drawn by
one of those novelties that are not often let for hire—a very fair
horse.

This curious little state is in its own way perfectly unique,
and its existence is the more singular from its being situated in
Italy, though for centuries in the Middle Ages that country was
the scene of an uninterrupted succession of wars. The hand
of every country was against its neighbours. Towns changed

---

[1] Saint Marinus, a stonecutter and Christian Deacon in Rimini
VENERATION: *great respect or reverence*
INOPPORTUNE: *inappropriate*
COHORTS: *divisions of about 500 soldiers*

owners every few years; states were swallowed up, conquered, reconquered, but San Marino has remained.

The law of strength was the only law recognized—that law which says he shall take who has the power, and he shall keep who can; for the weakest always went to the wall. It is then most singular that this little territory of about eight thousand inhabitants should have remained intact for more than fifteen centuries, and that now, while all its powerful neighbours have become merged into one great state, this tiny republic should be the sole portion of Italian soil possessing a separate autonomy.

History tells us that in the old Roman days, soon after the persecution of the Christians by the Emperor Diocletian[1] commenced, San Marino, finding that there was no rest for his people in Rimini, led his little flock out from that city and established a Christian colony at the summit of the highest and most rugged mountain in that part of the country, then probably a place surrounded by untrodden forests; and the little state thus founded has remained separate ever since.

The road to San Marino led across an undulating and very richly cultivated country, where the peasants were engaged gathering in the grape harvest, which that year, from the extreme dryness of the early part of the season, was the worst the people had ever known. They were also occupied picking the maize, which is so important an item of the Italian farmer's crop.

Indian corn is a little better known now in connection with its beautiful growth than when Henty paid his visit, but his description of what was to him almost a novelty is still pleasant reading. He tells us how the plants are thinned out as soon as they appear above the ground, and the blades are left to grow on about a foot apart in a climate where they spring up to the height of about six feet. The stalks, he says, "for the first two feet above the ground are about the diameter of a man's thumb, but towards the top they expand to a considerable extent."

[1] Roman Emperor from A.D. 284 to A.D. 305

SINGULAR: *exceptional*
AUTONOMY: *independence*
UNDULATING: *rolling*

He had seen maize growing in its early stage during his previous visits to Italy, but never before having passed the hot season there, this was the first time he had witnessed the harvest, and it was a matter of surprise to him that such thin stalks could support the weight of a head of maize. But now to him the mystery was explained. At about two feet from the ground, at the time the plant flowers, the stem increases in size, presently opens, and a thick shoot makes its appearance, apparently composed of a compressed bunch of leaves. This becomes larger and larger, the leaves expand, open more and more, and spread out like broad wavy blades of grass. The head or cob of maize swells out and forms at its summit a great silky pale golden tassel, while, as the cob becomes larger and larger, much of the upper part of the stalk in the process of the ripening dies and falls off. Then the lower leaves drop away, the grand beauty of the field of maize passes, and from the time the crop is ripe until the harvest the field seems to be composed of stumps with bunches of dead leaves at the top. These leaves, however, enclose the great solid, regularly formed or apparently built-up head of maize, which is left drying as it stands in the torrid sunshine, till it is cut off and carted to the farms. At this stage the Indian corn is taken in hand by the women and children of the family, and the separate grains are picked off and exposed on cloths to dry perfectly in the sun.

Passing the cultivated fields and crossing the little stream which forms its boundary, Henty learned that he was in the Republic of San Marino, that the circumference of the state was thirty-five miles, and that the mountain, or crag as it should rather be called, rose almost in its centre. With the exception of the rock itself, every part was extremely fertile and well cultivated, and of more value than land in the surrounding country, on account of the absence of taxation and other advantages peculiar to the republic, chief among which was the freedom from military conscription. Every male in San Marino is, it is true, a soldier, but soldiering involves no fighting or absence from home. Although all are liable to be called upon to serve in case of necessity, only those under a certain age are on ordinary occasions called out. The strength of this regular army of the republic is eight hundred men. Of these, seven hundred form the National Guard; the remaining hundred are the bodyguard of the president.

They have their uniform of blue, the National Guard having red facings, the bodyguard yellow, the band white. Then they have their national flag of blue and white; and a police force administered by a chief and five carbineers, whose uniform is dark blue with white cross-belts and grey trousers, so that they look on the whole much like the carbineers of the Italian service. These five are, of course, always on duty, and are regular salaried police. The army only appears in uniform upon Sundays and fête days, when the men are drilled; but the troops receive no pay.

"We arrived," says Henty, "at the village of Serravalle. Here the carriage stopped, and I had to take my seat in a little pair-wheeled trap drawn by a good-sized pony. These *berruchinos*, as they are called, are by no means comfortable, for instead of being boarded, the floor is composed of a loose network of cords, which affords little rest for the feet. They have no dash- or splash-board, and you are consequently in unpleasant proximity to the horse's heels, if it should take it into its head to kick. They have, besides, no rail or other rest for the back." It was an intensely hot day, and at the village from which he made his fresh start he was glad to accept the loan of an immense blue umbrella. And now began an adventure.

They had ascended a steep hill, so steep that the driver got down and walked, and he had not retaken his seat when,

MILITARY CONSCRIPTION: *being forced to serve in the military*
CARBINEERS: *soldiers armed with short rifles called carbines*
PROXIMITY: *nearness*

without the slightest previous notice of its intention, and presumably induced thereto by the bite of a fly in some more than ordinarily tender part, the wretched little pony started off at full gallop.

At this time Henty was sitting quietly under the umbrella, tranquilly smoking and chatting to the driver, when there was a sudden jerk. His feet having no hold and his back no support, the former flew up into the air and his head went back. Instinctively he made a desperate grasp at the side rail with his unoccupied hand, but it gave way, and in an instant he was on his back in the middle of the road with the blue umbrella perfectly shut up beneath him. Fortunately the trap was not very high, and his bones were at that period of his life very well protected, so in a moment he was on his feet again, much more astonished than hurt. Bearing the relics of the blue umbrella he pursued the trap, which in spite of the efforts of the driver was going on at full speed, dragging him after it, and it was three or four hundred yards from the place where the pony started before the man was able to bring it to a standstill.

A little scene ensued, for when he came up Henty found the driver looking pale as death, and so much scared that it was with the greatest difficulty he could be persuaded that his fare was not seriously hurt.

It was rather a remarkable escape; but Henty states that he was so little shaken that he did not even suffer with a headache from the effects. Of course, however, the principal damage was to the blue umbrella, and on his return to Serravalle he had a very lengthy amount of talk and argument with the old lady, its owner, as to the amount of compensation to be paid, for it was irretrievably ruined.

The rest of Henty's journey to the Burgo of San Marino, a village containing about seven hundred inhabitants, was uneventful. It is planted at the foot of a precipice, at the top of which the old town, which is populated to about the same extent, is perched. It is a remarkable mountain, rising as it does almost perpendicularly, and therefore being a very suitable spot for the erection of a fortress in the old dangerous times, for all around there lie nothing but softly swelling hills, no other so suitable a defensive place occurring until far back in the Apennines,[1] another twenty-five miles inland.

The rock is about half a mile long, and to the east the face is absolutely perpendicular, while to the west it has a gradual but still rapid fall, the land being cultivated up to the very walls of the town upon its summit.

There is no flat ground upon the top. It is a mere narrow ridge, the descent beginning from the very edge of the perpendicular east face. When looking up the rock from the road all that is seen of the town are three towers perched upon the three highest points, and the church. None of the houses is visible owing to their position upon the west slope.

Inquiries brought an introduction to one of the ancients of the place, who acted as cicerone to strangers visiting San Marino, and during a walk he was found to be charged with a pretty full description of the politics and history of the little state.

Everything was in a delightful state of innocency, honour more than money seeming to be generally the object sought. There were two captains-regent instead of presidents, who were allowed seventy-five francs each during their term of office of six months. The home and foreign ministers were each paid two hundred and fifty francs for office expenses, postage, etc. The commander-in-chief of the army got honour alone and not a sou besides, and apparently had to pay for his own uniform. Then came the highest paid officials of the republic. These were three, two physicians and one surgeon, who received

---

[1] A mountain range running along the center of Italy

CICERONE: *guide*
CAPTAINS-REGENT: *governors*
SOU: *a small French coin*

thirteen hundred and fifty francs, or fifty-four pounds a year each, and for this had to be at the call of all the citizens of the state, to whom they rendered their services gratis. The only patients who had to put their hands in their pockets were those who lived out of town, and they had also to provide conveyance.

There was a judge who went on circuit, and he was chosen for a period of three years, but might be reelected twice. To meet these stupendous demands, which meant an expenditure of about three thousand pounds a year, the government raised a revenue by the profits upon the sale of tobacco and salt, these being, as in other parts of Italy, state monopolies.

In addition to this a very small tax was levied on the landed proprietors, and the Italian government paid a sum of eighteen thousand francs a year, which was used for making roads, assisting the poor, giving aid in cases of loss by fire or misfortune, and repairing the public buildings. This sum was paid by the Italian government for customs dues.

Following his guide, Henty found the city to be a long narrow village on and below the crest of the cliff. It was enclosed by a wall some twenty-five feet high, surmounted by numerous round bastions. It showed every proof of having been very strong in former times, and even then, although the walls were very old and crumbling, it was evident that a thousand men could defend it for some time against a strong force, the rock falling so steeply away below it that it would be difficult to bring cannon to bear on it. Within the walls the houses were all crowded together; the streets, although they all zigzagged upwards, were so steep that no horse could draw a vehicle up them.

Among the antiquities of the place were the old Assembly Hall and the building which contained the rooms of the captain regent, displaying the arms of the republic—three towers with plumes on the tops and the motto "Libertas." These towers

GRATIS: *free of charge*
CONVEYANCE: *transportation*
BASTIONS: *fortifications that project out from the main wall*

represented the three which stood upon the highest points of the rocks. The view from the summit of the rock was superb. A thousand feet below lay the Burgo. Beyond that for miles upon miles spread a gently undulating country, dotted with innumerable towns and villages, stretching away to the seashore. To the north lay a perfectly flat marsh land through which the Po and Adige[1] find their way into the sea, this—the Adriatic—looking like a blue wall dotted with white sails. The guide assured the visitor that just before sunrise the mountains of Dalmatia, a hundred miles distant at least, were plainly visible.

Away to the west the Apennines shut in the view. Upon one of the spurs the castle of St. Leon was visible, where the celebrated Cagliostro[2] was imprisoned and died.

Henty observed upon his descent to the gate of the tower six strong posts, four being placed to make a parallelogram with cross pieces at the top, to one of which was attached a windlass. The remaining two posts were placed one in front and one behind, the whole suggesting the possibility that they had been used in former times in the defence of the tower. On being questioned, however, the guide explained that they were used for a much more matter-of-fact purpose. When oxen are being shoed they are not so calm and patient over the operation as a horse, generally objecting very strongly to the performance. Hence they were driven in between the posts, ropes were fastened to the cross-bar on one side, these were attached to the windlass, and when this was turned, the bullock was swung up into the air, and his feet fastened to the posts in front and behind.

It proved to be a delightful visit, the visitor ending by dining at a little auberge in the village at the foot of the hill, where to his surprise he found that they had an excellent cook.

[1] A large river in northern Italy
[2] Count Alessandro di Cagliostro (1743-1795)

WINDLASS: *a cylinder around which a rope is run*
AUBERGE: *inn*

CHAPTER XI

A LAND OF MYSTERY

HENTY, having been interested in mining early in life, was at any time eager to seize upon an opportunity to plunge into the bowels of the earth, and not long after he commenced as war correspondent to the *Standard*, that is, at the termination of the Italo-Austrian campaign, he took occasion when at Trieste to run up into the hill country for a few days and visit the three great sights of Carniola, namely, the Grotto of Adelsberg, the Lake of Zirknitz, and the quicksilver mines of Idria.

Here the man who had studied mining in his youth with the possibility of succeeding to his father's industrial occupation was in his element, and showed himself ready to study the country with an open and receptive mind. He was eager at once to investigate the mountainous and sterile country covered by the Alps and Tyrol, the vast forests and their timber, the transport, the burning of charcoal, and the general cheerlessness of a land of desolation often covered with huge boulders and scaurs of white stone. Quite the geologist here, he notes the hard white limestone of the secondary formation, quarried extensively, being excellent for building, and known through Italy as Istrian marble. He speaks of it as being the same stone which extends through Carniola and through Dalmatia into Greece, and here he seems to revel in a kind of exciting pleasure as

GROTTO: *cave*
QUICKSILVER: *mercury*
STERILE: *barren*
SCAURS: *rock banks*

he finds himself in a limestone formation somewhat similar to that of our own Derbyshire, asking to be explored and tempting him to excursions, honeycombed as it is with fissures and caverns.

Probably in no tract of country of equal size in the world are there so many singular freaks of nature. Rivers of navigable size and depth issue from its mountains—rivers which far surpass the subterranean streams of Central France—and these, after running for a few miles, enter a cavern and lose themselves as suddenly and mysteriously as they appeared.

It is a land of mystery and wonder, and, as if the spirit were moving within him to store up his mind with the natural wonders for attractive stories to come, such as would in some form or another fascinate readers yet unborn, Henty, with great eagerness, embraced the opportunity here offered to explore a wild land of savage sterility, where, as if to be in keeping with the "crag, knoll, and mound confusedly hurled, the fragments of an earlier world,"[1] terrible tempests sweep with irresistible force. In the fury which rages in this inhospitable region, horses and wagons are not infrequently hurled over precipices, and a foot passenger, surprised in one of the tempestuous mountain squalls, is forced to seek for shelter beneath the parapets that have been built along the road.

Here he found that he was in a country where the railroads were protected by strong stone walls ten or twelve feet high, or equally lofty wooden palisading supported on both sides by massive struts, so as to afford some shelter to the passing trains which, when the gales are at their worst, are quite unable to pursue their journey.

Here, too, the engineering difficulties encountered in the construction of one of the lines had the deepest interest for Henty as a mining engineer, for not only was he face to face

[1] Lines from the poem, *The Lady of the Lake,* by Sir Walter Scott (1771-1832)

FISSURES: *narrow cracks*

with the difficulties of the making of the railroad, but also with those of obtaining a supply of water at the various stations. Where the line ran, all was aridity and desolation. The water was below, requiring the help of powerful engines to raise it, and aqueducts over the surface to bear it along, one of these water-bridges being twenty-five miles in length. It was a very giant-land for a writer of fiction to fill with adventure.

Passing through this country of desolation, he at last reached the well-named village of Adelsberg,[1] which in a state of nature might very well have supplied the crags where the eagles built. This he found a comfortable well-to-do village, Swiss-like in appearance, with its chalet style of architecture; but he was bent on the works of nature, and drove out to the famed Lake of Zirknitz, a piece of water that has obtained fame through its peculiar habit of quitting its bed once a year for a few weeks and so supplying the natives of those parts with an opportunity for growing a crop of coarse grass and millet before its return. This is all a suggestion of the peculiar workings of the subterranean waters below, and the regularity is more or less wonderful.

About midsummer the waters of the lake begin to shrink, growing lower and lower, and so rapidly that, after about twenty days in July, the lake is empty, remaining so till September or October, according to the season. This is the rule; but as there is no rule without an exception, the lake sometimes remains full for three or four years together, to the great loss of the people of the stony neighbourhood, who depend upon the little crop of buckwheat and millet which they are able to grow in the muddy bed. They also look forward to another harvest given to them when the water dries away; for, strange to state, at this time a plentiful supply of fish that flourish in the depths of the lake is left high and dry, and forms a portion of the natives' food.

[1] "Noble Mountain" in German

ARIDITY: *barrenness*
QUITTING ITS BED: *draining*

Knowing the character of the lake, Henty on his visit had looked forward to finding the place empty; but it presented no attraction for the visitor, appearing to be only an ordinary sheet of water some four miles long by three wide. There were villages about its shores, and a few small islands dotted its surface; but no opportunity was afforded him of examining what to a mining engineer would have been a matter of intense interest, the natural machinery which operates in the remarkable process of emptying and refilling. For above ground the lake has neither outlet nor inlet; but the limestone which forms its bed contains a number of funnel-shaped holes communicating with the vast caves, grottoes, and reservoirs in the mountains, by which the water enters or is drawn off. Some of these act as ebbing-pipes only; by others the water both enters and retires.

Upon occasions when the lake is empty, and there has been a sudden storm in the mountains, the water pours into the dry bed with such wonderful force and rapidity that it is sometimes filled in twenty-four hours. The annual emptying of the lake, however, is observed almost as a fête by the surrounding villages. The church announces the strange phenomenon, and the inhabitants become fishers for the nonce. Nets are prepared, and every description of vessel is held ready for the capture of the fish left behind when the water retreats, the nets being principally used as the waters sink and the funnel-shaped holes can be reached by the fishermen, who endeavour to cover these orifices before the fish can descend through them into the natural reservoirs below.

As the waters gradually disappear, a certain number of little pools are left, each being the property of one or other of the villages, and bearing its name. These pools vary greatly in the extent of the harvest they yield the villagers. One year a pool

EBBING-PIPES: *drainage pipes*
NONCE: *moment*
ORIFICES: *openings*

will contain cartloads of fish, another year perhaps only a few dozen.

Henty gives a most interesting account of the strange phenomenon, but says nothing respecting the quality of the fish, except such as is conveyed by the eagerness of the inhabitants to obtain this natural yielding of the lake. They in all probability, however, belong to the *coregonus* family, a kind of lake fish which in variety haunt the lakes of Central Europe, and which one can answer for being very good eating, a quality not often possessed by fresh-water fish. In this case, as salt forms a large source of trade in the neighbourhood of Lake Zirknitz, the fish obtained from its waters most likely partake of the firmness and good qualities of those obtained from the sea.

In this mountainous region Henty's observation was always busy, and he notes everything, not forgetting the accommodation. He describes the inns as rude, but not uncomfortable, the cookery not bad, but considers the people display an undue affection for stewed apples, which they look upon as a vegetable to be consumed with meat of all kinds.

He was much interested, too, in the custom of the villagers of keeping bees. He noticed in some villages several long carts, upon each of which were placed some twenty or thirty beehives of the shape of fig-boxes, but about two feet and a half long by a foot wide and nine inches deep. These hives are the property of various villagers, who club together, take a cart, and send it from place to place, so as to give the bees a fresh hunting-ground and a change of blossom for their supply.

Of course it is in the nature of a bee to be busy. Here they all seemed to be very active and hard at work, but they were rather a nuisance in the villages by reason of their numbers. However, they seemed particularly good-tempered bees, a fact of which Henty gives an example, and were not so much a

RUDE: *crudely built*

nuisance through offering injury as from their habit of cluster-ing upon the grapes and other fruits exposed for sale.

Henty says he remonstrated with a market woman, of whom he was willing to buy a bunch of grapes, when she held it out to him with eight or ten bees upon it, busily extracting honey, whereupon she laughed at him, picked the insects off with her fingers, and held them out to him to show that they were not disposed to use their stings even when roughly handled. An interesting fact this in natural history, and one which Henty admired, though he preferred seeing it done with other fingers than his own, and was quite content that the woman should have a poor opinion of his personal courage. But there are bees and bees, some more aggressive than others.

We all know the qualities of our own native bee, and any bee-keeper, unless he has been stung frequently and become inured, will tell you that the bees imported of late years from Liguria, and now acclimatized, have a rather vicious disposi-tion.

These from the neighbourhood of Adelsberg are in all prob-ability the reverse in character. Certainly they seem to vary, for Henty describes the honey as by no means good, being very dark-coloured, and having a strong, unpleasant twang. On the other hand, the flavour depends upon the neighbouring growth of flowers, and the taste may be given by some nectary common to the neighbourhood, possibly by what Henty de-scribes when he says the fields were bright with purple crocus, which he had never before seen flowering at this time of year—October—evidently a mistake on his part, for the colchicum,[1] the producer of the old-world remedy for gout.

---

[1] The colchicum resembles the crocus but blooms in the fall.

REMONSTRATED WITH: *protested to*
INURED: *accustomed to it*
ACCLIMATIZED: *adapted to the climate*

Chapter XII

A Subterranean Excursion

THE next day Henty started for his eagerly anticipated plunge into the far-famed Grotto of Adelsberg, and he frankly declares at once that there are some sights of which it is impossible by mere words to convey any adequate impression, and to do justice to which it would be necessary to combine the epithets and imagery of a dozen languages.

"Foremost among these," he says, "is the Grotto of Adelsberg, and I had hardly entered it when I became painfully conscious that the idea with which I had come—namely, of writing a description which should give a vivid conception of the most beautiful and varied succession of grottoes in the world—was hopelessly beyond my powers."

The entrance to the caverns is about a mile from Adelsberg, and a little way up the side of a limestone mountain whose strata dip at an angle of about forty-five degrees. Immediately below the entrance a good-sized stream plunges into a low cavern and reappears only some ten miles distant in a direct line to the north. But some idea of the actual course of this river may be gained from the fact that pieces of cork thrown in where the river disappears do not emerge again for twelve hours, which goes to prove that the distance they have travelled is more than double the above. There are, it seems, two entrances, and in

EPITHETS: *descriptive words*
CONCEPTION: *picture*
STRATA: *rock layers*

the one followed, the path at first led through a passage or corridor of no great length, and then opened suddenly into a noble cavern known as the "Dome".

This was all that was known of the grottoes till the year 1819, when a workman accidentally destroyed a stalactite screen and discovered the entrance to the apparently illimitable series of caves beyond. Of these, five miles in length have been explored; but the end has not been reached, and they extend for unknown distances in several directions. The effect of the Dome is superlatively grand. It is three hundred feet in length and one hundred feet in height and width. The sides are quite perpendicular, and at about half their height a natural gallery runs partially round them. The view from this is magnificent in the extreme. The guides who accompanied the visitors placed candles at short intervals along the parapet, but their light barely pierced the gloomy expanse. Upward the roof loomed dark and vague. Beneath, the river, which had commenced its subterranean passage, rushed brawling among rocks, and was crossed by a wooden bridge lit up by two rows of candles, whose rays were reflected in broken flashes from the black tumbling water.

At the extreme end of this vast hall a faint blue light showed where the daylight beyond struggled in at the outlet of the river cave. Above and around the roar of the stream was re-echoed and answered by a thousand low reverberating murmurs. The whole effect was ineffably solemn and awe-inspiring. Henty and his companions having provided themselves with magnesium wire[1] at Trieste, this was now used, and the effect was absolutely startling. The light streamed out into the most distant recesses, the candles faded to dim red points, and the roof, which had before appeared of fabulous height, seemed now to be crushing down upon them, the stalactites of its rugged surface

---

[1] When burned, magnesium wire produces a bright white light.

ILLIMITABLE: *limitless*

GALLERY: *balcony*

REVERBERATING: *echoing*

INEFFABLY: *unspeakably*

standing out clear and well defined. Then, as the bright white light with its clouding smoke died out, the darkness deepened with oppressive heaviness. Everything had been so grand, that it needed all the persuasions of the guide, who assured the party that far more beautiful things were to be seen beyond, before they could be induced to leave this spot and to ascend the steps which led to the entrance of the inner caves.

The path which they followed then was upwards of three miles long, and so arranged that they returned by a different series of grottoes from those they had traversed. The variety of scenery displayed in these three miles was extraordinary. Sometimes the way contracted into low narrow passages, at others opened out into enormous halls. Chambers and corridors, fairy grottoes and gloomy caves, alternated with each other, and the principal halls were popularly named the Ballroom, the Concert-room, and the Calvary. The Ballroom was of nearly the same proportions as the Dome, except that the height was not so great, but its character was entirely different. It was graceful and airy, and was apparently illuminated with numerous chandeliers. The floor was perfectly smooth and level, and at one end an artificial orchestra had been erected in the midst of a group of crags and stalagmites. This, once a year, is really used as a ballroom for a dance, to which thousands of the surrounding peasantry flock. Nothing could be more beautiful than the way in which the walls are decked by nature. Everywhere from walls and roof depend masses of stalactites of the most graceful and elegant forms. Floating draperies are festooned around. Filmy, semi-transparent veils seem to wave gently to and fro as they sparkle in the numerous lights. Here appear drooping pendants and tapering spike-like projections; there, majestic pillars and clustering columns.

The Concert-room is similar in character, but larger and narrower, and hence issued an immense and gloomy corridor

DEPEND: *hang*
UNCOUTH: *strange*

more than a hundred feet high. The floor was covered with masses of loose rock, whose huge and rugged shapes loomed, distorted and uncouth, in the faint light of the candles.

From this abode of gloom they entered the Calvary, which appeared to be the largest of all the halls. It must have been three hundred feet long and upwards of two hundred wide. At one end rose a lofty heap of rocks that had fallen from the roof and been cemented together by stalagmites. It bore a resemblance to a great shrine, and was brilliantly illuminated, while the rest of the vast space lay in deep and mysterious shadow. From the lower end, where the observers stood, the floor sloped steeply up. It was composed of misshapen blocks of stone, for at some far-distant period the whole interior, now a flat bare surface, must have fallen with a mighty crash, brought down by the weight of the stalactites that had formed upon it. That the catastrophe happened long ages since was evidenced by the fact that the whole floor was covered with stalagmites of various sizes and heights, which looked as though a forest of great pines had once grown there, till their trunks had been snapped short off by the swoop of some mighty whirlwind.

There was a weird grandeur about this hall which was almost appalling, producing as it did questioning fancies respecting the possibility of a repetition of the old-world scene.

In the corridors and caves that intervened between these principal chambers and halls there was an infinity of fantastic shapes, in which fancy could trace almost every known form. A monstrous bee-hive, a Brobdingnagian tortoise, huge fallen trees covered with lichens growing rankly, half-rounded nodules, and great wart-like protuberances. In one place the roof would be supported by Gothic columns, farther on by unshapely props and buttresses. In one corner rough stems as of ivy seemed to be clinging to the wall, or the gnarled trunks of

BROBDINGNAGIAN: *gigantic*
RANKLY: *thickly*
NODULES: *lumps*
PROTUBERANCES: *bulges*

oaks thrust themselves up between the blocks. Above one cave it seemed as if a great tree were growing, whose twining roots hung down from the roof.

And so on, and so on, fancy helping the visitor to believe that he was gazing upon long ranges of organ pipes, upon stems of palm-trees with well-defined marks whence the broad leaves had sprouted, or upon basaltic columns, with wide steps slowly formed by ages, where water had trickled down. Farther on, too, at intervals, creamy-red couches seemed to be temptingly placed, with folds of a soft white material thrown carelessly over them, while long flags and fringed draperies of admirable texture and design drooped down from chinks and crannies in the roof, as if to form decorations for some fête in the world of the gnomes.

There was no end to the wonders wrought by nature's own sculptors—fonts, chalices, exquisitely chased imaged shrines, and strange confessionals; groups of statuary wrought in beauty, with roofs above covered with fretwork of the most delicate tracery; and in opposition there was the grotesque on every hand, with squat heathen idols, grim corbels, and in the darkness, with Doré-like effect,[1] diabolical-looking creations or works as of some enchanter's wand. In parts everything was so real, that it was impossible not to believe that that cascade, glistening as it did when the lights were turned upon it, was not deep water, but only stone, or that a fountain glittering with diamond spray in the passing light was not composed of liquid drops.

In one cave the wall seemed to be hung in ruddy masses of stalactite of so truly a fleshy tint that they seemed to be palpably strips of flesh, which carried the spectator back to old classic readings and the legends of the Latin ancients. For it seemed as if the cave might be the spot where Apollo

---

[1] Looking like the illustrations of Gustave Doré (1832-1883)

BASALTIC: *volcanic*

CHASED: *engraved*

FRETWORK: *patterns*

CORBELS: *decorative brackets*

had skinned Marsyas,[1] and Henty listened as if expectant of hearing the sufferer's howls re-echo through the vast labyrinth. For here seemed to hang his flesh—great strips of muscle and tendon, some looking cold and stiff, others soft and limp, with the glowing tint of life still warm upon them. It was terribly real.

Earthy solutions had stained some of the stalactites of a dirty grey hue, the material of the carbonate of lime being dull and coarse; but others again were white as alabaster, the carbonate giving place to the sulphate, and looking pure and semi-transparent. In many places the surface of the deposit of lime, slowly formed of nature's great patience, was smooth as polished marble, while in other places, suggestive of the more ready work of heated springs of water charged with lime, the deposit was uneven as masses of coral. The tints, too, varied from clear white to cream colour, orange, and red; and while in many places the drooping stalactites were dull and soft-looking, and reflected no light, in others they sparkled with myriads of coruscations as of diamonds, emeralds, and rubies; or rather, as they changed and flashed in the passing light, they resembled rocks over which a thin film of jewels was streaming, or a sudden blaze of sunshine upon hoarfrost.

And it was not only the eye that was dazzled and seemed to gather an imagination of its own; but there were wonders for the ear, for now and again there were hanging masses offering themselves to be struck, waiting there in the whispering silence of the vast halls of wonder, to give out a clear bell-like sound which varied from the sharp ring of a struck glass to the deep soft boom of some cathedral bell, the tone being invariably much purer and sweeter from the semi-transparent blocks than from those that were formed of material which was loose and coarse.

---

[1] According to Greek mythology, the god Apollo skinned the satyr Marsyas as a penalty for losing a musical contest with him.

PALPABLY: *clearly seen as*
CORUSCATIONS: *bright flashes*

Many of the caves that closely adjoined each other varied in the most extraordinary manner. Some seemed to be dark and murky, suitable homes for gnomes and evil genii. Misshapen monsters appeared to lurk, eerie and gruesome, in obscure corners; slimy and uncouth reptiles seemed to crawl and grovel in the damp mire, looking horribly real, though only fancy save in the solidity of stone.

And then, gloomily seen on high, weird, shadowy creatures, dank and bat-like with their dusky wings, appeared to be hovering just beneath the roof, till a nameless horror seemed to pervade the gloomy atmosphere, and the imagination peopled the place with unearthly creatures which the mind refused to believe were illusory, so real were they in their stony extravagance; yet all were the work of nature, formed through the dark ages slowly, drop by drop.

There they were in the dim nooks and recesses, seeming, as the smoking candles flickered upon their glistening surfaces, to beckon and grin, peering round twisted buttresses, gloating, vampire-like, on the passerby from behind the fallen columns, and producing a shuddering horror, as they seemed to be only waiting till the visitors to these awful shades had passed before they sprang.

It was here that even the brilliant rays of magnesium failed to dispel the gathered blackness, and the strange shapes stood out more spectral and awe-inspiring than before. And it was water—water everywhere, drip, drip, drip, never ceasing—the hardest of hard water, that the most thirsty in these caverns would shrink from drinking, for he would know that he was sipping liquid stone, the stone that had built up everything around, and which would go on almost silently building fresh wonders until Time should be no more. And in spite of the flash and brilliancy of beauty as opposed to the dull, glistening, slimy look of much of nature's work, there was something

ILLUSORY: *imaginary*
SHADES: *shadows*
SPECTRAL: *ghostly*

shuddering in its inspiration as he who gazed at the same time had what was going on conveyed to him through his ears—the drip of water never ceasing, and its feeble echoes seeming to rustle with mysterious whisper throughout these shadowy cells and proclaim the wonder-work in process of construction.

It was with a strange feeling of relief that they passed on out of these awe-inspiring caverns into a region where, in delightful contrast, the eyes were welcomed with a sight of what could only be the dwelling-places of the inhabitants of a kind of fairyland. Here all was graceful pinnacle, delicate spire, tapering point, and slender pillar, each frosted alike with silvery rime, which made the finger shrink when touching them; for it seemed, according to everyday knowledge, quite startling that these beautiful works of nature should feel cool and temperate; the visitor felt that they ought to sting the nerves with pain, for their sparkling effect looked so exactly as though it had been produced by frost.

Icy, too, appeared much of the beauty now—the sparkling fairy couches spread with frosty lace, the gauzy floating folds encrusted with gems. Everywhere the lights flashed and glittered, refracted in a thousand colours; for here, too, seemed to be the caves of crystal-land, the homes of the water sprites who dwelt where water had now become pure, solid, and perfect forevermore, where water had become pure ice that was not cold, where even the floor was white sparkling sand scattered with gleaming shells, above which the water fays floated, and the sea sprites played and chased fish in the ice grottoes.

Such were some of George Henty's impressions of the Grotto of Adelsberg, and he concludes by saying that any traveller who has ever had the opportunity of seeing that home of nature's wonders lit up as he had, would surely bear him out in saying that, so far from exaggerating, he has but touched upon a few of the varied and extraordinary beauties of the place.

RIME: *ice*
FAYS: *fairies*

CHAPTER XIII

MINING FOR MERCURY

STILL feeling his great interest in mining to an extent that makes one wonder that he did not make that pursuit the work of his life to the same extent as he made yachting the pleasure, Henty now made his way to Idria to make a careful examination of the quicksilver mines, the property of the Austrian government. The journey was undertaken partly from its being likely to form an interesting letter, but still more probably from a desire to foster his own inclinations. And no wonder! For it is not every man who could write in perfect sincerity, "My experience of mines is very extensive," and then go on to talk like a past master of mining in general, not in support of this assertion, but in proof of his general knowledge.

Reaching the quicksilver mines, which are, as is probably known, very few and far between upon the face of the earth, he gives a thorough description of the place. The workmen, he tells us, number some six hundred, the buildings connected with the mine are good and well kept, the posts and doors painted the familiar black and yellow of Austria, while the imperial arms, surmounted by the two crossed hammers, are fixed to the various offices.

In old works, accounts are given about condemnation to the quicksilver mines and the convict life of the unfortunates, but

Henty's account of the place seems to prove everything to be very businesslike and matter-of-fact, and the old descriptions that blackened the administration would appear to have been extremely highly coloured. The government has erected a theatre for the use of the workmen, and has in other ways laid itself out to study their comforts in a manner for which its habitual detractors would hardly have given it credit.

The pay of the miners is about eightpence a day, apparently a very small sum, but which is above the average gain in a country where the necessaries of life are extremely cheap. When they are ill, and this is not infrequently the case, for the fumes of mercury are extremely deleterious, they receive three-quarter pay, together with medicine and medical attendance, while they are provided for in old age.

After this brief socio-political statement, the businesslike miner and student of geology speaks of the formation of the country where the mines are situated. This is an oolite limestone, that is to say, the cream-coloured soft building stone so familiar in building, which hardens in time, and is generally dubbed Bath Stone.

He was rather surprised that a quicksilver mine should be here, and he made a careful examination of the surface of the neighbourhood before descending, but could discover no signs of the existence of a mineral vein, and so felt at a loss to imagine what induced the original investigators to set to work at that particular spot.

Here is his version of the old story which credits the discovery of quicksilver as being due to a barrel-maker who, after making a tub, placed it under a dropping spring to see if it would hold water. When he came to look at it again, he found it contained what he took to be a certain amount of glistening water; but on attempting to move the tub, he discovered it to be so heavy that

HIGHLY COLOURED: *exaggerated*
ITS HABITUAL DETRACTORS: *those who are always criticizing it*
DELETERIOUS: *harmful*
DUBBED: *named*

he could not lift it, the supposed water being the enormously heavy liquid, quicksilver.

Henty also relates that a spring that arose in Idria had been observed to deposit in the hollows of the stone small quantities of quicksilver. This came to the notice of a merchant from Trieste, who happened to be stopping in the neighbourhood. Being a businessman whose head was screwed on the right way, he came to the conclusion that this quicksilver must issue from the rock in company with water, and that if he sank to a sufficient depth, the source from which the spring drew the mercury would be discovered. Without any delay he obtained a grant from government, began to sink, and carried on quicksilver-mining for some years with success. But it soon became evident to him that the primary source of the fluent metal was much deeper down, and to reach it much larger capital was required than he could command; so, still acting as the businessman, he sold his works to the government, no doubt at an excellent profit, and by the government they have been carried on ever since. They are now the richest and most extensive of any in Europe, with the exception only of those at Almaden, in Spain.

Henty's stay in Idria was only short; but being furnished with a guide, and having put on the suit of miner's clothes provided for visitors, he commenced his descent. This was made by means of a number of inclined shafts of admirable masonry, worked in a perfect oval, and about seven feet in height. These can be best conceived by imagining a perfectly dry London sewer being placed nearly on end. In these shafts small stone steps were formed, by which the descent was made without fatigue or difficulty. He considered that these shafts were superior, both in arrangement and workmanship, to anything he had ever seen in his great experience.

On descending he noticed that the mine was worked, to speak technically, in five levels, and that in some places the quicksilver was in the familiar glistening globules in a soft and partially decomposed state. But the greater portion occurred in the aforesaid limestone itself, and even where it was present in the enormous proportion of eighty per cent it was not visible; but the ore resembled very rich brown hematite ironstone. In describing his visit, Henty goes on to write about the warmth of the atmosphere and the close mineral odour, and to relate how, in consequence of the deleterious mercurial fumes, the miners are unable to work in the richest parts for more than two hours at a time.

He continues, then, quite as a man accustomed to inspecting mines, declaring that the timbering, i.e. the supports, of the levels, ventilation, and other arrangements of the mine are good. But he never saw labour so completely thrown away in any undertaking of the kind he ever visited; for the miners were constantly employed upon poor barren-looking stuff, which the most unpractised mining man—including, of course, himself—might have seen would never lead to anything. Had their work taken the shape of small galleries for exploration, it might have been explicable; but the men were almost all engaged in greatly widening previously-made passages where nothing whatever had been found, nor was likely to be. He accounts for this, like a practical man, by supposing that, as a miner could only work for a few hours a week upon the rich spots, and as the management are obliged to keep a large succession of men for working continuously, they put the men to work in the barren places purely to keep them employed.

Satisfied with his inspection, he at last made the ascent, coming up a nearly perpendicular shaft, worked by water-power, in the large and dirty basket in which the ore is lifted to the

AFORESAID: *previously mentioned*
EXPLICABLE: *explainable*

surface. He then proceeded to the smelting-houses, where the quicksilver is extracted from the ore. These were about a mile from the town; but the furnaces were not at work at that time of year—October—on account of the fumes thrown off being so extremely deleterious to vegetation and to the cattle which fed upon it, as in grazing they, of course, took up a certain amount of the mercury deposited upon the herbage.

The smelting, or, as it might more properly be called, the distilling, of the mercury is only carried on in winter, when the fumes that escape from the furnaces fall upon the surface of the snow, which in that mountainous country covers the earth, and are washed away when the thaw comes in the spring. The poorer ores are crushed under stamps, and the mineral is separated by dressing and shaking tables. The richer stuff is at once carried to the furnaces, where it is roasted, and the mercurial fumes which are evolved by this process are collected in adjoining chambers. Henty goes on, like a mining expert, to criticize the imperfect way in which the processes are carried out, adjudging that under better management the fumes which spread over the surrounding country would be far less noxious.

The total amount of quicksilver produced by this one mine annually is about two thousand five hundred pounds, and this is exported in iron bottles for the use of the gold and silver mines of Mexico, Peru, and Brazil.[1]

Surprise was expressed at the commencement of this chapter that literature had not lost her able writer for boys by his being absorbed by the mining profession. His remarks concerning miners gained from his own observation pretty well justify this comment, for, moralizing upon the people under observation at the quicksilver mines of Idria, he says that among no class of the population of various countries is there so great a resemblance as between miners. However the peasantry in general

---

[1] Mercury combines easily with gold and silver and can be used to extract them from other minerals.

EVOLVED: *given off*
ADJUDGING: *declaring*
NOXIOUS: *harmful*

may attire themselves, the miner wears a universal garb. He shaves closely, so that the dust and dirt, which his occupation involves, may be the more readily removed when he returns to the upper air; and if the workers in the lead-mines of the island of Sardinia (where he had been, to study them), the Slav from Illyria, the Frenchman, the Belgian, the Cornish, Welsh and Newcastle miner, with all of whom he had made acquaintance, were massed together, the shrewdest observer would be puzzled to separate the men belonging to the different nationalities. They wear the same coarse flannel attire; they have the same loosely-hung limbs, the same muscular development about the shoulders, and the same weakness of leg; their faces are uniformly pale and sallow from working in places where daylight never penetrates; they are hard drinkers, strong in their likes and dislikes, very independent, and great sticklers for their rights.

Certainly, he continues, these Idrian miners are more fortunate in many respects than their fellows, for their houses are singularly large, clean, and commodious. Their government lays a considerable extra tax upon wine, because its use is very hurtful to the men engaged in the mercury works, but its price does not prevent the miners from partaking of it freely.

Henty slept in Idria but one night, and he found it very late before the little town settled into tranquillity. Every time he closed his eyes and endeavoured to go to sleep, a burst of discordant singing from parties returning from wine-shops reminded him unpleasantly that miners will be miners all the world over.

The next morning he left for Italy, and he amusingly describes his experiences of travel in a primitive conveyance hung very low, without any springs whatever. This should have been drawn by a pair of horses, but was actually only drawn by a

GARB: *type of clothing*
SALLOW: *sickly, yellowish*
GREAT STICKLERS FOR: *always insisting on*
COMMODIOUS: *spacious*

single beast trotting upon one side of the pole. The shaking upon the rough road traversed was something terrible, and in the course of a six hours' journey he was rather glad of a rest of half an hour and a relief from the shaking.

As the village inns were all alike, he describes one as a sample, in which he partook of some very weak, warm stuff which they called broth. The room set apart for the meal was low and whitewashed, crossed by the rough beams which supported the room above. In one corner was an immense stove, five feet high and six feet square, covered with green-glazed earthenware tiles. A seat ran round this, and upon the top a layer of maize was spread out to dry. In another corner was a small cupboard. But even there art was represented by roughly-coloured prints dealing with the Prodigal Son, in the attire of a Venetian senator of the Middle Ages. There was a crucifix with a small lamp upon it, a great clock like those seen in English country cottages, with a preternaturally loud tick, and there was a strange-looking table, which he found upon examination was a paste-board and flour-bin combined. Three puppies and two kittens scampered and played about upon the floor, which was of stone, but beautifully clean.

Reader, do you like struddle? Most probably you are quite ignorant of what the question means. Henty was in precisely the same mental condition when, after eating his soup, his hostess asked him if he would like some struddle.

Henty assented, without having the slightest idea of what struddle might be, and the hostess brought in a plate of what resembled boiled three-corner puffs; but, though sweet, they were not triangular jam tarts, for the contents were principally onions and parsley, and quite uneatable.

PRETERNATURALLY: *unnaturally*
PASTE-BOARD: *kneading-trough*

THE ABYSSINIAN CAMPAIGN

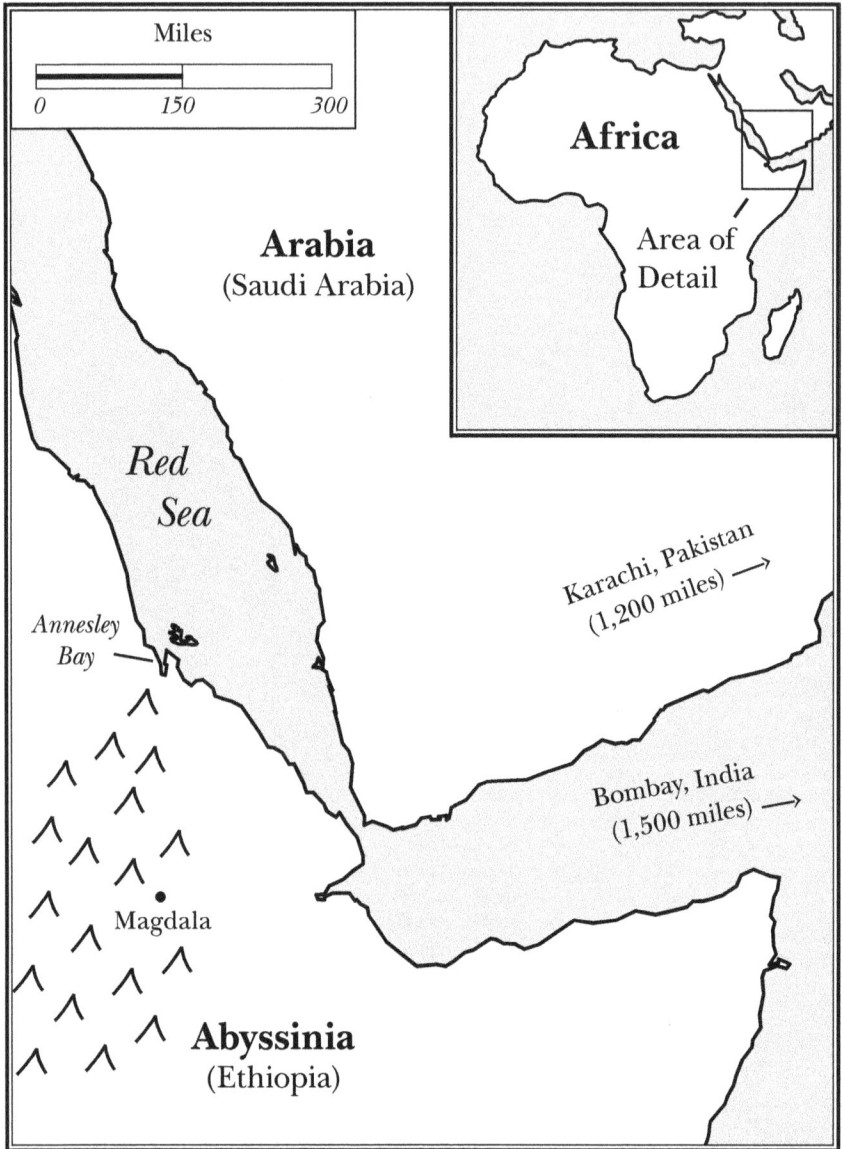

Miles

0   150   300

Africa

Area of
Detail

Arabia
(Saudi Arabia)

Red
Sea

Annesley
Bay

Karachi, Pakistan
(1,200 miles) →

Bombay, India
(1,500 miles) →

Magdala

Abyssinia
(Ethiopia)

CHAPTER XIV

THE ABYSSINIAN CAMPAIGN

HENTY was not one who, during a long life, indited many letters dealing with his ordinary social communings with his friends, from which chapters might be extracted concerning his thoughts upon political or social subjects, his leanings towards life in general, or his interest in some special subject. He rarely wrote home save, as has been before said, to tell of the state of his health, referring those he loved to his long professional letters in the columns of the journal he represented. But in justice to one of the most industrious of men, his family fared, as far as interesting and descriptive matter was concerned, much better than those connected with the most chatty of correspondents, who scatter manuscript as opposed to his print.

Autobiographies are few. There are plenty of the young and enthusiastic who begin life by writing a journal, but those who keep it up to the end are very, very rare. Unconsciously, however, George Alfred Henty pretty well passed his days in writing his own life, and, as it turned out, a life of the most stirring kind.

The letters he did write to his colleagues upon business, those of a social nature, or on matters connected with some literary transaction to a fellow club member, as well as those

INDITED: *wrote*

between editor and contributor, or with the positions reversed, were always the same—written in a minute neat hand upon small notepaper and in violet ink. But of the many possessed by the writer not one seems to contain material that would be interesting to the general reader. Owing, perhaps, to their want of egotism, they do not tell their own tale of the man's nature one half so well as the columns he wrote during his long connection with the newspaper press.

And thus it is that through his early manhood onward, through maturity to his thoroughly vigorous old age—if it can be termed old age when a man is robust and virile till beyond three-score years and ten—Henty's life formed so many chapters of energetic and active career, marked, as it were, by passages generally warlike, connected with the warfare of nations.

At the time of which one is writing, that is, the year following the freeing of Italy, he spent much of his time making tentative unofficial efforts with his pen; but this was prior to the commencement of the long series of novels and stories written especially for the youth of England. For the next year he began to devote considerable attention to his little yacht, finding exercise and refreshing peaceful life afloat. Yachting was the one hobby of his manhood, and a recreation in which he indulged himself at every opportunity, even to the very last. In this way he recouped himself, and made up for the worry and excitement such as falls to the lot of a war correspondent, who is never free from the strain of thinking out what will be the most interesting thing to record among the many incidents occurring around him. There is invariably anxiety about how to write and where to write, and when the account is written the additional worry of how to get in touch with the post and make sure that you have done everything possible to ensure the matter reaching its destination safely and expeditiously.

MINUTE: *very small*
WANT OF EGOTISM: *lack of an excessive focus on himself*
THREE-SCORE YEARS AND TEN: *seventy years*
EXPEDITIOUSLY: *quickly*

The year's comparative rest that followed the adventures in Italy was needed, for Henty was awaking fully to the fact that a war correspondent's life makes a heavy drain upon the stored-up forces of the Bank of Life; and it must not be forgotten that his health exchequer in youth was at a very low ebb.

It may have been instinct—the natural desire of the weak to gain strength—that induced Henty to direct his attention so much to the sea; and without doubt this favourite pursuit of yachting, which took him away from town life, from the strain of mind and the weary hours at the desk, to where he could breathe the free air of heaven and cast off care, strengthened him and prepared him for the next bout of duty that he would be called upon to undertake.

It was just a year after the conclusion of the Italian war when he was called upon to gird himself for another period of active service, and leave civilized Europe for the heats and colds of semi-barbarous mountainous Africa. The cry of the sufferers had awakened patient Britain to the fact that she could no longer stop her ears to the piteous plaint of the captives, no longer suffer the mocking insolence of the defiant ignorant ruler, King Theodore of Abyssinia; and Sir Robert Napier was preparing his forces for the invasion of that comparatively unknown and warlike land.

All this is well-recorded history. Henty's adventures begin with his start for the front, after reaching Bombay, where his first troubles commenced with the choice of attendants. Servants swarmed, but experience seemed to show that it was considered the correct thing to hire oneself out to a master bound for Abyssinia, and, just before he left, to disappear with his purse and any handy portable property.

Henty's first experience was with a mild Hindu, who directly after fell sick, while this man's brother, engaged by a colleague,

EXCHEQUER: *treasury*
PLAINT: *cry for help*

was at the last moment melted by the tears of an aged and despairing mother, and the two rogues decamped laden with plunder.

This difficulty got over, necessaries were packed, and a vessel was chosen in which Henty and a friend were to sail in company with some of the troops. They were a little disturbed, though, when they discovered that the only available bath below had to be removed to make room for three and a half tons of gunpowder. It was a change which by no means added to their comfort or to their feelings of security.

However, in spite of hindrances and delays, he, a brother special, and three officers made their start, choosing by preference to sleep on deck, partly because the nights *al fresco* were delightful, though rather cold, but more on account of the imaginary dangers that might arise from the monsters which haunted the berths below. It may have been the effect of imagination and extreme terror, but these creatures appeared to be as large as cats, and much quicker footed, probably from having more legs. Their horns resembled those of bullocks, and in their utter fearlessness of man they attacked him ferociously. Henty christens them vampires, though he does not record that they practised the bloodthirsty habits of those creatures, and then he comes down to plain fact and explains that his *bêtes noires* answered to the common name of cockroach.

One of his first experiences of sleeping on deck with his comrades was to be awakened by a splash of water in his face, and as the vessel was given to rolling he attributed this to spray; but only for an instant, for down came a rush of water as if emptied from a bucket. In a moment he was upon his feet to begin dragging his bed over to leeward. Then came a rude awakening to the fact that the splash and the bucketing were caused

DECAMPED: *left camp*
AL FRESCO: *out of doors; literally "in the fresh" in Italian*
BÊTES NOIRES: *"black beasts" in French*
OVER TO LEEWARD: *downwind*

by rain, which raged down as if pumped by a hundred steam fire-engines. There was nothing for it but to laugh, as the party gained the cabin floor drenched, and with their silken pyjamas clinging to their skins.

The customary troubles on board the small vessel, laden to a great extent with heterogeneous stores, came to an end, but not without incident, for navigation in the Red Sea is a most intricate and dangerous business, as its western shore is studded with islands and coral reefs.

The vessel was running along with a favourable breeze, and Henty had been watching the low shore with its stunted bushes and strange conical hills bearing a fantastic resemblance to haycocks, while a mighty range of mountains loomed up in the distance. The outlook was interesting enough, for this was his first sight of Abyssinia; but then came a very narrow escape. They were sauntering about, watching the land and listening to the calls of the sailor heaving the lead in the chains. First it was ten fathoms, then two minutes elapsed and the man cried five fathoms, whereupon a shout came from the captain: "Stop her! Turn her astern!" In the momentary pause of the beat of the screw the sailor's voice came again: "Two fathoms!"—a dire warning to those on board the steamer.

But the screw had been reversed, and the yellow water was foaming round them, showing that the sand at the bottom of the shallow water was being churned up as the steamer, still forging more and more slowly ahead, came to a standstill. Then the fact was patent that they were ashore; while thoughts of shipwreck began to be busy in the brain.

The customary business of trying to get the vessel off ensued; orders flew about; the vessel was driven ahead, then astern; but she remained fast, and seemed to be moving only on a pivot.

HETEROGENEOUS: *widely varied*
HAYCOCKS: *haystacks*
SCREW: *propeller*

The troops and crew were ordered up and tramped here and there—marching aft, then forward, but without result. They were run in a body from side to side, to give the vessel a rolling motion. Still no result. Then another plan was tried, so as to loosen the craft from the clinging sand and work out a sort of channel; and this was managed by the soldiers running to one side and then jumping together, then back across the deck and jumping again, the effort being made by every active person on board, till it seemed as if all were engaged in a frantic war-dance.

After this anchors were got out, and the men set to work at the capstan, the only result being that they seemed to be fishing for coral, pieces of which were dragged up looking ominously suggestive of what would happen if some of the glistening white dead rock pierced the vessel's skin.

There seemed at last to be no chance of getting off unless a portion of the cargo were discharged. Accordingly when an Arab dhow came into sight and dropped anchor, a bargain was made with the sheik, her captain, for him to come alongside and lighten the steamer by taking on board a portion of the cargo and the whole of the troops. This, Eastern fashion, took an enormous amount of talking, and when all was settled it was found that the water was too shallow for the big dhow to come alongside, with the result that this expedient was given up.

Then another dhow came and anchored at a short distance, presenting something novel to the traveller. This vessel proved to be bound for their own port, namely, Annesley Bay, and it was laden with a portion of the transport that was to help the expedition across the wild country towards Magdala, to wit, a herd of no fewer than twenty-two camels. The poor animals, the so-called ships of the desert, were packed together in a boat that did not look large enough to hold half that number.

CAPSTAN: *a device used to pull on ropes, in this case the anchor chains*
DHOW: *a sailing ship with triangular sails*
SHEIK: *an Arab leader or official*
EXPEDIENT: *plan*

At last real help came within signaling distance, and this proved to be one of the Peninsular and Oriental Company's big steamers.[1] She had half of one of our regiments on board, and was towing a consort with the remaining half of the 33rd Regiment from Karachi.

A boat was sent from the great steamer, and an officer came on board to examine the state of affairs. He very soon came to the decision that the water was too shallow for his vessel, the *Salsette,* to come within towing distance. As the grounded ship was in no danger, he was obliged to leave it to its fate; but to the great satisfaction of Henty and his colleague, on ascertaining their destination he offered them a passage for the rest of the way. In due course they arrived very comfortably at the starting-point for the expedition.

[1] An British shipping company founded in 1837, the Peninsular and Oriental Company primarily delivered mail in the 1800's.

CONSORT: *additional ship*

Chapter XV

Incidents of Transport

THERE was plenty to see at the far-from-cheerful place which was to become the depot of troops and stores. A pier was being run up for landing purposes, and vessels were discharging slowly, with the promise of a deadlock unless more convenience for landing the contents of the vessels that were lying idle was provided.

To all intents and purposes they were at the edge of a desert, and here everything that was necessary for the expedition had to be landed. An enclosure was filled with stacks of pressed hay for the mules and piles of grain and rice—goods that would be easily damaged, but were fairly safe, nevertheless, owing to being in a hot and comparatively rainless district.

Besides the regular labourers that had been engaged, brightly clothed women, looking particularly picturesque, had been sent over from India on purpose to grind the corn for the troops. Tents had arisen, forming quite a canvas town; and storehouses were being constructed by Chinese carpenters, so that the place was rapidly becoming busily populous. In addition to those at the landing-place, clusters of tents were scattered within a circle of a mile, while the main camp of the expedition was a mile and a half inland, consequent upon the scarcity of water. For at the beginning all living things, men and beasts, had to depend for the principal life-sustainer, water, on the supply obtained from the ships. Consequently every steamer in the harbour was at work night and day condensing, at a cost of twopence halfpenny a gallon for the coal consumed in the process.

Henty's senses of sight and smell were offended as they had not been since the Crimea. Dead mules, camels, and oxen lay everywhere about the shore, and attempts were being made to get rid of the offence by burning the carcasses. Wherever the poor brutes were lately dead, vultures were congregated, many so gorged with flesh that they could hardly rise when approached, while others, where some poor beast had lately expired, were walking about at a distance, as if not quite certain that the animal was dead.

It was a doleful picture—one of the accessaries of the glories of war. Here and there half-starved mules were wandering about, their heads down, their ears drooping, and their eyes growing dim with the approach of death; others staggered down to where the sea rippled on the sands, and tasted again and again the briny water; while others still, half-maddened by the heat and thirst, drank copiously, to drop dead where they stood, or crawl away to die miserably in the low desolate-looking scrub.

A man with a great love for domestic animals, Henty generally had about half-a-dozen dogs of the Scotch terrier and other breeds to share with him the quiet of his home study, supplemented by two or three cats which lived in fairly good harmony; the sight of these suffering dumb creatures therefore strongly moved his sympathies.

CONDENSING: *boiling saltwater to obtain fresh water*
ACCESSARIES: *partners*
BRINY: *salty*
COPIOUSLY: *deeply*

G. A. Henty's Dogs

Before his landing, his attention had been attracted by the cruel way in which the wretched, doleful camels were packed in the dhow, and the sight of these beasts of burden being disembarked drew his attention at once.

The native boats could not get nearer than two or three hundred yards from the shore, for the water was not more than three or four feet deep, and into these shallows the poor brutes were dragged and thrust, when, dazed by the novel position, they for the most part lay down, their long necks raising their curious heads just above the surface, while they made no attempt to make for the land. Some never did make any effort, and later their bodies would be seen drifting here and there, growing more buoyant under the hot sun as decomposition set in. Others, however, struggled to within fifty yards of the shore before lying down, to look, with their erect necks and partly submerged bodies, just like gigantic waterfowl. As for those that were driven ashore, want of food and the evil treatment received during their transit had reduced them to the most miserable plight. Their bones were almost starting through their skins; and while at the best of times, when well fed and watered, a camel in its utterances is a most doleful, murmurous creature, these poor brutes lay as if dead upon the sand, uttering feebly the almost human moaning and complainings peculiar to their race.

Whether from mismanagement or callous brutality, the treatment of the unfortunate mules and camels landed on these desolate shores was painful in the extreme, and droves of hundreds untended were wandering about, striving for a few days' existence by plucking scanty shoots, previous to sickening and dying.

The scenes, Henty says, were frightful everywhere, but worst of all at the water-troughs, where the half-mad animals, especially the mules, struggled for a drink at a time when water was almost worth its weight in gold. They fought wildly for a draught of that for which they were dying, biting and kicking till many of them in their weakness were knocked down and trampled to death, a fate which at least saved them from perishing miserably under their burdens upon the road.

Thoroughly angered by the neglect, and in accordance with the intense desire of the practical man to have everything done orderly and well, Henty busied himself and inquired why these scattered mules were left untended, to learn that nearly the whole of the mule and camel drivers had deserted. In fact, at the beginning of the arrangements in connection with the transport, everything seemed to have gone wrong. The mules and camels were dying of thirst and neglect; consequently the advance brigade could not be supplied with food. Someone was in fault, but, as is often the case, the mistakes of one are visited upon no one knows how many. But there, it is easy to find fault.

CALLOUS: *uncaring*

It must have seemed almost bliss to get away from the misery and confusion in the neighbourhood of Annesley Bay. At least there was the hope of ceasing to be tormented by the flies that were increasing and multiplying, as they did farther north in the old Pharaonic days.[1] There was the prospect of a weary desert journey over sand and rock, with a pause here and there where wells existed with their scanty supply of water, or others were being dug, but there was the promise of a pleasanter existence afterwards, since the camp station was nearly five hundred feet above sea-level, with a likelihood of comparative coolness.

It was a long and dreary ride, with nature apparently against the intruders. As a consequence, with animals as well as with man everything seemed to go wrong. One of Henty's principal complaints was still of the flies, which he considered to be, up to the present, the greatest nuisance he had met with in Abyssinia. He declared them to be as numerous and as irritating as they were in Egypt; but he consoled himself with the fact that they went to sleep when the sun set, and as there were no mosquitoes to take their place, he was able to sleep in tranquillity, that is to say, to lie down in the sand. Water, of course, was too scarce for a wash; but here again there was consolation—a good shake on rising, and the dry clean sand all fell away.

Still, there was a fresh anxiety for him in connection with the traveller's greatest worry, that is, luggage. He was much troubled by the fact that the troop of mules which bore the officers' necessaries had not turned up, and one of the missing animals was the carrier of his own luggage and stores.

On this march Henty had his first experience of the desert wells. These wells were dug in the bed of what in the rainy season must have been a mighty torrent fifty yards wide. He states that he had seen many singular scenes, but this was the strangest. The wells were six in number, about a dozen feet across and

[1] Days of the Pharaohs; referring to the plague of flies, one of the ten plagues which occurred just before the Jewish Exodus out of Egypt

as many deep. All the water had to be raised in buckets by men standing upon wooden platforms who passed the full buckets from hand to hand. The water was then emptied into earthen troughs, which soon became mud basins, and from these the animals were allowed to drink to the tune of a perpetual chant kept up by the natives, without which the latter seemed unable to work.

Round the wells was a vast crowd of animals—flocks of goats and small sheep, strings of draught bullocks, mules, ponies, horses, and camels, and about them stood the regular inhabitants of the country in their scanty attire, armed with spears, swords like reaping-hooks, and heavy clubs. The women among them were either draped in calico or picturesquely clothed in leather, and plentifully adorned with necklaces of seeds or shells.

Here, too, the trouble with the thirsty animals was often terrible, the camels being especially unmanageable. One of them, for instance, because its pack had slipped beneath it, began to utter strange uncouth cries, kicking and plunging wildly, until it started a stampede among the mules, many of which had probably never seen any of these ungainly beasts before.

When matters settled down, the little party made for the commissariat tent to draw their rations, and here a religious trouble arose among some of the Parsee clerks of one of the departments. They complained bitterly that there was no mutton, and that it was contrary to their religion to eat beef. The commissariat officer regretted the circumstances, but pointed out that at present no sheep had been landed, while the small ovine animals of the country were mere skin and bone.

Henty closes this little scene with the moral that Parsees should not go to war in a country where mutton is scarce, and he wonders how the Hindu soldiers will manage to preserve their caste intact.

UNGAINLY: *awkward looking*
PARSEE: *Persian*
MUTTON: *sheep meat*
OVINE: *sheep-like*

CHAPTER XVI

EN ROUTE FOR MAGDALA

THE famous march to Magdala had now begun, and Henty's recorded recollections are full of interest and observation.

At one time he came upon a party of excited soldiers who had suddenly disturbed a troop of the great baboons which haunt the stony mountains, and, with visions of specimens flashing across his mind, he joined in the chase, revolver in hand, racing and climbing among impeding thorns, compared to which an English quickset hedge was nothing at all. After a couple of hours' hunt, followed out as eagerly as when he was a boy, he found that the quarry was quite at home and that he was not, with the result that he thought he lost pounds in weight by his exertions, but that the toil did him good.

Before the starting of the expedition, the press had been full of the predictions of the busybodies who know all about everything, and had prophesied that those who went were to die of fever, malaria, sunstroke, tsetse fly, guinea worm, tapeworm, and other maladies. It was soon found, however, that everybody enjoyed vigorous health, and that though the army was in expectation of being hindered by, and of having to fight their way through, the forces of the petty kings or chiefs through whose countries they passed, very little of a serious nature occurred to hinder the advance to the stronghold of the stubborn monarch of Abyssinia.

EN ROUTE: *"on the way" in French*
QUICKSET HEDGE: *a hedge made of hawthorn bushes*
PETTY KINGS: *little kings*

Nothing seems to have been too small for Henty's observation, and his letters to the journal he represented teem with references to the various objects that caught his eye. At one time he was describing the appearance, uniforms, and physique of the Indian troops, the Beloochs, or the manners and customs of the scoundrelly camp-followers. Then he would descend directly afterwards to such minor matters in natural history as the feeding habits of the sheep ticks, which in places swarmed. In another place he discourses in a much more interesting fashion than a scientific student (for he omits the hard technical names) of the vegetation seen around, such as gigantic tulip trees, and a shrub of whose name he confesses his ignorance, though he considers it notable from the sprays resembling asparagus. He is attracted by plants of the cactus tribe, particularly by one that spreads out a number of arms pointing upwards, making it resemble a gigantic cauliflower. Then, evidently feeling doubtful about the suitability of so matter-of-fact a description, he makes a brave shot at the Latin name—almost the only one he records—the scientific italics, *Euphorbia candalabriensis*, looking novel and strange. Later, with a frank display of doubt, he declares that he does not vouch for the correctness of this name.

Onward still, hour by hour and day by day, we follow him, noting how eager and fresh he is in the morning, and how weary as the day's march approaches its end. At these times we find him recording the unpleasantnesses of the route, such as the influence upon the atmosphere of the dead carcasses of the worn-out animals, from whose neighbourhood the great vultures rise lazily and wheel away.

The heat of the sun was at times intense, but the nights were sometimes bitterly cold, too cold to sleep, and when at last sleep came, again and again the weary travellers were disturbed by the antics of one of the beasts that bear about the worst

DISCOURSES: *speaks*

character of any that have been brought into domestic use, and whose obstinacy has become a proverb. One of these mules would break loose from its head ropes, and, as if urged on by some malignant spirit of mischief, would nearly upset the tent by stumbling over the pegs and getting itself involved amongst the ropes, when, as if bitterly resenting the presence of their mischievous distant relative, the horses would seem perfectly savage, and threaten to break loose and stampede. Four or five times in a night Henty or one of his colleagues would have to get up and go out in the cold to stone the brute, while the grooms, who were sleeping for mutual protection close to the horses' heads, and who were rolled up in their rugs, wonderful to state, heard nothing.

But this was not the only manner in which the calm of the night's rest would be disturbed, for the native followers who acted as servants to the group of war correspondents seemed to have a natural proclivity for quarrelling among themselves, often rousing up their masters in alarm to find out what some outburst might mean. Long after his return from Abyssinia, Henty would amuse his literary friends by chatting over these troubles of the night.

As a change from this we find Henty noticing the beauty of the country, the picturesqueness of the narrow gorges through which they passed, and the profusion of wild figs, golden-blossomed laburnum, and acacias, the last white-flowered and with pods of the clearest carmine. Getting now upon colour, he describes the beauty of the numerous sun-birds and the gorgeous plumage of others of larger size that, startled by the strangeness of their visitors, perched at a short distance from the path. Again, the descriptions of the brilliant butterflies which flitted here and there among the flowers are strongly suggestive of the observant boy longing for a net and a few cardboard boxes and pins.

STONE: *throw stones at*
LABURNUM: *a tree or shrub with hanging clusters of flowers*
ACACIAS: *small trees or shrubs in the locust family*
CARMINE: *red*

These charming rides had to give way to work of a very different nature, which included dismounting, leading their ponies, and preparing to ascend the mountainside; for the valleys and ravines gave way to steep tracks covered with boulders, the tropical valley with its beautiful foliage was succeeded by stunted pines, and the sappers were set busily at work forming a track of zigzags for the force to ascend.

At times the store and ammunition-bearing mules had to ascend places as steep as flights of stairs, with the steps as much as three feet high; but, nothing daunted, the force pressed on.

Later, an ambassador from one of the local kings, whose country was being traversed, met the advancing force, and it was considered an act of wisdom to give him a sample of what our well-drilled troops could do, in the way of a little sham-fight. The display was so effectively carried out that this monarch considered it good policy not to support King Theodore with his army of seven thousand men.

At the first camp among the mountains the native Abyssinians, led by curiosity, or possibly with other intentions if opportunity served, swarmed around, exciting Henty's interest in their swords and spears. Certain specimens he managed to secure (not those of the poorer classes, but those of costly silver), and these he afterwards hung upon the walls of his study at home.

As compared with the slight bayonet of our men, fixed to the rifle barrel, the Abyssinians' spears were formidable weapons, from six to ten feet long, and weighted at the butt. Their bearers could throw them over thirty yards with great force and with no little accuracy, while in a hand-to-hand fight, or when offering resistance to a charge, they were dangerous weapons in the grasp of an active man.

At one time Henty records an unpleasant check to his proceedings in the shape of an order being promulgated that no

SAPPERS: *military engineers*
BUTT: *base*

correspondents were to accompany the expedition; but when another general took over the command, this embargo was removed, and we find him at the front again, after a long weary pause which had forced him into inactivity at the base.

In spite of obstacles upon obstacles the troops were progressing. The heavy guns surmounted the rugged mountain-paths, and the savage cruel tyrant passed from mocking defiance to alarm, as his scouts brought him tidings of the slow and determined march, higher and higher towards his stronghold, of the punitive force which conquered slowly and steadily every physical difficulty.

Then there were rumours that King Theodore was beginning to repent, and that he was ready to give up his many prisoners, releasing them from their long captivity. But the expedition still rolled onwards and upwards—cavalry, infantry, and the heavy and light mountain guns—ready to carry Magdala by *coup de main* if it were feasible, or bring the tyrant into submission by a prolonged siege.

Though everything seemed to be done very deliberately, the advance never stayed, with the troops still healthy and well, the losses only occurring among the transport animals as the result of accident, hard usage, and disease. It was a varied little army which composed this expedition, horse and foot—light-mounted Hussars, sturdy infantry, and dark-browed men of India in their picturesque uniform, green frocks, red sashes, and scarlet turbans. The picturesque was not lacking, either, in the work of surmounting the stern rugged passes, where the engineer officers with their sappers cleverly and speedily constructed bridges over gully and gash.

The progress by this time had become steady and methodical. The losses were terrible, but fresh animals arrived to take the place of those which were swept away by disease. The chief

EMBARGO: *restriction*
PUNITIVE: *punishing*
COUP DE MAIN: *quick action*
STAYED: *stopped*

halts were made at the stations formed at the wells, many of the latter being constructed on the new ingenious principle which came into note at that time.[1] These wells were afterwards familiar at home as Abyssinian wells. Thus slowly, but steadily, our lightly burdened troops continued on their way, each day bringing them nearer to where Theodore had gathered his forces in the mountain aerie, which he had believed impregnable.

---

[1] Wells made by driving a perforated pipe into the ground

AERIE: *fortress*
IMPREGNABLE: *unconquerable*

CHAPTER XVII

JOTTINGS BY THE WAY

DURING the advance Henty relates that three of the officers of the 4th Regiment of Foot were witnesses of a horribly barbarous custom practised among the natives of Abyssinia, a custom which shows the callousness of the natives to the sufferings of the animals in domestic use. The practise was recorded by James Bruce as witnessed by him during his travels in Abyssinia, towards the end of the eighteenth century, in connection with his attempts to discover the sources of the Nile. Upon his return, when he described the manners and customs of the people of Abyssinia, his narratives were received with mingled incredulity and ridicule, and the practise now in question was treated as an outrageous traveller's tale. Certainly the problem whether nature would readily heal the wound described gave some excuse for want of faith in what approaches the marvellous.

The operation described by Bruce, but which has been denied by all subsequent travellers, and by the Abyssinians themselves, probably through some feeling of shame at their own barbarity, was that of cutting a steak from the body of a living ox. Our officers came upon the natives just as they were engaged in the act. The unfortunate bullock was thrown down, and its four legs were tied together. The operator then cut an incision near

INCREDULITY: *disbelief*
MARVELLOUS: *incredible*

the spine, just behind the hip joint. Next, separating the skin from the flesh, he cut two other incisions at right angles to the first, this enabling him to lift up a flap of skin four or five inches square. After this, by cutting with his knife diagonally, so as to pass the keen instrument partly under the skin, he cut out a lump of flesh larger in length and width than the flap of skin. The hole made was then filled with a particular preparation, and the flap of skin was replaced and plastered over with mud. Finally, the feet of the poor animal, which had kept up a low moaning while the operation was going on, were untied, and it was given a kick to make it get up. It should be mentioned that the operator cut two or three gashes in the neighbourhood of the wound, apparently as a sign to show that the animal had been operated upon in that part. The officers observed that several of the other cattle of the same herd were marked in a precisely similar manner. It was remarked, too, that during the operation the poor animal bled very little, and half an hour afterwards was found walking about and feeding quietly.

Anatomists have denied, Henty continues, the possibility of an animal being able to walk after such treatment; but here was the indisputable fact. There is the possibility that the antiseptic nature of the huge plaster, used to fill up the vacancy from which the piece of flesh had been cut, was sufficient to make it heal in the pure clear air of mountain Africa.

Fortunately, from our few losses—unfortunately, from a scientific point of view—we have no record of how clean-cut wounds in the human being fared in Abyssinia. On the other hand, the rapid healing of flesh and muscle on the lofty tablelands of the Transvaal during the Boer War was almost marvellous.

Everywhere on his way to the front Henty found something fresh to describe. One day there was to be rocket practise, the operators being the Naval Brigade, with its frank-looking,

ANATOMISTS: *specialists who study how bodies work*
TRANSVAAL: *a region in northern South Africa*

free-and-easy Jacks, who were anxious to be ready to astonish the natives with their singular missiles. There was not room in the valley where they were in camp, so the plan was tried of drawing the tubes up one hill and firing across to the next hill, about two thousand yards away.

There were twelve mules, each with a tube and a supply of ninety rockets. There were four men to each tube, besides the one who led the bearer. At the word "Unload!" the tubes, each about three feet in length, were taken off the mules and arranged in line upon a sort of stand, with an elevator, which could be adjusted to any required angle.

The order first given was to try ten degrees of elevation, and at the command "Fire!" a stickless rocket rushed from the tube like a firework, and buzzed through the air to the opposite hill. Three rockets were fired at this elevation, and then three from an elevation of five degrees, all apparently passing to their mark in a way likely to strike terror into the hearts of the defenders of Magdala.

These men of the Naval Rocket Brigade, who had come up to join the military, proved to be an admirable body of men, ready to endure fatigue and hardship with the good temper peculiar to sailors. Contrary to what might have been expected, seeing how little marching a man-of-war's man is accustomed to get, they marched better than soldiers, and never fell out, even on the most fatiguing journeys. Their quaint humour provided great amusement to the troops, and the way in which they talked to their mules, which they persisted in treating as ships, was irresistibly comic.

Henty mentions one sailor who was leading a mule with a messmate walking behind, when they came to where a body of soldiers was stationed. This did not seem to concern the sailors, who had been given orders to carry out, and so they

FELL OUT: *dropped out of formation*
MESSMATE: *friend*
TARS: *sailors*

went straight on. "Hallo, Jack!" cried one of the soldiers good-humouredly. "Where are you coming to?" "Coming?" said Jack. "I ain't a-coming anywheres. I am only towing the craft. It's the chap behind who does the steering. Ask him." It was always the same with the tars. The mule's halter was either the tow-rope or the painter. They starboarded or ported their helm, tacked through a crowd, or wore the ship round, in a most amusing way. On one occasion an officer called out: "Sergeant-major!" There was no answer. "Sergeant-major!" (louder). Still no reply. A third and still louder hail produced no response. "Boatswain, I say, where *are* you?" "Ay, ay, sir!" was the instant answer from the man who was close by, but who had quite forgotten that in the service ashore of the Rocket Brigade he took the new rank of Sergeant-major.

The Jacks made curious friendships during the advance, and a good deal of comradeship soon existed between them and the Punjabis, although neither understood a word of the other's language. During a halt the cheerful sailors would sometimes get up a dance to the music of the band of the soldiers from the Five Rivers Region. The band played well, seated in a circle and looking extremely grave, while the sailors would stand up in couples or octettes and solemnly execute quadrilles, waltzes, and polkas, to the great astonishment of the natives, who crowded round looking on in wonder at what to them seemed a profound mystery.

The Punjab Pioneers seem to have been a splendid regiment, and their services under their gallant major proved to be most valuable during the expedition, for their leader divined the spots where water ought to be found, and it was dug for until a gushing supply of the precious necessary was forthcoming.

PAINTER: *a rope used to tie up a boat*
PUNJABIS: *natives from the province of Punjab in India*
OCTETTES: *groups of eight*
QUADRILLES: *square dances*
DIVINED: *identified*

Chapter XVIII

King Theodore at Bay

At last the spot was reached where the army could take up its position to look across at Magdala, which appeared like a three-topped mountain with almost perpendicular sides. And here the whole force rested and girded up their loins for the final struggle.

The advance had been long and wearisome; but as soon as the men were refreshed by a rest all was excitement, and the next morning the troops were again in motion. Henty started early in the full conviction that something would take place, while the men in his neighbourhood, who had been suffering after their last march the night before from want of water, were looking eagerly forward to reaching the welcome stream that could be seen flowing at the bottom of the ravine below.

Here, however, came a disappointment. There was abundance of water in a river eighty yards wide, and waist deep; but it was the colour of coffee with milk, and nearly opaque with mud. In fact, it was like a dirty puddle in a London street just after being churned up by an omnibus. However, there was nothing for it. All had a drink, and then the men filled their canteens before they prepared to wade across.

Later, the heat was terrible. Everyone was devoured with a burning thirst, and any money would have been given cheerfully for a drink of pure water. When, that afternoon, a storm

GIRDED UP THEIR LOINS: *prepared themselves*
OMNIBUS: *bus*

passed over, and they caught just the tail end of the rain which fell, Henty was glad to spread out his waterproof sheet, and he caught nearly half a pint of what he declared was the most refreshing draught he had ever tasted.

Matters now grew very exciting. Henty and his colleagues could see with their glasses the enemy's guns upon the fortifications, with artillerymen passing from gun to gun and loading them in succession.

Behind the spectators the troops were still advancing. The Naval Rocket Brigade emerged from the flat below and were joining the Punjabis, when, almost at the same moment, a dozen voices proclaimed that a large force was coming down the road from the fortress. Glasses were turned in that direction, and a large body of horse and footmen were seen hurrying down pell-mell. The question arose, did this mean a peaceful embassy or fighting?

All doubt was soon at an end: a gun boomed, and a thirty-two pound shot struck the ground in front of the Indian troops. It was war, then—defiance. King Theodore meant to fight, but not within the walls of Magdala; he was coming out to engage the British forces in the open.

The fight had begun; a steady fire was kept up from the fortress guns, and Henty says: "A prettier sight is seldom presented in warfare than that of the enemy's advance. Some were in groups; some were in twos and threes; here and there galloped chiefs in their scarlet cloth robes. Many of those on foot were in scarlet and silk, and they came on at a run, the whole force advancing across the plain with incredible and alarming rapidity. It was for some time doubtful whether they would not reach the brow of the little valley, along which the Rocket train was still coming in a long single file, before the infantry could arrive to check them. After a few minutes, however, the infantry came up at the double, all

PELL-MELL: *in reckless haste*
TRAIN: *procession*

their fatigue and thirst having vanished at the thought of a fight.

Almost immediately the enemy had their first answer to the guns of the fortress in the shape of a rocket whizzing out upon the plain, for Jack was alive, and a cheer rang out as other rockets followed in rapid succession, making the Abyssinians stop short in utter astonishment at this novel way of making war. But the chiefs urged them forward, and they advanced again, being now not more than five hundred yards from where Henty and his colleagues stood watching them.

With his glass he could distinguish every feature, and as he looked at them advancing at a run with shield and spear, he could not help feeling pity for them, knowing what a terrible reception they were about to meet with; for in another minute our line of skirmishers had breasted the slope and opened a tremendous fire.

The enemy, taken completely by surprise, paused, discharged their firearms, and then slowly and doggedly retreated, increasing their speed as they felt how hopeless was the struggle against antagonists who could pour in ten shots to their one.

Meanwhile the infantry regiment advanced rapidly, driving the retreating men before them. The native regiment followed up, and the lookers-on could see the battle was almost won, for the troops advanced so rapidly that the Abyssinians could not regain the road to the fortress, but, chased by the rockets, were driven to the right, away from Magdala.

All this time the guns from the fortress kept up their fire upon the advancing line, but most of the shot went over the men's heads. So bad was the aim of the king's gunners, that he himself was nearly killed while superintending the working of one of his big guns by his German prisoners.

BREASTED THE SLOPE: *reached the top of the slope*

In another portion of the field a more desperate fight was being carried on by the defenders, and step by step Sir Robert Napier's forces were developing the attack. The mountain train of steel guns got into position and sent in a terrific fire, speedily stopping the head of another of the enemy's columns, while the Punjabis poured in a withering fire and afterwards charged with the bayonet. As a result King Theodore suffered a crushing defeat, for upwards of five thousand of his bravest soldiers had sallied out to the attack, while scarcely as many hundreds returned.

All this took place in the midst of a tremendous thunderstorm, with the deep echoing roar of the thunder completely drowning the heavy rattle of musketry, the crack of the steel guns, and the boom of the enemy's heavy cannon upon the heights.

A tremendous cheer rose from the whole British force as the enemy finally retired, and thus terminated one of the most decisive skirmishes which had perhaps ever occurred; it was memorable, too, as being the first encounter in which British troops ever used breech-loading rifles.

CHAPTER XIX

THE FALL OF THE CURTAIN

THE eventful day was now closing in, and everyone was glad to wrap himself in his wet blanket and to forget hunger and thirst for a while in sleep. Strong bodies of troops were thrown out as pickets, and the men were under arms again at two in the morning, lest Theodore should renew his attack before daybreak.

Then news was brought in that there was plenty of water to be had in a ravine near at hand, and the Indian bheesties were sent down with the water-skins, in company with soldiers with their canteens. But the water was worse than any they had drunk before, for the place had been a camp of Theodore's army. Numbers of animals, mules and cattle, had been slaughtered there; the stench was abominable, and the water nearly as much tainted as the atmosphere. Still, there was no help for it; all had to drink the noxious fluid. After obtaining a little food, Henty rode over to where he could leave his horse and go down into the ravine. Here fatigue parties were engaged in the work of burial; and in plain simple words Henty describes the scene as shocking—certainly his picture is too dreadful to be dwelt upon.

In good time that morning there was a tremendous burst of cheering, for two of the prisoners had come in with proposals

UNDER ARMS: *prepared for battle*
BHEESTIES: *water carriers*
FATIGUE PARTIES: *work parties*

from the king; and the embassage reported that Theodore had returned after the battle to say to them with a noble simplicity: "My people have been out to fight yours. I thought I was a great man and knew how to fight. I find I know nothing. My best soldiers have been killed; the rest are scattered. I will give in. Go you into camp and make terms for me."

There was something almost Scriptural in the tone of resignation these words breathed—words which invited the sympathy of all thinking men for the conquered. But this feeling was deadened directly news arrived of the horrors that had taken place in Magdala on the very day before the arrival of the British. Theodore had ordered all the European captives out to be witnesses of what he could do, and before their eyes he put to death three hundred and forty prisoners, many of whom he had kept in chains for years. These included men, women, and little children. They were brought out and thrown upon the ground, with their heads fastened down to their feet, and the brutal tyrant went among the helpless group and slashed right and left until he had killed a score or so. Then, growing tired, he called out his musketeers and ordered them to fire upon the crowd, which they did until all were dispatched, when their bodies were thrown over a precipice. His usual modes of execution were the very refinement of cruelty, the sufferers being tortured and then left to die.

With this knowledge Sir Robert Napier declined to grant any conditions whatever, demanding an instant surrender of the whole of the European prisoners and of the fortress, promising only that the king and his family should be honourably treated.

The two captives who had borne the king's message returned with this answer, to come back in the afternoon with a message from Theodore begging that better terms might be offered him; but the general felt obliged to refuse, and the

EMBASSAGE: *ambassadors*
DISPATCHED: *killed*

ambassadors departed once more amid the sorrowful anticipa-
tions of the camp.

To the great joy of all, however, Mr. Flad,[1] one of the messengers, again came to camp with the joyful news that all the
captives would be with them in an hour. This proved correct,
and with the exception of Mrs. Flad and her children the whole
of the captives were released.

Meanwhile the king was allowed till noon the next day to
surrender Magdala, otherwise the place would be stormed,
and the making of scaling-ladders was begun; long bamboo
dhooly poles were utilized for the sides, and handles of pick-
axes for the rungs.

Within the next few days Mrs. Flad and her children were
brought into camp, and several of the principal chiefs came
in and showed that Theodore's strength was crumbling away,
for they declared their willingness to surrender; but the king
held out. The storming parties were arranged, and the cavalry
were sent out to cut off the tyrant's retreat. Meanwhile a great
exodus of the people was going on, the fortress being cleared
of the non-combatants.

During the attack which followed, while the garrison kept
up a scattered fire with bullets, none of which reached our
troops, there were not wanting signs to indicate the despair of
the partly-forsaken monarch. Driven frantic by his position, the
wretched man could be plainly seen galloping about with some
half a dozen of his chiefs in a sort of aimless frenzy.

At last the storming party advanced, the defenders of the
gate were cleared away after a feeble defence, and the fighting
was over, with none killed on the British side and only fifteen
wounded. The remaining inhabitants, rejoicing that the days
of the tyranny were over, crowded out to offer the conquerors
refreshing drink, while Theodore was discovered lying dead.

---

[1] German missionary Johann Martin Flad (1831-1915)

DHOOLY POLES: *poles taken from the dhoolies, or stretchers*
EXODUS: *departure*

Henty's task was done, and not choosing to wait for the slow return of the troops, he, together with three others, making with the ten servants, syces and mule-drivers, a formidable and well-armed little company, started on the way down. It was a bold undertaking, nevertheless, for they had to pass through a disturbed country where convoys were being constantly attacked and muleteers murdered, and where scarcely a day passed without outrages being committed by the Gallas, the inhabitants of Northern Abyssinia, who were always upon plunder bent.

Their servants were all armed with spears, the baggage mules were kept in close file, and Henty and another rode in front, the two others in the rear, with cocked rifles and revolvers ready to hand. Owing to their state of preparedness, and the fierce look of the well-armed English leader, though they passed a party or two of sixty of the Gallas, equipped with spears and shields, and a desire to use the former if they had the chance, these rogues sneaked off among the bushes, and the war correspondent and his colleagues reached the depot and port in peace. But not entirely, for, to use Henty's own words, "When coming down country from the Abyssinian business the Gallas stopped us on one occasion and proposed to loot the entire caravan, but I was able to half-choke the life out of the gentleman who tackled me personally." In fact, the party had ample opportunity of realizing the risk and danger to which a war correspondent is exposed.

SYCES: *Indian stablemen*

CHAPTER XX

THE SUEZ CANAL

UPON Henty's return from the Abyssinian campaign in 1868 his active busy mind incited him to take a calm home rest from his warlike labours by writing one of his first books, based upon his correspondent letters, and entitled, *The March to Magdala*. This, published towards the end of the year, was full of vigorous description, and as an epitome of the war it achieved a very fair success. In addition it served to make the reading public better acquainted with a name already familiar to the newspaper world.

Very shortly after this essay now, he wrote and sent out through the same publishers, Messrs. Tinsley Brothers, his second three-volume novel, *All but Lost*. This was in 1869, and long before the days when he devoted himself to the young readers of his works of adventure.

At the end of the year he undertook another expedition. This, however, was of a peaceful nature, to wit, the task of describing the epoch-marking inauguration of M. Ferdinand de Lesseps's *magnum opus*, the Suez Canal. It was a pleasant duty, for the correspondent was practically a privileged visitor, and one of the representatives of civilization who had come to partake of Ismail Pasha's[1] munificent hospitality, in company with other guests who may fairly be classed as representing "the world".

---

[1] Khedive, or ruler, of Egypt and Sudan from 1863 to 1879.
INCITED: *encouraged*
EPITOME: *summary*
EPOCH-MARKING INAUGURATION: *introduction of a new era*
MAGNUM OPUS: *greatest work*

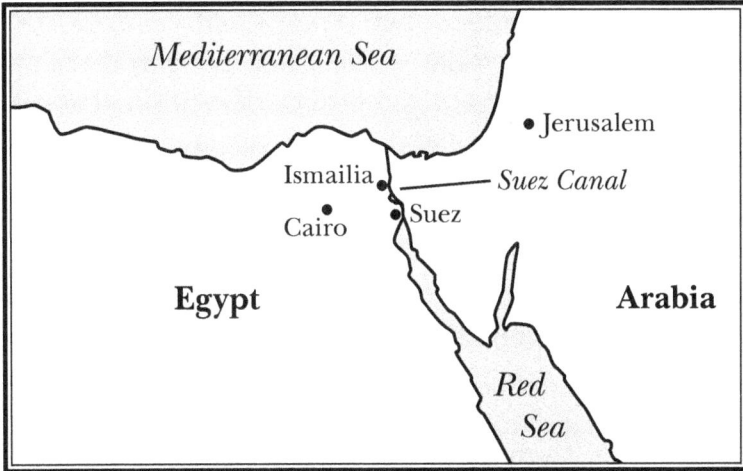

The Suez Canal

He wrote a series of letters full of vivid word-painting, descriptive of Cairo *en fête*, of ball and banquet, of the illuminations, and of the state of the ancient city—of the Egypt where of old the children of Israel were enslaved, and helped to build the monuments which still remain. He also touched on the homes which were raised and built with the straw-mingled clay that ages ago crumbled into dust, and is now being excavated and basket-borne to spread upon the agricultural land as an extra fertilizer of the almost too fertile earth.

Henty had a great opportunity here for his descriptive pen, and his letters abound with pictures of the Aladdin-like state of the place, of the way in which money was lavished to provide a grand reception for empress and emperor, viceroy and prince, and the rest of the distinguished guests whom the Khedive delighted to honour. Cairo presented such a scene, that the writer felt that he could readily imagine himself transported into the times of the *Arabian Nights* as it might have been on

MUNIFICENT: *extremely generous*
VICEROY: *governor*

the occasion of the marriage of Aladdin to the princess of his heart, one Badroulboudour. The illuminations in the soft transparency of an Egyptian atmosphere presented a fairy-like aspect. Flags of all nations hung perfectly still in the soft air, side by side with lanterns and decorations of a more national kind. There were fireworks everywhere; rockets ascended with a hiss and roar in rapid succession, while dazzling fires of every hue that chemistry has won from earth's minerals threw broad floods of colour like nocturnal rainbows, only more iridescent in their mingling, along the street and across the square. Noise was not wanting, for petards exploded with unpleasant frequency; and as the salvoes died out there was constantly arising the peculiar dull subdued roar of the thronging multitude in ecstasy at the unwonted sight.

In the side streets the crowd was strangely novel to the eyes of the foreign visitor, and as carriages crowded with spectators made their way slowly through the throng of the ordinary Egyptian city dwellers, strongly reinforced by the inhabitants from all the country round, the eyes of the stranger were constantly attracted by the silent, solemn-looking, white-turbaned Mussulman, and the dark, blue-robed, muffled, and yashmak-wearing women—all eyes for the looker-on. It was a strange and constant change from light to darkness in the generally ill-lit city. One minute the spectator would be traversing a street that presented the appearance of a long ballroom, with lines of chandeliers running down the centre only a few paces apart. From these hung festoons and garlands of coloured lamps, while several lines of lanterns ran along the houses on either side. Then a few steps and the visitor plunged into a narrow way, sombre, suggestive, and gloomy, possibly illumined only by the glow-worm-like rays of a single lamp, with a few slippered people

NOCTURNAL RAINBOWS: *rainbows in the night*
IRIDESCENT: *rainbow-like*
PETARDS: *firecrackers*
SALVOES: *rounds of explosions*
UNWONTED: *rare*
MUSSULMAN: *Muslim*

hurrying softly, almost shadow-like, as they made their way towards the line of illuminations.

In the brightly lighted streets the looker-on from any elevation gazed down upon a perfect sea of turbans and also at a long line of carriages, each preceded by its wand-bearing runners shouting boisterously to the crowd to clear the way. It was one long festival for rich and poor alike, and the variety of the scene was wondrous. The occupants of the carriages, whose drivers forced their way through the good-tempered crowd, were often the closely-veiled inhabitants of the harems of the rich, not as a rule the harem of the Eastern story, the word harem now more truly meaning simply the ordinary home. But in many cases these were guarded jealously by attendant eunuchs, and preceded by runners bearing braziers or cressets of flaming wood.

But the houses on either side were not occupied merely by flaming lamps, for from the latticed windows over the shops the female inhabitants of the city, eagerly throwing off the customary reserve, peered down upon the passing throng. Colour in the lighted streets and diversity were everywhere in company with rampant irregularity, for each decorator had worked according to his own sweet will. No two streets were alike either in occupants or in decoration. Sombre and sordid buildings crowded close upon palaces, and while one street was dark and empty, with its sporadic lamps, the next was crowded with a dense mass listening to the plaintive music of the native bands discoursing wild and, possibly to the hearers, delicious strains, but strains containing too much bagpipe and cymbal for the foreign ear. In another, as if it were some gigantic old-world fair, the merry-featured, strangely robed throng was clustering round a knot of dancing girls, Egyptian Terpsichoreans. These

YASHMAK-WEARING: *veil-wearing*
BRAZIERS OR CRESSETS: *metal pans or cups*
SPORADIC: *widely spaced*
PLAINTIVE: *sorrowful*
DISCOURSING: *uttering*
TERPSICHOREANS: *dancers*

displayed their ideas of the poetry of motion in a singularly wild and picturesque manner, and were evidently frantically admired by the holiday-keeping lookers-on.

By way of change, after hours of wandering through the crowded and illuminated streets, Henty describes one of the palaces where the principal guests were accommodated by the Khedive. This was reached after a quiet drive to its site, a short distance from the town. Here in the soft darkness of the Egyptian night the illuminations were superb, and the description exemplifies the lavish recklessness of the host on behalf of his guests. In front of the palace was a space forming a parallelogram of considerably over a quarter of a mile long by some three hundred yards wide. This was surrounded by an arched trellis-work, resembling somewhat in its detail the delicate tracery of a cathedral cloister. The wooden structure was literally covered upon both sides with illumination lanterns, and looked like some gnome or fairy fabric of fire. Round it was a carriage drive which passed between it and the palace, and against the walls of the palace itself glittering lights were fixed in the same order as upon the wooden framework, so that to the spectator it was as if he gazed down a vista of two interminable walls of fire connected by arches of coloured lamps. The effect was exquisite, heightened as it was by the ascending rockets which burst and showered down coloured stars in constant succession. Pyrotechnic fires burned here and there, and threading as it were the falling stars, the strains of band after band of music blended their enchantment with the beauty of the scene.

This is but a slight description of one of the many sights embraced by the enormous fête provided for the Khedive Ismail's world-invited guests, and picture after picture Henty painted of these scenes by night and by day. He also visited the various points of interest in the neighbourhood, notably the Pyramids,

---

LAVISH RECKLESSNESS: *careless extravagance*
CLOISTER: *courtyard*
INTERMINABLE: *unending*
EMULATE: *rival or surpass*
CUI BONO?: *"For whose benefit?" in Latin*

going by the road to these ancient monuments which had been slave-constructed by order of the Khedive, as if in a fit of lavish recklessness he had determined to emulate the doings of some Pharaoh of old, so that his French empress visitor should have a special way made smooth across the desert to the old world-famous pyramidal tombs. Visitor and special correspondent Henty was, but he spoke out as the quiet, thoughtful Englishman in translating the words of the wise old Orientals who thoughtfully shook their heads and added their quiet *Cui Bono?* over the thriftless wanton expense. There was banqueting and feasting, and all at a time when the treasury was depleted, when the civil and military forces had their payments in arrear, and when national debt heaped upon national debt. All this could only end in the bankruptcy which too surely came.

Most of this renowned spectacle was preliminary to the long-expected opening of the canal, and, ignoring the head-shaking of the thoughtful, the great mass of the light-hearted Egyptians, rich and poor alike, went to see and share in the festivity, and took no thought of the future. The world had come to see the opening of the canal, the finish of a stupendous undertaking, the inception of a clever western, but thoroughly Egyptian and Pharaoh-like in its audacity. At last the shovel and basket of the drudging slaves as well as workers for hire, were cast aside, and the waters flowed through what American visitors sardonically styled "the ditch," opening nearly a hundred miles of waterway extending from Suez to Timsah, now rechristened, or Mahommedanized into Ismailia. Along this "ditch" there was a grand procession of state barges, steam launches, and visitor-bearing craft, all made the more imposing by the presence of a squadron of British battleships, whose approach to the entrance with the saluting thunder of their great guns Henty dwells upon, though, apparently with a grim

THRIFTLESS WANTON: *wastefully extravagant*
IN ARREAR: *overdue*
THE INCEPTION OF: *begun by*
SARDONICALLY: *scornfully*
MAHOMMEDANIZED INTO: *given the Muslim name of*

chuckle of British irony, he relates how two of the marine monsters got aground.

The procession, however, seems to have been petty in comparison with the innate grandeur of M. de Lesseps's enterprise and what it meant to the future of the civilized world. Later, as if to make up for his words respecting the grounding of the huge iron-clads, which were doomed to flounder like whales in a rivulet before they got off, Henty hastens to paint vividly and evidently with a feeling of pride the aspect of the ships of war of every European nation, the dark line of sailors who manned the yards, cheering vociferously, the clouds of powder smoke mingling with the volumes from the funnels drifting slowly across the water, the lofty lighthouse, and the populous town which had sprung up as if under the wand of a magician. And that magician was M. de Lesseps, the sun of whose greatness sank in sadness years after, when, as if vaulting ambition had overleaped itself, he died half-forgotten and broken-hearted at the temporary failure of his other great venture, the canal to join Pacific and Atlantic, which, these many years after the great man's death, promises to be the accomplished fact of the twentieth century.[1]

George Henty was always a sailor at heart, and never happier than when, hatless in a brisk breeze, he was watching the easing off or the tightening of a sheet, while his hands played with the spokes of the wheel which governed a vessel's course. So it is not surprising that in his description of the grand fêtes and rejoicings over the opening of the canal he should find a businesslike corner at the bottom of one of his letters to talk about the chances of a vessel passing easily through the sand-bordered ribbon of water which joined the Mediterranean and Red Seas. He says: "I have been favoured with a log of the soundings taken on board the *Cambria* during her passage through

---

[1] The Panama Canal was completed by the American government in 1914.

MARINE MONSTERS: *giant ships*

RIVULET: *small stream*

YARDS: *horizontal poles used to support the sails*

the canal"—he speaks like the man in his element—"and I am bound to say that they are far more favourable than from all other accounts I could have believed possible. The total number of soundings were seventy-six. They were taken, with the exception of the passage of the Bitter Lakes, during the whole passage at intervals of a nautical mile, and of the seventy-six soundings no fewer than fifty-six gave a depth of twenty-seven feet and over, while of the remaining twenty only four were below twenty-two feet, one only giving as little as nineteen feet of water. This table of soundings shows that the canal is upon the average of a depth of twenty-six feet; and although it is unquestionable that the vessels drawing only eighteen feet did scrape the ground in several places during their passage, the soundings taken by Mr. Ashbury showed that these must have been, with the exception of the lump of rock at Serapium, mere accidental mounds and banks which had been left in the process of dredging."

And here, too, it will not be out of place to add a few words written after the inauguration, and *finis coronat opus* had been added to Henty's descriptions of the great event. Just overleaf it was the sailor speaking upon the achievement and the canal's possibilities of carrying out the objects for which it was designed. He is now speaking as the thoughtful leader-writer, and somewhat in these words he begins to count the cost of the entertainment provided by the Khedive. "Admitting," he says, "that the cost of all this enterprise has been enormous, amounting as they say here to two millions sterling, to what good has this sum been spent? For it is not the viceroy's private money, but the national revenue, and one feels in the position of the guests of the directors of some public company. One says, 'Yes, it is a splendid banquet; but what will the unfortunate shareholders say?' I can reply that the shareholders do not

VOCIFEROUSLY: *loudly*
SOUNDINGS: *measurements of the depth of the water*
DREDGING: *digging out the channel*
FINIS CORONAT OPUS: *final word; literally "crowning end" in Latin*
JUST OVERLEAF: *on the previous page*

like it at all. Why should French journalists, German professors, and English heads of chambers of commerce be taken up
the Nile at the expense of the people of Egypt?"

But it is only fair to say that this was not written in a grudging
spirit, for Henty had found time to praise warmly the admirable management and kindly welcome given to the Khedive's
guests, and his final remarks were veined with a feeling of sor-
row that the hospitality should have been so profuse.

At the dispersal of the crowd of visitors it seems as if it occurred to Henty that this would be a most favourable opportunity, after making himself acquainted with the land of the
captivity and the ancient works in Egypt, to take in reverse the
journey made of old in the days of famine, and visit the Holy
Land. This happy thought he put into execution, and making
a tour through the Holy Land, he ended by visiting Jerusalem
before his return to England.

VEINED: *marked*

THE FRANCO-GERMAN WAR

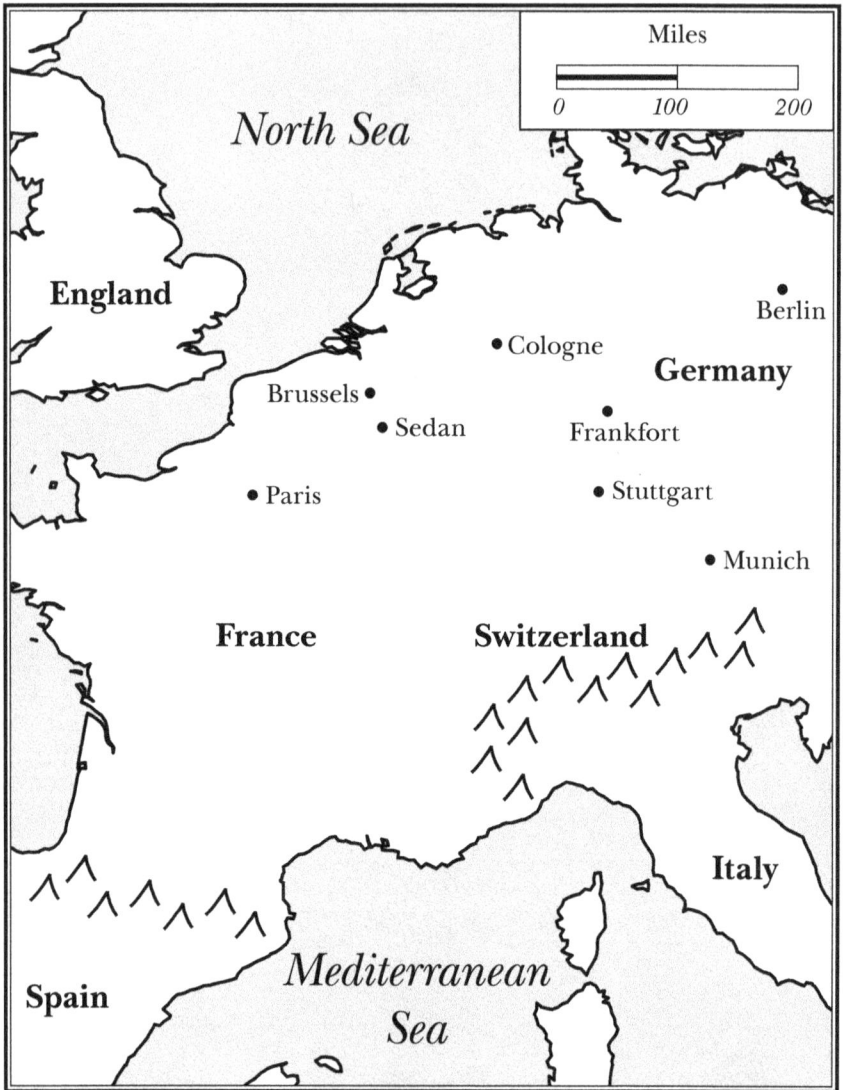

Miles

0   100   200

North Sea

England

• Berlin

• Cologne

Germany

Brussels •

• Sedan

Frankfort

• Paris

• Stuttgart

• Munich

France

Switzerland

Italy

Spain

Mediterranean Sea

CHAPTER XXI

THE FRANCO-GERMAN WAR

THERE was very little time for rest in this life of work between the Egyptian festivals, Eastern travel, and the terrible European disaster looming ahead, the crisis which culminated in the declaration of war between France and Germany in the June of the year following his return home. But somehow or other, before starting for Berlin Henty contrived to have one of his first boys' books[1] upon the stocks, and this was published at the end of that year—1870—during his absence.

Meanwhile he started for the front, and on his way he writes: "We had a break of nearly two hours at Cologne before the departure of the train for Berlin. Here for the first time I had before me the actual preparation for war. In France, in Brussels, and at various stations along this line, soldiers in uniform had been conspicuously absent. Here they were everywhere busy. Baggage wagons moved hither and thither loaded with stores; tumbrels with ammunition rumbled along the streets. Here was a company of soldiers each with two new needle-guns upon his shoulder; there another party was dragging stores in hand carts. Going onto the bridge and looking down onto the river, I saw a steamer with some field-gun carriages packed on her deck, while a gang of men were loading her with countless coils of field-telegraph wire. Upon the walls was a notice that

---

[1] *Out of the Pampas*

UPON THE STOCKS: *in progress*
NEEDLE-GUNS: *German guns with a firing pin shaped like a needle*

two thousand labourers were required on the following day for work upon the fortifications. Judging by the number of troops I saw about, the garrison of Cologne must at present be very large indeed, and every hour must increase it as the reserves flock in. All the young men are leaving."

The waiter at the hotel where he dined, a delicate-looking young fellow, told him that he was off directly to join the infantry, while a comrade who came in to say good-bye was on the point of starting for the cavalry. There was no brag or pretence of indifference about any of the young fellows. The country required them, and they were perfectly ready to go, and, if necessary, to die for her.

At the station the confusion was tremendous. Trains had come in, and other trains were starting. The one for Berlin was of enormous length, and literally crammed. Cheers and counter cheers were being exchanged by the occupants and the people on the platform. Hands and handkerchiefs waved adieux, which in many cases would be for long indeed. There was but little weeping on the part of the women, of whom only a few were present. No doubt they had wept over the parting ones, and blessed them when they left, remaining behind to pray rather than shake the confidence of their loved ones at the start. As the train moved slowly out of the station, across the bridge, and out into the level country beyond, the darkness was falling and the mist rising; but on through the night they went, stopping occasionally, taking in men and more men, adding carriage after carriage to an already enormous length, until, had not the line been perfectly level, the two powerful locomotives could not have drawn the load. Trains were waiting at the various junctions, all crowded, and at every halt, as daylight came, labourers were seen gathering to work upon the fortifications, showing that Germany meant to be fully prepared for

ADIEUX: *farewells*

the worst, while side by side with the manifold preparations for war there was smiling peace, with the crops extending as far as eye could reach. The wheat was ripe and ready for the sickle, the oats and barley coming on, while the ground was covered with the blossoms of the poppy and the bright yellow of the lupins. The crops were unusually heavy over the whole of Prussia, and there were to be no hands to gather them, save those of the women and old men, for the whole country was joining the ranks of the able-bodied and marching for the seat of war.

At length he was in the city which the French anticipated entering when in their mad enthusiasm they paraded their own streets, shouting "A Berlin!" and from here, now grown to be one of the band of trusted war correspondents, Henty writes to the journal he was again representing of the wild state of confusion and growing excitement connected with the Prussian preparations.

Matters, moreover, did not work easily for the war correspondent, for he had to pass his time in Berlin in a series of attempts to obtain permission to accompany the Prussian army to the front. Delays and promises followed each other, and he was kept eager and fretting with disappointment like a hound in the leash, hoping and yet doubting, till at last all he could get was an official reply to his application, stating that it had been decided to follow the example of the French and refuse permission for correspondents to accompany the army, or even to hover after it to pick up information in the rear.

To hesitate and not take action in some shape Henty felt might prove loss of time, and perhaps the missing of some vastly important piece of news for the journal he represented, and this at a time when rumour was quietly whispering that before long a mandate would be issued from headquarters that postal

MANIFOLD: *many and varied*
PRUSSIA: *the largest kingdom, or state, in Germany at this time*
A BERLIN!: *"On to Berlin!" in French*
MANDATE: *order*

as well as travelling communication would be almost entirely cut off.

Henty was a thoughtful man of stern determination, and once he had made up his mind he satisfied himself by making a final application to the authorities. All he could learn though was that his requests were under consideration, and that a decision would be given later. This decision, he felt sure, would be in the negative, and he determined to return to England for the purpose of making a fresh start.

He made for the station at once, to find that the difficulties had already begun. A fierce struggle for tickets was going on among those who wished to leave the city, and he was informed by a clerk that tickets were only issued for a short distance on the way. This, of course, meant that the railways were already in the hands of the government for the conveyance of troops, and pretty evident proofs of this change in the state of affairs were all around him in the shape of piled rifles ornamented with *pickelhaubes*, the spiked helmets of the Teutons.

It would be of no use, he felt, to wait the pleasure of the stolid, head-shaking Germans, fretting and worrying, while possibly he would be receiving from his own headquarters, from an angry editor, letters asking what he was about in keeping him waiting for that which is the very life-blood of a newspaper in time of war.

It was all plain enough, that he had come to a wise decision. The great dislocation of the German railway system had begun, and ordinary passengers were having to make way for the movements of troops. In spite of his energy he was stopped again and again, before finally reaching Frankfort, whence he gained England, and in roundabout fashion crossed to France, where after endless difficulties he managed to get pretty close to the French army, and saw what he could of the war.

STOLID: *unemotional*
SOJOURN: *stay*
DASH AND GO: *spirited action*
RÔLE: *role*
ACQUIESCENCE: *agreement*

During his enforced sojourn in Berlin, and while waiting impatiently for his official permit to accompany the German army, the soldier within him was not idle, and, doubtless with a map at hand, he began to make his notes, in the shape of a letter dwelling upon the position, and the possibilities of how the men would fight. He dwelt upon the dash and go of the French in the rôle of invaders, and came to the conclusion that if France took the offensive, crossed the Rhine, and struck first at Stuttgart and then at Munich, the Prussians would be at their best, for they would be fighting in defence of their native soil.

These conclusions were come to at a time when he was still waiting, for he writes: "To my application to be allowed to accompany the army I have as yet received no reply." In the event of an acquiescence to his request, he says: "I shall have no further difficulty, but shall go where the army goes. In the event of a refusal, my object will be to gain some central point and then wait events."

All these surmises were followed by the stern refusal, as aforesaid, which turned him back, to learn afterwards how futile were the conclusions to which he had come, for, as will be well remembered, the battle-cry of the French, "A Berlin!" proved to be so much vanity, the Germans themselves assuming the offensive and sweeping everything before them almost from the first.

Afterwards he was one of the lookers-on when maddened France was in the throes of those wild scenes which are history now—times of disorder and disorganization, of brigades being marched here and there in purposeless movements until, when at last they did encounter their foe, defeat followed defeat; the civilized world meanwhile watching with bated breath for the next news of disaster till there came *la débâcle*, the crowning horror of Sedan,[1] and the surrender of the emperor.

---

[1] The Battle of Sedan ended with the capture of Emperor Napoleon III and his army of over 100,000 men.

SURMISES: *ideas*

BATED BREATH: *their breath held*

LA DÉBÂCLE: *"the disaster" in French*

Chapter XXII

The Commune

EARLY in the year 1871, after the signature of peace, Henty in pursuit of his journalistic duties entered Paris, and during the wild days of its occupation by the Commune he passed a life of adventure of which volumes might be written, for, in brief, he saw all the fighting very closely. It was a wild time, in which no man's life was safe, and in the absence of law and order an Englishman bound to investigate and report upon the proceedings of the ill-governed city dare hardly call his soul his own.

During this period Henty's letters teem with information, all showing his keen observation of minutiæ. He describes the gathering and marching down the Rue de Rivoli of one of the first armies of the Commune, an army the more dangerous to the republic through so many trained fighting men of the regular army having joined its ranks. The determination and hatred of the settled government of the motley company made up for their want of uniformity. With respect to their weapons, he describes how a great many in the ranks, numbering in all some ten thousand, were armed with the chassepot rifle, but the majority had old muskets converted into snider breech-loaders,[1] while a certain percentage had nothing better than the old muzzleloader. It was an armed mob, though mingled

---

[1] This conversion was invented by American Jacob Snider.

MINUTIÆ: *small details*

CHASSEPOT RIFLE: *a breech-loading rifle invented by Antoine Chassepot*

with it were battalions of the National Guard in the pay of the Commune. Later, when encountering the forces of the regular army, the solidity of the much-talked-of fraternity was exemplified at the first encounter, for, amidst cries of "Vive la Republique!" and patriotic outbursts, one side would appeal to the other with a touching cry: "Surely you will not fire on your brethren!" The answer to this would be a volley, with the weaker side making a rapid retreat in search of shelter.

Henty was very soon saying to the newspaper he represented: "I write my daily letter in doubt as to whether it will ever come to hand. The post has ceased to run, and we are cut off from all news from the provinces. The gates of Paris are closed, we are in a state of siege, and the passengers of such trains as are running are told that they will not be allowed to return." The misery and suffering connected with the great siege were quite forgotten, the fighting began again, and once more the streets of the brilliant city were echoing with the rattle of musketry, a sound punctuated with the sharp thud of the field-pieces that were more and more brought into action, and whose shells in the early days had a startling effect upon the insurgent members of the Commune. For Henty observed the steadiness of the National Guards, who remained at their posts and showed no signs of flinching, while on the other hand the inexperienced, undrilled men of the insurgent ranks were prone to throw themselves down flat in the road at each flash of a cannon and remain there until the shell had burst, perhaps three hundred yards away.

In these early revolutionary days, sometimes a strong body of the Communists, in a state of wild excitement, would be on their way to attack the regulars and carry all before them, when one of the forts would open fire and send shells among them. To use the writer's words, "The effect was magical." About

VIVE LA REPUBLIQUE!: *"Long live the Republic!" in French*
INSURGENT: *rebel*

one-half of the column "skedaddled back to Paris." It was not a retreat; the war element had evaporated much more quickly than it had been generated, and doubtless if the leaders of law and order had been more energetic, the Commune would have been crushed in its infancy. Indeed the men of the lower orders from the wildest parts of Paris were so utterly cowed, that they gave up their muskets, refusing to have any more to do with the business. One man was heard to remark naïvely, "If you call this fighting, I have had enough of it," while one of the leaders of the mob, a self-dubbed general, an enthusiast and a fanatic, but a man of courage, a *rara avis* in the party which his mania induced him to join, was seen no more. Presumably he was shot, and died a soldier's death. Throughout his descriptions of the fighting, of the firmness and pluck of the trained men, and of the cowardice and shuffling of the mob, eager for plunder and rapine if they could get the upper hand, and only too ready to escape into shelter, Henty seems to consider the Commune as a thing gone stark-staring mad, while its leaders were incited at this critical juncture by the ill-judged articles that fulminated in the Red Press.

As an example of the state of affairs in these early days of the Commune, and of the way in which he did his duty as a correspondent, whatsoever the risk, Henty once related to a friend a couple of the most exciting incidents in his life, which took place soon after his arrival in Paris on account of the proclamation of the Commune. The first occurred in the Place Vendôme, which was being held by the National Guards, just at the time when the headquarters of the Insurrection were at the Hôtel de ville. The latter had been strongly fortified with barricades and was held by thousands of the Communists, who had strengthened their position by a battery of field-pieces. Matters had arrived at a pass when a strong feeling of bitterness existed

COWED: *frightened*
RARA AVIS: *"rare person" in Latin*
RAPINE: *robbery*
FULMINATED: *thundered*

between the body of order and those who were in favour of an entirely new form of government, and the general feeling prevailed that unless the insurgents realized the futility of their aims, bloodshed would ensue. In his search for information Henty had learned that the loyalists were about to make the first advances in the shape of a peaceful demonstration in order to point out that matters might be easily settled if the insurgents would listen to reason. But on going into the streets and studying the appearance of the rough-looking mob that had gathered in the neighbourhood of the Hôtel de ville, the result of this inspection was so unsatisfactory, that Henty felt full of doubt as to whether the peaceful demonstration would have a peaceful end.

The demonstrators would have to come in procession down the Rue de la Paix, and, wishing to have a good view of what would take place, he chose a position near the Vendôme Column, so as to see whether the body of Communists who held the place in military force would allow them to go by. After a time the head of the procession was seen approaching. It appeared to be a well-dressed crowd selected for the occasion— people of repute, in black coats and top hats, many of them even in evening dress, and the most striking point of all, as evidence of their peaceful demonstration, was that they were all unarmed, while in their midst a white flag was carried, bearing the words, "Vive l'ordre!"

Apparently the party, about five hundred strong, were members of the business classes, and in this form, that of a large deputation, they began to descend the Rue de la Paix. But immediately upon this, indications as to what their reception was to be began to be heard. Directly after, sharp military commands rang out from the lines of the defenders who held the Hôtel de ville, on the Place Vendôme bugles were sounded, and a body

REPUTE: *good reputation*
VIVE L'ORDRE!: *"Long live order!" in French*
DEPUTATION: *delegation*

of the National Guard advanced at the double and formed four deep across the end of the Rue de la Paix. This thoroughly blocked farther advance, while, to form a reserve, the Place was occupied by a strong body of nearly three thousand National Guards, who stood looking calm and determined and ready to prevent the party of order from passing. Looking more peaceful than ever, the demonstrators came steadily on without the slightest suggestion of military formation.

Henty relates that he did not anticipate trouble, for he felt sure that the demonstrators would not attempt to force their way through the solid body of Communists, and, satisfied with his excellent position as spectator and gatherer of news, he stood fast.

As the black-clothed body of men drew near the line of National Guards they began to wave their handkerchiefs, shouting, "Vive la Republique!" or "Vive l'ordre!" and then, seeing that the Communists stood firm, they distributed themselves across the street and began to enter into conversation. They formed an irregular group some five or six feet deep, and everything appeared as if it would come to an amicable conclusion. The excitement of the gathering of armed men had passed away, and nothing was heard but the murmur of conversation. So far from anticipating danger, Henty had joined the demonstrators, and was standing in the second row facing the Communists, when all at once something occurred which was like the dropping of a spark into a heap of gunpowder. A musket went off. The Communist who held it had fired in the air, whether accidentally or of malice intent it is impossible to say. The result was that, startled by the report, the lines of unarmed men who faced the Communists took a step or two backward; then, as if ashamed of their alarm, in the silence that followed, a cry arose that it was nothing, an

AMICABLE: *peaceful*

accident, and directly after there was another shout, that of "Vive la Republique!"

But the spark had fired the mass. Another shot was fired. A sensible and visible thrill ran through the front line of the Communists, they levelled their guns, and the next moment, as if without orders, they commenced a heavy fusillade upon the unarmed lines in front. The French citizen who stood next to Henty, and with whom he had just been in conversation respecting the probable termination of the affair, fell dead at his feet, and many of those in the front row met the same fate, for they were so near the Communists that the latter's muskets almost touched them when the firing began.

There was utter paralysis for the moment, and then a wild rush began, men turning upon their heels and running straight up the Rue de la Paix along which they had approached, while others, Henty included, turned off to the right down the first street, a short distance from the entrance to the Square. It was a state of wild excitement, a *sauve qui peut*, men stumbling and tripping over each other in their desperate haste to escape the storm of bullets that were whistling by them, too many of which reached their mark, probably without aim in the excitement of the discharge. It was a matter of minutes, but the time seemed long enough before the angle of the street was turned and the retreating crowd were in comparative safety, though all were in full expectation, as they tore on, of hearing the Communists' advancing tramp and halt as they stopped to fire down the street. This did not follow, for the insurgents were too busy in expending their cartridges upon the flying men who were running straight up the Rue de la Paix, giving Henty and those with him time to escape up the next street before they fired in their direction. How many were killed was never exactly known, but it must certainly have been sixty

A SENSIBLE AND VISIBLE THRILL: *a thrill able to be felt and seen*
FUSILLADE: *simultaneous firing of guns*
SAUVE QUI PEUT: *"every man for himself" in French*
EXPENDING: *using up*

or seventy; and he recalled, long years after, the rage of the peaceful demonstrators against their cowardly assailants. This was undoubtedly the match that fired one of the long trains of disaster that ran through Paris during the holding of the Commune.

It might have been supposed that, warned by the risk of mingling too much with the excited people, Henty would have held aloof and avoided too near proximity to the explosive race, ready to take fire without a moment's warning. Yet his thirst for news would not allow him to stay in the background when information reached him a couple of days later of the possibility of there being a regular battle in the streets.

At this time the quarter of the Bank was strongly held by the National Guard of that *arrondissement*, and every approach was thoroughly guarded. A messenger came to Henty at the hotel where he was staying, with the information that the Communists were astir in earnest, and had sent two battalions of their infantry with a battery of artillery to seize the Mairie of the First Arrondissement.

Hurrying off, he reached the entrance to the Place St. Germain l'Auxerrois as the head of the column of Communists came up, to find themselves much in the same position as their victims of the peaceful demonstration had occupied two days before, for they were immediately facing a strong party of the National Guard, who were faithful to the body of order. These men were drawn up eight deep across the street, the windows of the houses on either side were also filled with men who commanded the approach, while the main body of the Reserve occupied the Place.

Everything looked threatening in the extreme, for upon this occasion it was not the armed against the unarmed, but two

QUARTER: *area*
THAT ARRONDISSEMENT: *that district within the city of Paris*
MAIRIE OF THE FIRST ARRONDISSEMENT: *the town hall of the First District*

strong bodies of determined men face to face. The Communists as they marched up filled the whole street; and while their officers advanced and began to parley, their battery of field-pieces was brought forward and took up position threateningly in front of the attacking party.

There was an excited interval. The defenders of the Mairie absolutely refused to give way, and the angry conference went on, for the Communists were determined to carry out the orders they had received from headquarters and to obtain possession of the place.

At length, after angry debate, fierce bluster began, and the commander of the Communist force shouted to the gunners in front to load with grape—an order which was immediately carried out. Henty states that, in his eagerness to see and learn everything that passed, he was standing on the footway with a couple of civilians in a line with the officers parleying. He now shifted his position a few yards to an open door leading into one of the houses, which was held by the party of order, so as to be able to rush into shelter when the first shot was fired.

Still the excitement grew. Nothing could have exceeded the calmness and determination of the defenders who stood facing the loaded cannon ten paces away. Meanwhile, though, their comrades who occupied the houses on either side of the line had their pieces levelled in readiness to shoot down the artillerymen as soon as matters came to the worst and the officers in front had withdrawn from their conference. So firm and commanding, indeed, was the position of the defenders, that Henty felt convinced that, in spite of the field-pieces, had the orders to fire come, although outnumbered by fully two to one, the scowling ruffians bent on advance would have been driven down the street, leaving their battery in the hands of their foe. This, however, could only have been a short-lived success, for there were thousands of their comrades at the Communists' headquarters, with several batteries of cannon.

Be that as it may, the tension was extreme. The defenders of the Mairie stood silent and waiting for the worst, whilst a roar of angry denunciations and revilings came from the Communists. In spite of the threats levelled at them, the defenders of the Mairie stood fast, waiting for the orders to be given, and this without even attempting to load. Their instructions were to fix bayonets ready for the order "Charge!" and there they stood with their pieces levelled, waiting for the signal before springing forward with a dash to clear the Place and street with the bayonet; the signal was understood to be the firing by the enemy of the first gun. It was, as has been said, a time of extreme tension, and the firm aspect of the defenders had its effect upon the insurgent mob.

The blustering on the part of the Communist officers was succeeded by thought. These men, these leaders of the Communists, were the noisy demagogues and declaimers of the various cabarets; they were men selected not for political knowledge, nor for military instinct, nor for ability as men of brain, but entirely on account of their policy of bluster, their savageness of language, and their denunciation of everything that was opposed to decent policy and order; and now they felt that they were face to face with defeat and probably with their own death. They were being put to the tests and it was no time for carrying matters with words.

They gave a look round, and at the first glance saw muskets at all the windows aimed at them as well as at the gunners at their posts, and the sight of these menacing muzzles made such courage as they possessed begin to ooze. They fully realized that their notion of being able to overawe the defenders by ordering the field-pieces to the front and having them charged

DENUNCIATIONS: *condemnations*
DEMAGOGUES: *people who gain influence through emotional speeches*
DECLAIMERS: *speakers*
CABARETS: *taverns*
OVERAWE: *intimidate*

was a failure, and they felt pretty certain that were a field-piece discharged they would be among the first of the victims of the defence. Accordingly the leaders gathered together and exchanged whispers, the result of which was that the parley which had come to an end in a fierce bullying way was reopened in a much tamer spirit. There was no shouting, no gesticulation, and at the end of a minute or two these self-constituted heroes of the moment issued fresh orders to their followers, with the result that the battery of field-pieces was run back about a hundred yards. Henty and his companions, who were standing, as it were, strung up and waiting between two fires, now began to breathe again, seeing as they did that the threats of the Communists upon that occasion were empty wind, for the latter had backed down and dared not carry out their threats. The struggle with all its horrors was averted for the time, and to the intense satisfaction of the civilian spectators, the Communist infantry fell back level with their guns; mounted officers who acted as aides-de-camp to the leaders of the enemy cantered to and fro to the Hotel de ville with messages and fresh orders, with the result at last that each party agreed to hold its own till after the elections that were about to take place. Henty, who had stood fast through all, narrates that of all the episodes he witnessed during the Commune, these were the most exciting incidents through which he passed.

SELF-CONSTITUTED: *self-made*
AIDES-DE-CAMP: *assistants*

Chapter XXIII

The Vendôme Column

O F course there were patriots and patriots, but, as an observer, Henty's intercourse with those who vapored under the self-assumed title seems to have aroused in him scarcely anything but scorn, and more than once he attaches the adjective drunken to the savage barricaders with whom he came in contact during his busy watching of proceedings and his visits to barricade and trench. He describes vividly the state of the streets which had been under fire—shop fronts smashed in, windows shattered, gables and roofs riddled with shrapnel, trees splintered. Every second lamppost lay a battered wreck on the ground. Here and there a yawning hole revealed a gas-pipe laid open. In another place there would be a pit made as if by pickaxe and shovel, showing where a shell had plunged into the soil, and where the earth had been thrown up as if by some internal revulsion. And everywhere, when firing had ceased, spectators collected to see what mischief had been done where shells had entered and shattered walls. In one spot, where there was something to attract the curious seekers after novelty, upwards of fifty people had collected like a London crowd at an accident, risking their lives as they watched a foolhardy fellow who was digging out a bomb

INTERCOURSE: *interaction*
VAPORED: *boasted*
REVULSION: *tearing*
SAMPHIRE: *an edible plant*

which had not exploded. It was exciting in the extreme, and the spice of danger added to the interest, though the people were so crowded together, that if, as the man dug, the bomb had exploded, the tale of killed and wounded must have been awful. Shakespeare writes of him who gathered samphire halfway down the Dover cliffs, and speaks of it as "dreadful trade,"[1] and this man's occupation of gathering shells, though profitable, was full of risks. Still it went on, and in spite of the horrors connected with these revolutionary times there were plenty of quick-witted men ready to speculate and take their chances of making an honest penny. Planted in spots where they were out of fire, telescopes were propped up on the side-ways, offering views of the enemy at work in the forts. There was a busy time, too, for the French representatives of the owners of Pantechnicon vans, which bulky vehicles were drawn up at many a door for the removal of the furniture where the houses were within reach of shells.

Horrors were plentiful, and among the statistics gathered by the learned in such matters Henty mentions the fact that the mortality in the National Guard during this stupid civil war was greater in fifty days than for the entire period of the Prussian investment.

Apropos of the mock patriots of the Commune engaged in this imbecile insurrection, Henty with his military instincts and contempt for vanity has a word or two for a great soldier. Bonaparte, he says, has left a name that is imperishable in the annals of his country. He fought for France at the head of the French armies. He was the idol of the people, and, dying, his last thoughts were of France. "I desire," he said, "that my ashes shall be laid to repose on the banks of the Seine, in the midst of the people I love so well;" and his remains were brought

---

[1] *King Lear, Act 4, Scene 6* by William Shakespeare (1564-1616)
SIDE-WAYS: *side streets*
PANTECHNICON VANS: *moving vans*
INVESTMENT: *siege*
APROPOS OF: *regarding*
ANNALS: *historical records*

back from St. Helena to be interred as he had asked. Yet his people assisted at the degradation of the memorial raised to his fame—not all the people, but the very dregs of it. "I am no convert," says Henty, "to the faith of conquest as foreign policy, and an autocracy as the best of domestic governments, but I avow it did cost me, a stranger, something like a pang to see the Vendôme Column fall down on a litter of stable dung, amidst the obscene ribaldry of a mock patriotic rabble and the unmusical fanfares of a make-believe soldiery. Out of the purest love for the nations, they pretended this was done, and as a gage of amity to the world all round. These hypocrites seized a moment when their country was prostrate and galled by defeat in a war with a foreign invader as the fit one to kindle the flames of civil war! They profess that when they rule there shall be no more bloodshed. It shall be the millennium. And yet at the same moment they condemn the generals of the Second Empire for not having overwhelmed the hordes of the German army, and they press their own unwilling fellow-citizens, under pain of court-martial, to go into the ranks to slay or be slain by their brothers. With all their declarations of attachment to the Goddess of Peace, they would be ready to bow to the popular clamour if it took up again the shout, 'A Berlin! A Berlin!' sooner than lose the power they have momentarily succeeded in clutching within their grasp, and this while they jabber of despotism, and swear they have pulled over the pillar to Bonaparte because he was a despot. The circumstance that the tricolour was hoisted on the column before it fell, and waved so that all might see it, is safe evidence that these ignorant Frenchmen knew not what they did. For the tricolour is the national emblem, and these harlequins desired that this national symbol should go down into the dust with the emperor's statue before their sheet

INTERRED: *buried*
AUTOCRACY: *a government ruled by one person with unlimited power*
RIBALDRY: *vulgar speech*
GAGE OF AMITY: *token of friendship*
THE MILLENNIUM: *a reign of peace*
DESPOTISM: *tyranny*

of unhallowed crimson. It was but a poor victory to raise the red flag of the Commune over the tricolour in the heart of the disarmed city, while the same red was retiring before the tricolour in the outskirts. As I looked on at this sorry spectacle from the head of the Rue de la Paix, I overheard a Forfarshire man remark in Doric English to an acquaintance among the bystanders, 'I am not sanguinary, but I own I would not weep if a volley were fired into those blackguards.' Neither am I sanguinary, but I own I could almost sympathize with the Scotchman's wish.

"As soon as this piece of vandalism had been perpetrated a picket of cavalry some score strong, which had been keeping the ground, trotted backwards and forwards for a few minutes to prevent the mass of spectators from pushing on to the scene where the colossal memorial in bronze and stone lay like a corpse. When the crowd found there was no danger, it streamed along the thoroughfare, and the members of the Commune yielded to the desire of the public to walk by the fallen monument. As soldiers are marched by the dead body of a comrade who has been shot, the Parisians that chose had the privilege of penetrating into the Place by batches, and leaning over the fallen Cæsar. National Guardsmen stood on either side on the top of the barricade, barring the entrance, and behind them on the crest of the work were ranged masquerading mariners, some with revolvers in their belts and cigars in their mouths, a few gaping miscreants in the uniform of soldiers of the line, and of course the Paris urchin with his bold, merry face, who turns up in every scene of popular commotion. The base of the column was still erect on the Place, its jagged surface, where the shaft had broken off, covered over with plaster dust as if snow had fallen there recently.

TRICOLOUR: *the French flag of red, white and blue*
HARLEQUINS: *comic actors*
DORIC ENGLISH: *rustic English*
SANGUINARY: *bloodthirsty*
MASQUERADING MARINERS: *men pretending to be sailors*
MISCREANTS: *evildoers*

Red flags had already been fixed on cross poles on the platform it afforded, and captains of the staff, with the inevitable *vivandière*, lounged in graceful attitudes, looking on the world beneath from their novel and unaccustomed elevation. The capital of the column seemed to have turned in the fall, for the figure of the emperor lay buried in the litter with the face to the sky."

Some of those admitted to the spectacle of great Cæsar low had the bad taste to spit on the face, thus proving how thoroughly justified was the English correspondent's feeling of utter scorn for mob patriotism. Henty ends his description of the fall with the words: "I should have mentioned that the only display of bunting in the Rue de la Paix during the fête of the rabble was on the houses of the British and American residents, and their flags were floating merely to signify that the property beneath was foreign. One flag peculiarly suited to the Commune at the time was conspicuous by its absence—the black flag of death."

VIVANDIÈRE: *women who accompany the army and sell them food*
CAPITAL OF THE COLUMN: *decorative top of the column*
BUNTING: *colored cloth*
REPRISAL: *retaliation*
FELINE: *catlike*

Chapter XXIV

The Days of Reprisal

THE day which marked the fall of the Vendôme Column heralded the coming of the end, the termination of the short-lived triumph of the Commune. For the party of safety was fully awake now to the necessity of saving France from what threatened to prove a perhaps more bloody repetition of the Revolution of 1793.[1] MacMahon's[2] commands came sharp and to the point, and every week made the position of the Communists so desperate, that it seemed as if in feline rage they had determined to die fighting, marking their end with every mischievous piece of destruction they could effect. Hence it was that not only was fire set to buildings, but the destruction was rendered more furious by the application of mineral oils. Civilization shuddered as reports were sent in of the work of the petroleuses, which seemed to indicate that the fairest city of the world was doomed to become a heap of ashes. In these latter days Henty writes that "never since the days of St. Bartholomew[3] has Paris passed through such a terrible twenty-four hours as those which I spent there. I question if even that famous massacre was more terrible. I do not remember the number of victims which history records to have fallen then, but since the troops entered Paris seven or eight thousand of the Communists were estimated to have been shot, and to this

---

[1] The Reign of Terror during the French Revolution
[2] Patrice MacMahon, a French General and future President
[3] During the St. Bartholomew's Day Massacre in 1572, thousands of French Protestants were killed by Catholic mobs.
PETROLEUSES: *women accused of burning down houses with petroleum*

slaughter must be added the horrors of the conflagration. To make a comparison, it was a mingling of the great Protestant massacre and the burning of Rome. The smoke of the blazing city, after hanging like a pall, as if to hide the horrors, drifted slowly away, and flakes of incandescent paper, which fluttered down in the suburbs as thick as snow, were some of them carried a distance of fifty miles away. At this time it was apparently lawful for anyone to shoot his neighbour. An unguarded word, a movement which an excited man might consider suspicious, and a cry was raised, 'A Communist!' The voice of the accused was drowned in the tumult, and the unfortunate man was lucky if he was not at once held up and shot by the first armed men who came upon the scene. Innocent and guilty alike fell victims; and, as instancing the risk of strangers being about, two of our English officers, not being in uniform, had got as far as the Louvre just as the troops were about to advance against the Hotel de ville. They were at once seized and questioned. The answer was: 'We are English officers. We have our papers to prove our position.' The reply to this was: 'Messieurs, we have no time to examine papers now. Fall in behind, and if you attempt to escape you will be shot.' There was nothing for it but to obey. The regiment went off at the double; the officers followed. Another regiment seeing these two officers in mufti running behind the troops, at once seized them. Question and explanation were again postponed, for there was no time to talk. 'Put these fellows in front,' said an officer; and this time in front of the troops they went forward under a tremendous fire, until, the insurgents falling back, there was time to inspect papers. This is the sort of thing," Henty concludes naïvely, "to which one was every moment exposed in Paris. I can assure you that a special correspondent's duties were no sinecure."

CONFLAGRATION: *large, destructive fire*
PALL: *a cloth for spreading over a coffin*
INCANDESCENT: *glowing*
TUMULT: *commotion*
MUFTI: *regular clothing*

For the fighting in Paris was now going on more fiercely than ever. Grape-shot and shell from the batteries of field-pieces, from the various barricades and the forts engaged, worked dire havoc, and just at this time in particular, Henty relates the fact that from nearly every house and almost every window in the better streets hung the gay tricolour flag, in proof that the occupants were anti-Communists, and opposed to the red. In the boulevards and elsewhere the openings, whether gratings or windows, were all covered up with heaps of wet sand or mud, or by tightly-fitting boards. This precaution was taken on account of the fiendish women belonging to the Commune, who were going about pouring petroleum into the cellars and then throwing down lighted matches. On one day alone, marked by fresh fires constantly breaking out, Henty saw lying on the pavement the bodies of two women, who had just been taken in their deadly pursuit and shot. Six more were lying close to the ruins of the Palais Royal. The death sentence had been promulgated by MacMahon, not only for the protection of the city, but of the lives of the troops as well, for the Communists were desperate, and again and again wires laid for communication with mines were torn up; this saved the principal buildings. Despite all the horrors of destruction and the retribution that followed, it was necessary for orders to be issued as to the early closing of public buildings. Something had to be done to put an end to the sightseeing of the people who were prowling about, eager to get a glimpse of a stray corpse or a pool of blood, or to follow the troops leading off a prisoner, man or woman, to be shot; any sensation, no matter how terrible, was followed up with the same eagerness with which at home in England people would hurry to a race meeting or to some royal event.

That monstrous cataclysm, the Commune, was in its last throes, though dying hard. Its lurid sun was setting in blood.

NO SINECURE: *not a position requiring no real work*
RETRIBUTION: *punishment*
CATACLYSM: *violent event*

Retribution was falling heavily and sensational reports were in the air. One of the Parisian papers that had shown a ghoul-like thirst for blood, and had exhibited the desire further to inflame the fury of the victorious party, asserted that a hundred and fifty firemen had been shot at Versailles on the date previous to its appearance. This, on authority which Henty considered unimpeachable, was utterly false, for there had been no summary executions there. Soon after, as a special correspondent, he had to read a communication addressed by a Frenchman to one of our English papers, charging his colleagues with exaggerating their accounts of the wholesale and summary executions which they witnessed, and with feeling undue compassion for the men, women, and children thus butchered. In reply to this Henty says: "No correspondent that I am aware of has ever regarded as other than inevitable the fury of the troops whose duty it was to avenge the burning of the Tuileries[1] and the murder of the hostages. That they would give no quarter was what everyone supposed. Such deeds done in hot blood, horrible as they may be to witness, are common incidents in warfare, and though the correspondents might regret to find a regular army so entirely beyond control, they would hardly be surprised. But that which the correspondents saw with feelings of horror and disgust was people arrested on a mere hue and cry of their being insurgents or having thrown petroleum, and then dragged away amidst showers of blows from the ruffianly middle-class mob that had tamely put up with the Commune, and shot down like dogs. To make my meaning clear, I will give you a couple of instances. At the corner of one street there was a barricade. The insurgents had run away when the troops came up and carried it. It was not until the following morning that the neighbouring houses were searched for fugitives. Six men, and a boy in the uniform of the National Guard, were

---

[1] The Tuileries Palace was destroyed by the Commune.

UNIMPEACHABLE: *completely reliable*
SUMMARY: *hasty*
HUE AND CRY: *outcry*

found. The men pleaded piteously for their lives; the boy, who had retained his musket, resisted to the last, and wounded two men before he was disarmed. Then all the seven were put up against the barricade and shot. This is bad, but it is not what my colleagues or myself mean by atrocious reprisals. But what will the French writer of the letter to the English press say to this. At a house in the Faubourg St. Germain there was a native of Chaillot, who fled thither with his family to escape being forcibly incorporated in the troops of the Commune. He had belonged to the National Guard during the first siege, and had retained the *képi* which most Frenchmen then wore. The troops searched the house, dragged the man down into the street, and without listening to a word of explanation blew out his brains. In the wholesale razzias that were made, prisoners overcome with fear and falling down from utter nervous exhaustion were dragged out, shot, and left lying in the road. As regards the women supposed to be going about with bottles of petroleum to set houses on fire, all I can say is that I have seen what has made me understand the old cry of 'A witch! a witch!' with us. Any ugly old crone, who might be mingling with the crowd, was liable to instant execution, and many were thus butchered. I will only add that so far as I have seen, the correspondents of the English press have rather underrated than overstated what took place, and so far as I am concerned, I have never reported what I did not see myself, and have even carried my scruples so far as not to mention the wholesale butcheries of which a well-known general was guilty, and from which a former officer in our artillery was rescued by something little short of a miracle. As for the troops, they did not, that I ever saw, exhibit any ferocity. They left that to the cowardly curs who were crying 'Vive la Commune!' the very day before the Versaillais came in. Had all the insurgents been put to death, I should not say a word. Such

KÉPI: *a circular cap with a flat top and a visor*
RAZZIAS: *"raids" in French*
CURS: *worthless dogs*
VIVE LA COMMUNE!: *"Long live the Commune!" in French*
VERSAILLAIS: *government soldiers stationed in the town of Versailles*

atrocities are part of the business of war. But what I do say is, that thousands have been sacrificed without their executioners taking the trouble to ascertain their identity. The clamour of the mob was considered to be sufficient proof of guilt."

Henty was very reticent about a good many of his adventures in Paris and just outside the Ville Lumière during those days streaked with political trouble and dire calamity which followed the close of the war. He looked on at the Commune just as a soldier thoroughly accustomed to *horrida bella* might, and what is more, he saw through its egotism and hollow pretence, and criticized its *opéra bouffe* absurdities and its crimes. When the Commune was at its height, however, he got out of Paris and set out to join the investing Versaillais. From the vantage point of Meudon he and one or two other correspondents used to watch the firing of the Communists, and came to entertain a very poor opinion of it, except from a spectacular point of view. To the uninitiated, shell-firing seems a form of warfare of the most deadly kind; but that is where the mistake comes in, for, as Henty says, "in no case is artillery fire really dangerous except at point-blank range." With elevation, a shell, to do great damage, must "drop straight on top of you." Then, of course, the effect is bad; otherwise there is a good deal of sound and fury signifying the vagaries of shells, and with a properly constituted *obus* the looker-on has time to decide, as he watches the firing, which way he had better go to avoid any unpleasant consequences. Henty seems to have rather enjoyed the sensation, as a matter of fact, and he pricks the bubble—of the cannon's mouth, as it were—by destroying a popular delusion as to the awful results bound to follow from heavy shell-fire. To read what he says, one is driven to the conclusion that the projectiles in question have been masquerading as far more dangerous than is really the case, in the same way as the Russian has built

RETICENT: *silent, reserved*
HORRIDA BELLA: *"horrid war" in Latin*
OPÉRA BOUFFE: *"comic opera" in French*
VAGARIES: *whims*
OBUS: *"shell" in French*

up a bogus reputation for fearsomeness on the strength of the big boots he wears. "Why, in the Turco-Servian War," Henty writes, "I was with some four thousand men on a knoll twice the size of Lincoln's Inn Fields. Into that space the enemy dropped three thousand shells in eight hours, and killed—three or four men!" One chance in a thousand was fairly small.

But to return to that charming spot, Meudon, at the time when it was residentially risky. What is the sensation like of being under fire? Henty, of course, was fortunately constituted, and did not mind little things. "At first," he says, "you are too flustered to be really afraid, and when you get used to that you've got your business to think about. You're there for a purpose, you must remember. Besides, use enables one to estimate danger very quickly, and often that estimate reveals the fact that there is no danger at all."

He gives a vividly interesting, and yet a matter-of-fact impression of watching shell-firing. "When the flash showed at the far-off battery, one listened for the missile—that horrible whistle, growing louder and louder as the shell travelled towards one. Until it was about thirty yards away it was impossible to tell whether it was coming within dangerous proximity or not. Thirty yards off, the sound altered if it was moving at an angle that would carry it out of range. If the sound didn't alter, one fell flat on one's face; if it did, one stood still. A matter of nerve, perhaps, but nerve backed up by knowledge." Familiarity, of course, produces an easier way of looking at such things, but viewed in this way the ordinary everyday idea of artillery fire has to be considerably altered. Henty's observations might well be incorporated in some little manual on etiquette when meeting shells.

BOGUS: *false*
RESIDENTIALLY RISKY: *dangerous to be a resident*
ETIQUETTE: *proper behavior*

CHAPTER XXV

A WORD ABOUT POLITICS

IT is impossible not to admire the single-mindedness and directness of purpose which characterize Henty's letters from Paris written at this period of dire trouble, when chapters which rival in tragedy and sadness any of those that have gone before were being added to the history of France. He viewed this time of heart-stirring crisis in a matter-of-fact style, such as was to be expected from a man of his temperament and business-like attributes. He went straight forward with the work of the day, chronicling details which came under his notice, and keeping to hard plain facts at a time when visionary speculation was the rule, and when all those who followed the prodigious happenings in France were amazed and bewildered by the complexity of the situation, and by the startling suggestiveness of what the morrow might have in store for the high-strung and imaginative French people. He kept sedulously to the point, in spite of all, notwithstanding the rumours concerning what Thiers[1] meant to do, and what Marshal MacMahon had said to the Comte de Chambord regarding the possibility of the latter being received at Versailles as "Henri Cinq".[2]

Outside the heated arena of politics in Paris there were all these larger issues of extreme importance, issues of such

---

[1] Adolphe Thiers, president of France from 1871 to 1873
[2] MacMahon supported the Comte's claim to the French throne.
SEDULOUSLY: *carefully*
HENRI CINQ: *Henry the Fifth*
SALONS: *large rooms for entertaining guests*
ADVENT: *arrival*

significance that they brought into the tumult of that day the quieter spirit of the old past. At the dinner tables, and in the *salons* of Paris, and elsewhere as well, even up to 1875, the talk was of the coming of Henry the Fifth, the king of the old line, the great-nephew of his majesty, Louis the Sixteenth, and of King Louis the Eighteenth, and the grandson of Charles the Tenth. Such an advent would have been in curious contrast to the wild "chicken-and-champagne" days of the corrupt and materialistic Second Empire, for the Comte de Chambord had lived in monastic seclusion ever since his protest in the early "fifties". Maybe in his mimic court at Frohsdorff, surrounded by all the respect and divinity of a prince who represented an illustrious tradition, and who found in religion his greatest solace, the heir to the French crown was nearer to happiness than he would have been had he boldly come forward and assumed the reins of power, as he might have done had his character been of blunter fibre. If this had occurred, the change for Paris from the red dominion of the Commune to the white lilies,[1] with all they signified, would have been another strikingly dramatic episode in the chronicles of France.

All these things Henty saw and lived among at that time when people were disgusted with the preceding twenty years, and wished for something which was better and more earnest, though precisely what was desired it would be hard to say. Side by side with rank, uncompromising Anarchism, were the echoes of an old and aristocratic regime, and learned theorists were busy weighing the various proposals in the balance, while a sort of hybrid military republic kept the lists. And all this at a time when the streets of the capital were perhaps the most dangerous of any in the world, and social order had gone by the board. At one time it really seemed as though the spirit

---

[1] When offered the French throne, the Comte declared that he would only accept on the condition that a white flag, with the fleur-de-lis, a symbol of the French monarchy, be adopted.

MONASTIC SECLUSION: *seclusion like that of a monastery*
ANARCHISM: *the belief that all government is evil*
KEPT THE LISTS: *managed the scene of conflict*

of the older France would prevail, that certain incontestable rights would come up for final adjustment, and that a thread of policy, of which sight had been lost for some years, would be finally resumed.

Vague speculation about matters which lay outside his immediate purview was, however, never Henty's method, but here and there a "newsy" item crops up in his correspondence, such as that the Prince of Orleans politely saw Thiers to his carriage, and that people were talking of the Duc d'Aumale, also that the Princes of Orleans, who had always followed social and military things rather than political, would abide by what France said. Of course this was rather a doubtful policy, for France sometimes speaks with an uncertain voice. The demagogue shouts enough for a hundred, but the silent thinker who disdains noise would be better worth hearing. That Henty followed all these things we know, and his real views crop up here and there; but he was a narrator, not a commentator. The empire was dead. As an actual political power it died in 1867, and however much Napoleon the Third might protest against his deposition, the fact that he had finally lost the throne was there patent to all. Even the statement of the astute M. Pietri, the secretary of the disinterested ex-monarch, that his master had not one centime in foreign funds, seems to have had no effect on the course of events.

Henty was only a bird of passage, an observer of Paris during a few moments at a period when the influences of centuries were at work, and his was by no means exclusively a political view. Empty theorizing or the peering into empty houses did not lie his way; but maybe for this reason more than any other is it most interesting to con over his lengthy contributions to the newspapers of that time. The almost photographic

INCONTESTABLE RIGHTS: *rights that cannot be challenged*
PURVIEW: *concern*
HIS DEPOSITION: *being deposed*
DISINTERESTED: *indifferent*
CENTIME: *a small French coin similar to a penny*
CON OVER: *study*

minutiæ give the reader a vivid impression of the crucible period, for everything was in the course of remaking. There was the first review after the Germans had packed up and gone away, the recoming of the martial spirit under the leadership of MacMahon, who turned in his saddle with a "There, gentlemen, what do you think of that?" as the battalions of cadets, the future officers of the armies of France, came swinging by before the staff and the foreign attachés. There was the bright spot of the Belfort incident, when the devoted garrison marched out with all the honours of war. It was a great and stirring time, when every moment was lived at fever heat; and Henty looked on as a soldier as well as a correspondent.

Very soon the French were beginning to look up again. "We have an army of 450,000 men," was the cry. There were a few pride-saving laurels won in the defeat of the Commune, civil war though it was. Then we see the recommencement of the social life of the capital. Wonderful was the exhibition of recuperative power. The broken bits of civic life were put together, and an order sent to the factories for a new outfit, as it were. The Comédie Française Company[1] toured in London, and refilled the empty exchequer; the loan necessary to pay off the more urgent demands was easily subscribed; and Henty fills in the picture with the unerring touch of a master hand. It is a pen such as his—dispassionate, observing, restrained—on which the historian rightly relies.

[1] An acting company established in 1680 by King Louis XIV
CRUCIBLE PERIOD: *time of severe trial*
MARTIAL: *warlike*
ATTACHÉS: *diplomats*
LAURELS: *honors*
DISPASSIONATE: *calm*

CHAPTER XXVI

ON THE LIFE OF A WAR CORRESPONDENT

EUROPE being once more at peace, with France settling down, Henty turned from fact to fiction, producing *The Young Settlers*, and later a book for boys, *The Young Franc Tireurs and their Adventures in the Franco-Prussian War*, the source of his inspiration being evident.

Little more than a year though elapsed before the cry in the north and east was again havoc. The dogs of war were let loose by Russia, and Henty's pen was again busy for his paper. This was in connection with the restless Turkoman dwellers in Khiva,[1] a name which brings up recollections of Captain Burnaby, who described his solitary ride to that city, and graphically narrated his extraordinary journey upon a camel in love.[2] Burnaby was a thorough specimen of the *beau sabreur*, as well set up and muscular as any Lifeguardsman (or Blue)[3] in his regiment. He was good company, and a very welcome guest at Henty's club, where he came one evening shortly before his departure for Egypt. His fate was that of a gallant soldier. Dismounted, he stood warding off the spear-thrusts of the Mandi's followers with his sword, what time they had succeeded in breaking the British square at Abu Klea,[4] and he held them back until he received in his neck the fatal thrust which robbed the service of a brave soldier.

---

[1] Russian soldiers conquered the city of Khiva in 1873.
[2] In his famous book, *A Ride to Khiva,* published in 1876
[3] Elite British cavalry troops
[4] A group of wells in northeast Ethiopia
BEAU SABREUR: *"handsome swordsman" in French*

Upon Henty's return from Russia the preparations for another campaign were not far distant, for the Ashanti expedition had been decided upon, and in September 1873 he sailed for Cape Coast Castle in the *Ambriz*, with Sir Garnet Wolseley.

In speaking of a correspondent's duties he tells us how, when at home, he receives a telegram saying, "Come up to the office at once," he knows that it means that there is something serious on the way, and from general knowledge of what is going on abroad he is pretty well aware why his services are required. On reaching the room of the manager of the newspaper, or that of the editor, he is told that he is to accompany this or that expedition, and most probably he is informed that he must be off the very next day.

If the journey is by rail, it may be that it has to be commenced at once, or if by steamer, it may depend upon when the vessel starts east, west, north, or south, and he learns that it will be better to go and take his passage at once.

If the conversation is with the editor, there are many things to be discussed, such as the length of the letters he is to send, the people he is to see; there is talk about passports, discussion on letters of recommendation, and hints about the political line he is to take, while various little ins and outs have to be dwelt upon. In fact, editors have special ideas of their own, and often *in petto* a disposition to come to conclusions as to what is about to take place.

At the end of the business discussion the correspondent receives a big cheque, and what remains to do is soon got over. The passage to wherever it may be is taken, and the adventurer—for such he is—hurries home to make the preparations which experience has taught him are necessary. The fewer things he has to lumber himself with the better, but stern necessity has taught him that certain provisions must be made; and when a man

LUMBER: *burden*

has followed the headquarters of an army time after time, he knows that he must have with him, to face heat, cold, and storm (often in extremes), a stock of clothes suitable for all climates, saddle and bridle of the best, revolvers, and a tent. The reader may raise his eyebrows as he reads this list of "necessaries" and think of the amount of luggage. Pooh! One has not half done. Our correspondent has to look after his health and strength, and the chances are many that he will starve if not provided for the worst. He has to take cooking apparatus for field work. He must be provided with waterproof sheets to spread on the damp ground and supplement the canvas of his tent. He has to take a portable bed, three or four blankets, and much other *impedimenta* which experience has taught that he *must* carry with him if he is to be in condition to write "good stuff" when he wants to commit the information he has learned to paper.

With regard to Ashanti, Henty says in addressing an imaginary person who wants to know what it is to become a war correspondent: "You will probably pause, after visiting the bank, to buy a case or two of spirits and one of cocoa and milk, a few pounds of tea in a tin, and if you are a smoker—and I don't know any special correspondent who is not—a good supply of tobacco, also in tins."

Then there is the health to be considered; and a man of experience knows how necessary it is to nip any threatening of disease in the bud. He must take remedies which suit his constitution in an ordinary way, and certain others which are bound to be wanted by a man who is about to cross rivers and swamps, and force his way through tangled forest and the other strongholds of jungle and malarial fever.

"Bless the old Jesuit fathers," he says, "for their grand discovery of quinine!"[1] as he fortifies himself with that most wonderful of discoveries, as useful in India and in Africa as in South

---

[1] Quinine, an extract of the bark of the cinchona tree, was a common and effective treatment for malaria.

IMPEDIMENTA: *baggage that slowed him down*

America, its ancient home. He provides himself, too, with little blue hexagonal bottles of chlorodyne.[1] He takes aperients also, but not in paper boxes such as a doctor uses, with the contents to be taken two at bedtime, but safely garnered behind tin or glass to preserve them from the mould produced by damp.

Then, too, there is the remedy against one of the most lowering of diseases, dysentery—ipecacuanha, and in addition, as a warming tonic, a bottle of essence of ginger, and another of that valuable corrective that is so strongly suggestive of a draught from a very soapy wash-tub, ammonia. Thus provided with these absolute necessaries for use when the doctor is not within reach, he may feel that he has done what is necessary to guard against any trouble that may come. And is that all? Not quite. A war correspondent is a very expensive luxury to his employers, though the British public obtains the results of all that he has done for the homely penny. He is a costly luxury, and he must be taken care of, even though his necessaries possess height, breadth, and weight.

He receives hospitality and protection and permission to accompany an army, but this does not include anything in the nature of a tent. "My own," says Henty, "which accompanied me in many campaigns, was about seven feet square. It was a *tente d'abri*, to which had been added a lower flap about two feet high, giving it a height in the centre of some four feet and a half. The two poles were joined like fishing-rods, and the whole affair packed up in a bag and weighed about thirty pounds. Of course the bed was on the ground and occupied one side of the tent, serving as a sofa by day as well as a bed at night. There was a passage left down the centre of the tent, whose other side was occupied by my trunks, which were, of course, small in size for facilities of transport. Here, too, were my other paraphernalia."

---

[1] Chlorodyne was a popular remedy for cholera and many other ailments. Its ingredients included alcohol, opium and chloroform.

APERIENTS: *laxatives*
GARNERED: *stored*

Thus provided for service in the field, the correspondent, as it will be seen, is pretty well burdened; but during his travels he is always independent, for he has a home where he can write and rest and recruit himself against hunger, albeit his cooking has to be done in the provided apparatus in the open air.

For warmth in the bitter nights there is a watch-fire; but in some instances Henty depended upon his own natural warmth and a wonderful coat of sheepskin tanned, with the thick wool on. He sometimes came to the club in this in the winter, looking feet more in girth than was his natural size.

One of the first things to be done on arriving at the scene of action is for the correspondent to apply at headquarters for a form of permission to accompany the army, a general permission having been obtained from the home authorities before starting. With regard to this, Henty did most of his campaigning in the days before generals had begun to grow more and more strict and reticent, until now they go so far as to refuse permission altogether. In the case of the Russo-Japanese War, the British correspondents on the Japanese side were, in spite of every civility and attention, so hindered and obstructed, under the pretence of being protected from danger, that one of Henty's colleagues, E. F. Knight, gave up the duty in disgust.

But to return to a war correspondent's necessities: his next task on reaching the front is to buy a good dependable horse to bear the saddle and to be guided by the bit and bridle with which he has come provided. In addition he should have a couple of ponies, or two of the patient but hardy obstinate animals known as mules, to bear the whole of his baggage and stores. Lastly comes one of the most important businesses, that of hiring a couple of servants, one as personal attendant and general factotum, the other to attend to the horse and baggage-animals. Great things often depend upon little, and there is a

IN GIRTH: *around the middle*
FACTOTUM: *a servant who does many different types of work*

little matter called experience upon which depends not merely a man's comfort and convenience, but also the success or failure of his campaign.

Henty praises warmly a class of men who seem to have devoted themselves to the profession of serving, and have earned for themselves the credit of being the best men for the purpose in the world. These are the Goa Portuguese men, with European features, but looking as dark as other natives of India. For many years they have been accustomed to furnish all ships trading in the East with stewards, and as a consequence most of them speak English fairly well.

Henty speaks of having been fortunate enough to obtain two such men at different times—one accompanied him from Bombay on the Abyssinian expedition, the other on the Prince of Wales's tour through India. Here is the admirable character he gives them: "Both were excellent fellows, always ready and willing, and absolutely uncomplaining whatever happened." And much did happen, of course.

To a young man of energy who longs to change some ordinary humdrum career for one of excitement, there is something wonderfully attractive in the career of a war correspondent. Certainly the army always offers itself as a life full of wild episodes, but then there is something deterrent in the forced and severe discipline, as well as in the dangers which a soldier has to face. The risks an energetic war correspondent takes are of course many, for he is often compelled to be under fire, and if matters are adverse he may be taken prisoner; but there is great attraction in being a witness of the moves in the great game of chess played by nations in stern reality, though there are innumerable troubles to be encountered that are terribly irritating in their pettiness, and this makes them seem exasperatingly far-reaching and vast. For instance, it is maddening,

STEWARDS: *servants*
ADVERSE: *unfavorable*

when wearied out with a long day's march, to have to be called by necessity to help the baggage man in the constant readjustment of the animals' loads, which always seem to be slipping off through the ropes coming untied. This is bad enough with ponies, but it is very much worse with mules.

The Yankees have one particular way of tying the hide lariats, or ropes, that secure the burdens upon a mule's back. This knot, or series of knots, they term the diamond hitch, perhaps from its value or its shape; both may be applicable. The Goa men have ways of their own, but these grow useless with the cunning animals. Sundry awkward packages have apparently been made perfectly secure on a mule's back, but almost directly afterwards they become loose, owing to the fact that the animal had swelled himself out when the ropes were being hauled tight, and then drawn himself in till everything seems to have shaken loose. The whole burden then starts to slide sideways, and threatens to glide under the little brute, so that he begins to stumble and trip. Much of this soon becomes galling to a weary man, and one has heard of people under such circumstances who vow that, as soon as they begin to pull upon the loose rope to make all taut again, a mule will draw back his lips and show his teeth in a hideous grin, as if he were looking upon the whole transaction as the best of fun.

Then, too, there is the misery attending the arrival at the camping-ground and the selection of the place to set up the tent to make things comfortable, perhaps with the rain pouring down. A pleasant accompaniment this last to the lighting of a fire and the cooking of a dinner, while ultimately the correspondent may be able to get no tent erected, and may be forced to lie down in the open, wrapped in a blanket and a waterproof sheet.

This was not one of his troubles in the Abyssinian expedition, for there Henty encountered but little rain; but he and his

TAUT: *tight*

companion, who represented the *Morning Post* and who travelled with him, met with plenty of petty troubles consequent
upon the behaviour of one of the servants, an Indian syce. This
fellow looked after the horses, but especially after himself, for
he was always provided with the one great excuse to avoid his
work, that he was not well. He ended by coming one day to
announce that Abyssinia did not agree with him, and that he
must go down to the coast and return in some ship that was
sailing for India.

When accompanying a British force on an expedition like
this, a correspondent is allowed to draw the same rations as
those served out to officers and men—meat, biscuits, preserved
vegetables, and a certain amount of tea and sugar—while in
the Abyssinian campaign, possibly owing to the presence of a
Naval Brigade, who worked the rockets, rum was served out
regularly. This, however, was given only very occasionally in
Ashanti, where, Henty says, "it was much more necessary. A
small quantity of spirits served out to be taken at the evening
meal is considered a very great benefit to men who arrive utterly exhausted after their march in a tropical climate."

Henty goes on to add that the meat served out in the Ashanti
campaign was either that of some freshly-killed bullock which
had accompanied the march day after day, and whose flesh was
as tough as leather, or else it was tinned meat, upon which after a short time everyone looked with loathing. This had to be
washed down with a decoction of the commonest and worst
tea, perhaps made with muddy water, and to an exhausted man
it was well nigh impossible. But in that awful climate the addition of a small quantity of spirits to the tea acted as a restor-
ative, giving the stomach a fillip, and enabling the food to be
eaten and digested.

Fortunately, upon the Ashanti expedition the correspondents had clubbed together and taken with them a small

FILLIP: *stimulant*

supply of wine, which proved invaluable in bracing them up to do their work, when but for it they would have been incapable of doing anything at the end of some of the specially hard and exhausting marches. It was to this claret that Henty largely attributed the preservation of his health, when so many not thus provided were prostrated by the deadly effects of the climate.

In a hot country like Ashanti it might have been supposed that native fruits and vegetables would be plentiful and easily to be purchased of the people at the various villages; but nothing of the kind was obtainable, and the correspondents had to depend entirely on the stores they carried with them upon their ponies or mules. The commissariat supply was not abundant or appetizing: for breakfast, oatmeal, eaten with preserved milk; but before that, at daybreak, they always contrived a cup of chocolate and milk. Dinner consisted of a banquet of tinned rations and preserved vegetables, made eatable by being flavoured with Worcester sauce or pickles, and when things were at the worst and appetite rebelled, there was an occasional addition of boiled rice with preserved fruit from their stores. Altogether, the weary correspondents were so lowered by exhaustion that they came to look upon their meals with utter disgust, consequent upon the heat and terrible nature of a climate which, higher up at the coast, was looked upon by old writers as the white man's grave.

Matters were very different in the breezy, bright uplands of Abyssinia, where, owing to the difficulties of carriage, the correspondents were only allowed to carry with them a very small quantity of stores. Here, however, they were generally able to eke out their rations by making purchases from the natives, who, as soon as they found that they could receive honourable treatment in the way of payment, and that they were not dealing with an invading army who confiscated everything in the

CLARET: *red wine*
EKE OUT: *stretch*

way of food, began to bring to market capital additions to the correspondents' fare. Now it would be eggs, now chickens, or the meals were truly sweetened by the contents of a jar of honey. It was a land, too, of flocks of sheep, which were purchased by the commissariat, and the heads, which were looked upon by the officers who superintended the rations as what is technically termed "offal," and not to be served out as rations, could often be obtained by the correspondents' cook. He was able to make of them a dainty dish, although he had probably never heard the Scotchman's remark that there was "a deal of meescellaneous feeding" in a good sheep's head.

There was shooting, too, with an occasional present of guinea-fowls or a hare shot by friends; and on these occasions they generally had a small dinner party. So famous was the cooking of their servants, that one day when Lord Napier asked Henty and his companion to dine with him he said: "You will have to put up with plain fare for once, for my staff tell me that when any of them dine with you they fare infinitely better than they do with me."

Henty gives an example of one of the menus on a festive occasion: Soup; slices of sheep's face, grilled with the tongue, and brain sauce; a joint of mutton, jugged hare; and an omelette with honey—a proof that during the Abyssinian expedition the special correspondents fared well.

OFFAL: *the waste parts of a butchered animal*
JUGGED HARE: *hare cooked in a jug which is placed in boiling water*

CHAPTER XXVII

A RISKY CRUISE WITH H. M. STANLEY

To come back, after this long digression on the life of a war correspondent, to the Ashanti campaign, upon which the subject of this memoir had now embarked, it may be taken quite as a matter of course that two such men as Henry Stanley[1] and George Henty, bound on the same mission on behalf of the *New York Herald* and the *London Standard*, should be on intimate terms together, the more especially as they were both men who loved being afloat, and in the pursuit of business let nothing in the way of danger stand in their way.

It was not surprising then that when the war correspondents were impatiently waiting for progress to be made by the expedition, such as would call them to the front and give stirring work for their pens to record, Stanley, with his customary defiance of risks when attempting an adventure, and being in want of a companion, should turn to his colleague Henty and ask him if he would take a turn with him along the coast in his yacht. It need hardly be said what was Henty's answer. The very word yacht was sufficient to make him accept eagerly, and he immediately acquiesced, delighted with the chance of a run of some seventy miles along the African shore from Cape Coast to Addah. At the time he was only aware that Stanley had brought out a small vessel at the cost of his newspaper,

---

[1] Henry Stanley (1841-1904) was a well known journalist writing for the *New York Herald*. He is most famous for his expedition to find Dr. David Livingstone.
DIGRESSION: *departure from the main subject*

THE ASHANTI CAMPAIGN

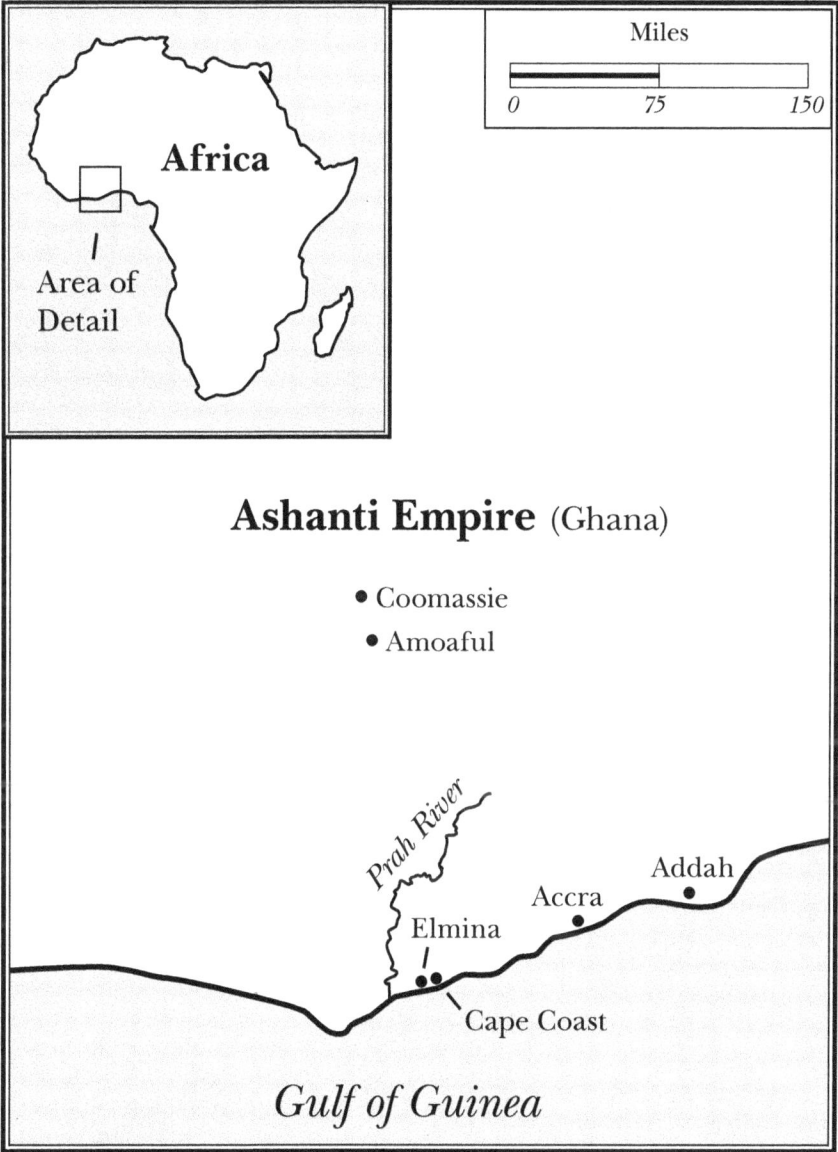

Map of the Ashanti Campaign showing Africa with Area of Detail, the Ashanti Empire (Ghana) with Coomassie and Amoaful, the Prah River, Elmina, Cape Coast, Accra, Addah, and the Gulf of Guinea. Scale in Miles: 0, 75, 150.

expressly so as to enable him to take runs up the West African rivers, and penetrate where he pleased in comparative independence. The use of a boat among the great flooded rivers was no novelty, of course, to the famous African explorer, and at the first blush, and with such an experienced pilot, there seemed to be no cause for hesitation, although at the time Henty was not aware in what kind of boat he was to be a passenger. All he knew was that the vessel was called the *Dauntless*, and that it was a Thames pleasure yacht which had been brought out by Stanley under the mistaken idea that Lord Wolseley's advance upon Coomassie was to be made by way of the river Prah.

Now, for the river Thames, where it was first launched, or for the river Prah, the *Dauntless*, which proved to be a little steam pleasure yacht, or launch, about thirty-six feet long by six feet wide, would have been admirably suited; but it suddenly began to dawn upon Henty that the craft in which he was about to take his trip, sailing in the evening and through the night, was about as ill-adapted for ocean work as any vessel that ever put out of port, and most particularly unsuited to sail out upon an ocean so wholly devoid of harbours as is the Atlantic upon the West African coast.

He must have known, though possibly it did not occur to him for the moment, that he was in a district where landing on the surf-bound shore was only possible with the aid of specially built boats rowed by the experienced natives, who are thoroughly accustomed to the huge breakers that come rolling in. Their light boats are as buoyant as corks, and the rowers take a capsize and the filling of their craft as merely an excuse for exercising their great swimming powers, regarding it as an easy task to right their surf-boat and row on again. Stanley's steam launch, however, was made heavy and unsuitable

EXPRESSLY: *for the specific purpose*
AT THE FIRST BLUSH: *at the first glance*
DEVOID OF: *free from*

by the dead weight of its engine and machinery, to which for a long run would of course be added heavy clumsy coal by the ton.

In describing his trip, and speaking as a man who is no mean sailor, Henty says that he is bound, in justice to his own character as a man who preferred to take reasonable care of his life, to say that when he accepted the offer he had not seen the boat. It was then lying moored up the Elmina river, and soon after, when entering into conversation with friends, who began to expostulate with him about the risk he was going to run, he felt disposed to laugh at them. One said it was madness, another that it was folly, and that it might be all very well for a reckless, venturesome man like Stanley, who dared go anywhere to find Livingstone, or penetrate the dense forests of Central Africa, but that the expedition was not one on which a sane man should embark. To quote the words of the counsellor, "You are an ordinary Englishman, and father of a family. Take care of yourself and your paper; for if you go out to sea in that little miserable tea-kettle of a thing, you will never come back; and we can't spare our colleague."

Expostulations from other friends followed, in the shape of prophecies of all sorts of evil things, and matters began to shape themselves in a manner that was not likely to prove encouraging. In his quiet way there was an enormous amount of firm determination in Henty; but it is not too much to say that he began to pass through a phase of indecision, and to wish that he had not given his word. Certainly he would much rather not have gone, but he was not the man to throw a friend over by breaking his promise at the last moment. All the same, though, he began to think and to turn matters over in his mind. Assuredly the *Dauntless* was a thoroughly non-seagoing boat; but if Stanley could go in her, why he, Henty, could go in her likewise,

---

MEAN SAILOR: *second-rate sailor*
EXPOSTULATE: *argue with the intent of warning*
VENTURESOME: *daring*

and he was perfectly aware that Stanley had at once started for Elmina to bring the boat down.

He felt himself nevertheless in a very different position from that which he would have occupied at home when calculating whether he should go out in his own fore-and-aft-rigged boat, in a sea whose currents he understood, and whose waters he knew how to sail.

But, Englishman-like, as the hours glided by he grew more firm and determined, and was almost ready to accuse himself of cowardice; so that when about ten o'clock at night he was joined by Stanley, who announced that he had brought the launch round, that the men were busy coaling, that the moon was up, and all would be ready for a start at midnight, Henty assumed a cheerful and gratified expression of countenance and promised to be there.

Now it may not be out of place to say that even in the calmest weather the breakers that come booming in upon that coast are quite sufficient to shake the nerves of even the most stoutly built, and to put out to sea in a Thames steam yacht, specially built for smooth water, was enough to make a brave man think twice of what he was about to do.

However, Henty put together a few necessaries, and was prepared for the start when some friends dropped in ready to shake hands with him, and to assure him encouragingly that this was a final goodbye; then he started for the beach, with the roar of the breakers thundering in his ears.

There was a little delay as he joined Stanley at the place from which the surf-boat was to start, to be rowed out to where the steam yacht was lying, for the coal had not yet all come down; but after about half an hour the final sacks were brought down and placed in the bottom of the boat, he and Stanley took their places, the rowers ran the light craft out, sprang aboard, and began to paddle, and fortunately they got through the line of breakers without a wetting. Then they made towards the tiny launch, which, as they rose high upon the swell, before dropping down into the trough of the sea, they could perceive showing a light about a quarter of a mile off the shore.

And now it was that Henty could see clearly what manner of vessel it was in which he was to make his voyage. For about six feet at either end she was decked, with the engine and boiler taking up half the remaining space, but just leaving a cockpit of about six feet long at either end.

When Henty boarded her he found that these open spaces were for the time being piled full of coal, of which ponderous awkward lading the little vessel had somewhere about two tons on board, and this was quite enough to bring her down within a few inches of the water. In fact, when steam was turned on, the water was awash over the after-deck, a state of affairs pretty startling for any but the most reckless.

As a matter of course, Henty (a businesslike and thorough seaman, who knew what he was about in the management of a sailing boat) must have set his teeth hard; but war-correspondent-like, he was ready to make the best of things, and after running his eye over the little steamer in the moonlight, he cheered himself with the thought that, as they went on, the weight of the coal would gradually grow less, and the launch become lighter in the water.

It was past the time for starting, so the anchor was soon drawn up, the little engine commenced to pant and rattle away merrily, while the lights upon the shore began to grow faint, for, in spite of being heavily laden, the steam launch showed herself worthy of her name, rising easily over the long heavy Atlantic swell. To Henty's great satisfaction it seemed to be time to enjoy a calm and thoughtful pipe, for it was at once apparent

LADING: *cargo*

that unless the wind freshened and made the sea get up, and this was only probable in the event of a hurricane, there was no cause for any uneasiness as to the safety of the little yacht.

In about half an hour they had settled down, for Henty was thoroughly at home on board the smallest of craft, and loved to see things shipshape. Thick mats were spread over the blocks of coal, rugs were unrolled, and preparations were made for indulgence in the ever-welcome cup of tea.

The crew, all told, were only six in number. Stanley, the skipper; an English lad, who acted as his amanuensis and general help; the engineer, two boys, who acted as servants and assistant stokers; and Henty himself. The last mentioned immediately began to talk business, and was for the time being the most important man on board, for it was not in him to be aboard a vessel of any kind without being ready to consider where their bearings lay and what effect the local currents would have upon their course.

Things were a little haphazard on board a vessel made only for steering by the shore, for the most part at the mouth of a river, so they had only a pocket compass. Quite nautically, Henty says that he knew that their course was slightly to north of east; but all the same it seemed extremely doubtful whether they ought to steer by such bearings, for they had no means of knowing how far the iron of the engine would affect the compass; "and besides, as there was a strong set of the current on the shore," he continues, "we agreed to steer by the land."

He goes on philosophically to say that steering by the land is simple enough by daylight, but at night, situated as they were, it was no easy matter, for though the moon was up, the customary African haze hung on the water and rendered the outline of the coast so indistinct that it was difficult in the extreme to judge the exact distance. Sometimes, too, the land lay so low

FRESHENED: *strengthened*
GET UP: *become rougher*
AMANUENSIS: *someone who takes down dictation*
STOKERS: *those who feed fuel into the engine*

that they could see little besides the white line of the surf, with here and there the head of a palm tree. Once or twice, feeling that it was necessary to go cautiously, steam was turned off, and they stopped a few minutes to oil heated bearings or to tighten a nut; and then in the stillness of the night the loud roar of the surf seemed startlingly near.

Then on again and on, not knowing what was to be their fate, for there was always the possibility that they might be carried by a current too near one of the breakers and then be caught up, borne along at a tremendous rate, till, striking upon the sand, the little vessel would be rolled over and over, prior to being cast ashore a complete wreck.

In this way they steamed through the dull half-transparent haze, a feeling of ignorance and helplessness troubling the man to whom the navigation was most strange.

They took it in turns to steer, and the one who was off duty was supposed to take a nap; but Henty says quietly, "I do not think there was much sleep on board the *Dauntless*, and there was a general satisfaction when the morning broke."

The general idea of a reader is that the West Coast of Africa is a land where the surf rushes in over the cast-up sand to where the dull olive-green of the weird-looking mangrove fringes the shore. But between Cape Coast Castle and Accra, although the seashore lies flat for a few miles inland, it, for the most part, impressed Henty as a beautiful undulating country, with the hills rising occasionally from the very edge of the sea and attaining at times a thousand feet in height, the highest eminence in the neighbourhood being double that elevation.

And yet, he says, this beautiful hilly portion of the coast is as unhealthy as, if not worse than, the low shores with their mango swamps. This evil repute is said to apply most strongly to parts where the land is rich in gold, and it deters the adventurous who are disposed to exploit the precious metal. There is no doubt about its presence, and abundance might be had, but gold is too dear at the cost of life; and though it might be considered that the native black would prove immune if employed at gold-digging, it has been demonstrated again and again that the fever—the malaria—that is set free as soon as the earth is disturbed, is just as fatal to the black as to the white. The latter, with a smattering of science, attributes it to the disturbance of the soil and the setting at liberty of the germs of disease buried therein, and points to the fact that where new plantations of coffee, cinchona, or India rubber are being made almost anywhere in the Malay Peninsula, the effects are, at the first cultivation of the soil, precisely the same, though in time, when the ground has been stirred again and again, it becomes healthy.

The West Coast black, however, has a very different theory, which he will freely impart, but with an almost awestricken whisper. Death comes to anyone who digs for gold, because it is fetish. It is of no use to laugh at his superstition. He knows that this is the case, and if any careless, contemptuous personage ridicules his superstition, he is angered; if a more rational explanation is propounded, he pities the inquirer's ignorance. It is fetish, and fatal. Fatal enough, but unfortunately the horrible fetish belief is utilized in connection with poison and the destruction of an enemy. Hence the power of the Obeah man, the impostor-like native priest, witch-doctor, or medicine man. This fetish idea lingers still in the West Indies, where it has been handed down by the early unfortunate slaves from the West Coast, who formed the trade of the old plantation times.

This by the way. There were no further troubles about the steering in the bright morning sunshine, and Henty spent his

FETISH: *magical*
PROPOUNDED: *presented for discussion or consideration*
BY THE WAY: *as an aside*

time probably dreaming of future stories and mentally describing the beauty of the plains and hills. Birds abounded as they drew near to Accra, and they caught sight of little African antelopes dashing across the plains. For in this neighbourhood horses, mules, and oxen can live; and, in fact, the town itself is one of the most healthy along the coast, while, strange anomaly, it is one of the filthiest.

Upon reaching Accra in safety the engineer discovered that the intense saltness of the water had encrusted up the gauge, rendering it necessary to blow out the boiler, allow it to cool, and fill it again before proceeding. So the *Dauntless* was moored to a hawser from the stern of one of the ships at anchor. While leaving the engineer to put all right, the two correspondents prepared to go ashore and see what the town was like. Henty found time to note the tremendously rampant population of pigs, which, with the help of dogs and fowls, were the scavengers of the place. He makes no allusion, however, to the quality of the pork, but goes on to discourse upon the intense love of the women of the place for beads. These ranged from the tiny opaque scraps of all colours used by children for their dolls, to cylinders of variegated hues, yellow being the favourite, which were sometimes as long as the joint of one's thumb and as thick round. The women wear these round the wrist, round the neck, and round the loins, while the occupation of threading the lesser beads is one of their greatest pleasures.

At seven the next morning they started back, congratulating themselves that they had met with no serious accident. But they were not to escape scot free, for on their return journey it was found that the rudder was gradually losing its power, proving at last to be broken, and when at length Addah was reached, and the *Dauntless* made fast to the stern of one of the vessels, they had to whistle for nearly half an hour before any

HAWSER: *large rope*
VARIEGATED: *multicolored*

effort was made to send out a surf-boat. When at last one was on the way, they began to understand the reluctance of the boatmen to make the trip, for over and over again, as the boatmen strove to cross the breakers, their vessel was thrown almost perpendicularly into the air, so that only a foot or so of the end of the keel touched the water. To quote Henty's own words:

"As we watched she still struggled on, though she was so long in getting through the hurtling foam that we began to fear that the men would give it up as being impracticable; but at last they got outside the surf, to lie upon their oars, utterly exhausted and waiting to recover from their exertions, when they rowed out to where we lay and took us on board.

"Nothing could have been better than the way in which they managed the landing. They hung upon their oars as we watched them breathlessly, and then, keen-eyed and watchful as they waited their time, they caught the exact moment when one of the breakers was, as it were, balancing itself as if waiting to pounce upon the surf-boat and its occupants.

"It was a race between man and nature, and man won, for the black boatmen seized the exact time, and then went at it with racing speed. Their steersman was one of the finest specimens of the African I have ever seen. Nothing could be finer than his attitude as he stood upon the seat in the stern, one hand resting upon the long steering-oar, while in the other he held his cap.

"For some time he stood half-turned round, gazing keenly seaward, while the boat lay at rest just outside the line of breakers. Then all at once he waved his hat and gave a wild shout, which was answered by his crew, and every man plunged his oar into the water, rowing desperately, while their helmsman cheered them on with his frantic shouts.

KEEL: *a ridge or fin running along the underside of the boat*
IMPRACTICABLE: *impossible to accomplish*

"How they pulled! And it seemed in vain, as if we had started too late, for a gigantic wave was rolling in behind us, looking as if it were about to curl over, break into the stern, and sweep us from end to end.

"But the boatmen knew what they were about. They rose upon the wave just as it was turning over, and in an instant they were sweeping along a cataract of white foam with the speed of an arrow. The next wave was smaller, but it carried them onward, and before a third that had been pursuing them hard could reach the boat, they were run up on the dripping sand.

"Just then a dozen men rushed out to meet them. The occupants of the boat threw themselves anyhow upon their shoulders, and directly after they were high and dry upon the sands."

CATARACT: *waterfall*

CHAPTER XXVIII

THE "WEAKER SEX" IN ASHANTI

ALMOST at the start of his campaigning in Ashanti Henty found himself confronted with a serious problem, and anyone who, like the present writer, had known him intimately for years will find it easy to imagine the look of annoyance, puzzlement, and wrath that his features must have displayed upon waking up to this fact. He was bound upon an important mission, one which compelled him to keep in company with the expeditionary army, or portions of it, just about to start from Cape Coast Castle[1] for the river Prah, in order to follow its windings through the dense tropical forest; he was a thorough athlete, and ready to make any shift to forward his progress that was possible, but he was now brought face to face with the unexpected. An expedition, he found, would start upon the following day at three, and as a matter of course, in spite of experience and the knowledge that he must not burden himself with what the old Romans so aptly called *impedimenta* during a campaign—a knowledge which had made him cut down his luggage to the narrowest limits, in fact made him take nothing more than he was obliged to take—he found to his dismay that it was impossible to procure hammock-bearers. It was not that he wished to travel in luxurious style, but nature had ordained that, to a European, walking through the prevalent intense

---

[1] A fortified castle originally built in the 1600's by Swedish traders

heat was an impossibility; not because of the intense sunshine, for the way for the most part was through the shadow of the dense tropical forest, but because of the strange lowering prostration which followed the slightest exertion and compelled the most robust, able-bodied men to throw themselves down and rest after walking a distance that was absurdly short.

Hammock-bearers, however, he found it impossible to procure. He had engaged eight men for the purpose, but they had all been summoned by their chiefs the night before, and the whole of the men in the neighbourhood who were not under arms as combatants were engaged by the government as porters. In his ignorance of what he had to contend with, he was ready to abandon the idea of having hammock-bearers, and prepared to trust to his own walking powers and start afoot; but matters looked very serious when he was informed by the native merchant he had employed that it was impossible to find even four men to carry his tent and necessaries. Four women could be obtained, and that was all!

Women! Henty indignantly declined, and turned over in his mind what he should do. Then the idea struck him that the Army Control Department might have more men than they wanted, or would possibly spare him a few. Going up to the Castle Yard he found all in a state of animation and bustle, with plenty of labourers rolling casks and carrying cases up from the beach; but to his utter astonishment there were a hundred women working with them, chattering and laughing, as they worked more vigorously than the men. A few questions to one of the Control officers brought the explanation that they were short of hands in consequence of the number of men at work upon the roads and at the various stations, while numbers more had obeyed the summons of their chiefs and deserted to go to the war. There was a vessel laden with war stores that must be

PORTERS: *servants who carry baggage*

unladen, and consequently the Control had been driven to enlist women carriers to take up the bales of military greatcoats, blankets, and waterproof sheets, in addition to other stores.

Henty began to think, urged on as he was by dire necessity, what is sauce for the goose under certain circumstances may be sauce for the gander. In other words, if it was not undignified for her Majesty's officials to make use of women labour, he began to see that it ought not to be bad form for him at such a supreme moment to follow their example. So under these circumstances he went back to the native Whiteley and accepted his offer to supply female bearers, and very shortly afterwards four women were brought forward for him to inspect. He objected to two of these at once, for one of them had what must be a great drawback to her power of carrying a load, in the shape of a child of two years old clinging to her back. The other was similarly circumstanced, but her little one was a mere infant. It was, however, these or none; and as the other two were smart good-looking girls of about sixteen years old, and as many of the women working for the Control were handicapped with children, he made no further demur, in spite of a lingering feeling of doubt about the banter which he would receive from his colleagues and the officers with whom he was brought in contact. It was so evidently the fashion, however, to employ women, that he hoped to escape scot free. But it was not so, for Henty's *Standard*-bearers became one of the jokes of the expedition.

Sir Evelyn Wood, in his exhaustive and chatty work, *From Midshipman to Field-Marshal*, alludes to the state of affairs in connection with bearers at the same time and place. He says: "The women have most of the qualities which are lacking in the men. They are bright, cheerful, and hard-working, and even under a hot fire never offer to leave the spot in which we place

HANDICAPPED: *burdened*
DEMUR: *objection*

them, and are very strong. As I paid over £130 to women for carrying my loads up to Prahsu, I had many opportunities of observing their strength and trustworthy character, for to my knowledge no load was ever broken open or lost. They carried fifty or sixty pounds from Cape Coast Castle to Prahsu, a distance of seventy-four miles, for ten shillings, and the greater number of them carried a baby astride of what London milliners used to call a 'dress improver'." High praise, this, for the weaker sex, when Sir Evelyn describes the male bearers as being prone, as soon as they came under fire, to throw their loads down on the ground and run for their lives.

M<small>ILLINERS</small>: *makers of hats or other fancy clothing*
D<small>RESS</small> I<small>MPROVER</small>: *a bustle*

Chapter XXIX

Warfare in the Bush

IT was only natural that wherever he went for an expedition there were two points to which Henty made frequent allusion. One was hospital practise and the care of the sick and wounded; the other the Commissariat Department and the supply of wholesome drinking water.

Plenty of such references are found in his account of the march to Coomassie. There is mention of the women bearers rolling the water-casks, and the native bearers, as they came in sight of one of the village markets, depositing their burdens upon the ground, to make a rush to the stores to lay in an extra supply for their wants during the tramp through the forest, these supplies consisting of native bread and dried fish. A rose by any other name, it is said, may smell as sweet; so it may be taken for granted that the native name for bread—"Kanky"—may not seriously affect its qualities. But when it comes to the dried fish, of which the blacks are very fond, Henty has some remarks to make. It is, though, by the way, rather curious what a liking the natives of some countries have for preserved fish. For instance, in the Malay Peninsula the natives have a great fancy for a concoction which they term *blachang*, as an appetizer to flavour the dull monotonous tameness of the ever-present boiled rice. This *blachang* is compounded of shrimps, saved up till they are in a state of putrefaction, and then beaten into a paste, the odour of which puts the ripest snipe to the blush.

The dried fish of the West Coast of Africa are to an Englishman (unless he has learned to like the flavour of asafoetida from long experience of the smoked dainties called in India Bombay ducks) excessively nasty, being smoked with some herb strongly resembling foetid gum in smell and flavour.

But to turn from fish to soup. Henty discourses very wisely about the latter in connection with the weariness and exhaustion consequent upon a long tramp through the forest. After an experience of ten miles or so of the hot, oppressive air there is no desire for eating, only a longing for a cup of hot cocoa or tea, as soon as a fire can be set going—not always an easy task in a land where the tropical downpours are tremendous, saturating everything and rendering the superabundant wood unfit to burn. Hunger, even after many hours' march, is completely quenched, and it might be expected that the weary traveller would be prone to fly for a stimulus to the commissariat rum. But to quote Henty's own words, spoken from experience, "Soup is undoubtedly the thing in this country;" and it grew to be the custom on the march, for the first party who arrived at the halting-place to start a fire and prepare what the soldiers spoke of as a jorum of hot broth, ready for the next comers. "After a fatiguing day's march one has no appetite for solid food, but a basin of soup sets one up at once."

This march to Coomassie was a dreary tramp through a jungle. The way being along a narrow native path, the progress was so slow, encumbered as they were with the necessaries of the journey, that on one occasion it took more than two hours and a half to accomplish four miles, for the heat was terribly trying. Yet to an observant eye the vegetation and the mighty trees were most attractive. The undergrowth of the

PUTREFACTION: *decay*
ASAFOETIDA: *a strong-smelling, bitter plant resin*
BOMBAY DUCKS: *a kind of strong-smelling dried fish*
FOETID GUM: *asafoetida resin*

forest consisted of broad-leaved plants, sword-bladed flags and the like, above which the great plantains, looking like Brobdingnagian hart's-tongue ferns, spread their great green, often split and ragged leaves, while every here and there the cotton-trees, lovers of moist swampy land, rose to an immense height. The heat all the time gradually increased, and the men suffered severely during the delays caused by difficulties with the baggage, or from the column having to climb over trunks of trees that had fallen across the path, while sometimes it was necessary to pass through swamps in which the water varied from ankle to knee deep.

On such occasions the halts were most trying, for a small obstacle caused considerable delay in the passage of a column in single file. Men would pause for a moment to pick their way before entering the swamp; others would stop to turn up their trousers; and so the stoppage would often accumulate until what was merely a second's wait of the leading man became five minutes with the five hundredth. A wait of even two minutes in the sun when there was not a breath of wind was most trying, for great as was the heat, it was not felt so much while moving, partly, perhaps, because the attention was directed to picking the way, but more because of the profuse flow of perspiration. In reference to this, though, Henty adds: "We did not suffer so much from the heat upon this coast as we do in parts of India; but this was because there was always either a sea or a land breeze blowing, which kept down the temperature in the shade to 84 or 85 degrees, which was by no means' unpleasant. But when the sun blazed down the heat was really intense. A thermometer placed in the sun upon the wall of the hospital marked over 150 degrees for some hours three or four days during the week, and I should say that the heat of the bush, where there was no shade, was fully as great. Under these circumstances it was not to be wondered at that a certain number

JORUM: *large bowl*
FLAGS: *tall wetland plants*

of men at the end of each day's march were found unfit for further work, and had to be sent back in hammocks. Still, the number that fell out was very small indeed, for men struggled to the last rather than give in."

When the men broke down, the officers noticed the poor fellows' flushed faces and dull eyes, and said that they could only speak coherently with an effort. These were cases of attacks by the sun, not of sunstroke, for they were not sudden. The doctors called them sun-fever, and the cure adopted was for the poor fellows to be sent back in hammocks to the coast and placed on board ship, where in most cases the sea air restored them to health.

Henty is pretty severe in his description of the Sierra Leone men, the over-civilized and spoilt blacks with whom he came in contact during the advance. He describes them as "the laziest, most discontented, most self-sufficient and most impudent set of rascals the world contains. They are no more," he says, "to be compared with the Fantis, or any of the other native tribes, than light is to darkness."

In one case they started a mutiny, refusing to work unless money was paid to them instead of stores; but they had Englishmen to deal with, and when two of the ringleaders offered to strike the Control officers, the latter at once seized them single-handed, forced them apart, and treated them with firmness. Subsequently, as the men grew more threatening and determined in their refusals to work, one of the naval officers of the expedition, Captain Peel, interfered, and in true naval fashion threatened that the first man who refused to obey orders should be had up to the triangles and receive three dozen lashes. If the fellow resisted after this, he declared he would summon his sailors on shore, take him on board ship, and give him five dozen; while, if his companions and fellow-mutineers attempted any violence, he would

COHERENTLY: *clearly*
HAD UP TO THE TRIANGLES: *tied to a tripod made of wooden beams*
SUFFICED: *was sufficient*

without hesitation give orders for the sailors to fire. The threat sufficed.

Night in the jungle produced its memories. After his day's tramp with the troops and bearers, nine o'clock in the evening saw all but the sentries lying down, and Henty retained for many years very vivid recollections of these nights in the forest on the way to Coomassie—close nights, with scarcely a breath of wind stirring. Somewhere outside the hut where the correspondents sheltered, a native would be demonstrating that chest troubles are not peculiar to our bronchitic, foggy isles, for here in the midst of this tropic heat one of the blacks would keep up a perpetual coughing that made sleep next to impossible; next, a legion of rats could be heard gnawing and scratching, as they tore about the shelters and raced in every direction over those who were seeking for rest; and then there were the insects. The mosquitoes would begin, and it seemed as if they knew the command in the old opera "The Siege of Rochelle"[1]— "Sound the trumpet boldly!" Every now and then, too, upon fell intention bent, they would make a raid from above on some unprotected face, while, to supplement this trouble, a colony of the wretched insects which make their attacks from below— thin, flat, silent, and secretive—carried on their assault, and retired afterwards singularly misshapen, grown, to use the old countrified expression, "quite out of knowledge."

"Now," says Henty, "I imagine that here were assembled all the elements which make night horrible, with the exception only of indigestion after a heavy supper. Had I been in any other country, I would have moved my rug outside and slept there, but here such a proceeding would have entailed an attack of fever. Consequently I had nothing to do but lie still till morning."

Henty relates a sad incident in connection with the encounters with the warlike Ashantis. He tells how the first of their

[1] An opera by Michael Balfe (1808-1870)
BRONCHITIC: *having a tendency towards bronchitis*
FELL INTENTION: *some dreadful purpose*
QUITE OUT OF KNOWLEDGE: *unrecognizable*

merry party on the screw steamer *Ambriz*, the vessel on which
Sir Garnet Wolseley went out to take up his command, had fall-
en, and "as usual," he says, "death had taken one of the most
gentle, brave, and kindly spirits from among them." Lieutenant
Wilmot, of the Royal Artillery, had fallen, fighting like a hero,
and the news of his death, when it was brought in, produced
the keenest regret among those who knew him. A promising
young officer, attached to his profession, a zealous worker, and
a favourite with all because of his quiet cheerfulness and modest unassuming manner, he was one of the leaders in a reconnaissance that had been thought necessary. The force consisted
of a hundred of the West India Regiment, nine hundred native allies, and some of the Hausas with rockets, the last being
under the command of the young officer. It seems that when
he approached the Ashanti camp an alarm was given, and the
fight began at once. The bush was extremely dense, and from
out of its shelter the enemy poured a fierce fire, and in those
short minutes the British officers had a severe lesson in the
amount of confidence that could be placed in the native allies.
Out of the nine hundred levies only about a hundred stood
firm, and these might, for all the good they did, have followed
their king or chief. This "noble" warrior headed the party who
took to flight, and he, with his company, did not cease to run
until they were safe back at camp, while many did not even
stop there, but continued right on till they reached their own
villages. Those that did stand fast made use of their muskets
in the wildest and most useless manner, in contradistinction
to the West India Regiment, which behaved with great steadiness and gallantry, and for two hours kept up a heavy Snider
fire at their invisible foes, the Ashantis. Lieutenant Wilmot had
dependable men in the Hausas, who had been well trained in
the use of rockets, weapons formidable and awe-inspiring to
natives; but early in the fight he received a severe wound in the

SCREW STEAMER: *a steamship driven by a propeller*
RECONNAISSANCE: *scouting mission*
LEVIES: *men forced into service*
IN CONTRADISTINCTION TO: *in contrast to*

shoulder from one of the Ashanti bullets fired from the bush, and this tore through flesh and muscle and narrowly missed the bone. The wound was bad enough to have necessitated immediate retirement; but it meant the loss of their leader to the Hausas, and in spite of the severity of the wound and the acute pain, he held on to his task, encouraging his men for two long hours, during which time the rockets discharged against the enemy dislodged them again and again from their strongholds. At last, when the gallant young officer's work was pretty well done, another bullet struck him down, and this time it was no mere painful flesh wound—the missile found its way straight to his heart, and he fell back dead. With the exception of one native, poor Wilmot was the only man killed. But the Ashantis had stood their ground well, and the wounds of the attacking party were many. So vigorous indeed was the defence of the brave Ashantis, that just about the time when Wilmot fell, Colonel Festing, who was in command, and was also hit, seeing that an attempt was being made by the enemy to cut off his retreat, fell back upon the village from which the attack had been made. The many wounds were for the most part very slight; for though put down as severe because they were received in spots where a rifle bullet wound would have been a serious matter, they were mostly inflicted by slugs from clumsy muskets. These pellets only penetrated a short distance, with the result that the injuries only entailed a day or two's confinement.

The death of poor young Wilmot moved the whole camp to deep feeling, and the funeral took place at the cemetery of Cape Coast on the following day. Sir Garnet Wolseley and the staff and nearly every officer in the town attended, while the navy was represented by the officers from the fleet. The procession was solemn and impressive, bringing to the minds of many the sad little poem which recounts the burial of Sir John Moore.[1] The body had been brought down from Prospect

---

[1] Sir John Moore (1761-1809), was a British military hero killed in northern Spain while fighting against Napoleon's troops.

RETIREMENT: *withdrawal*

House, to which it had been first taken, and was placed in a room of the General Hospital. A gun was brought, dragged by a party of marine artillerymen and marines, who, commanded by a naval officer, had come ashore for the purpose. An officer of the Royal Artillery superintended the preparations and followed as chief mourner. As the coffin, covered by a flag, was brought out and placed upon the gun carriage, all the officers saluted their dead comrade, and then fell in behind at a slow march.

"Not a drum was heard, not a funeral note."[1]

There was no military music, but Henty says: "I think the slow measured tramp was more moving than any pomp or military display could have been. Never before has such a procession of officers been seen on the Gold Coast; and a crowd of natives assembled to look on."

The road led by the sea, and the dull moan of the surge was more appropriate music than any made by mechanical instruments. A quarter of a mile brought them to the cemetery, and as they stood around and listened to the solemn words, Henty reflects, "It is, I trust, no derogation to our manliness to say that many a lip was bitten hard, many a hand dashed across the face to hide that emotion which, however great the cause, Englishmen always strive to conceal.

"During his month's stay at Cape Coast, Lieutenant Wilmot had assisted Captain Rait to turn the wild Hausas into steady gunners. He had won all hearts, and among us there was but one feeling—that of deep regret for the unselfish young fellow who had left us but a few days before in high health and spirits, and who was brought back only to be laid in his lonely grave by the never-ceasing surf of the Atlantic Ocean."

---

[1] A line from the poem, "The Burial of Sir John Moore after Corunna," by Charles Wolfe (1791-1823)

POMP: *showy display*

NO DEROGATION: *no dishonor*

CHAPTER XXX

THE MARCH UP COUNTRY

THE lessons learned in dealing with the native allies in the attack upon the daring savages who had set the British forces at defiance were too sharp to be neglected. There was, of course, something very attractive and cheering about being backed up by some hundreds, or even thousands, of well-armed, fierce-looking, stalwart natives. They were wonderfully skilful in performing upon the tom-tom, or in producing thunder from the war drum—sounds which could be kept up, suggesting dire threats, all through the night, and were often accompanied by yells and shouts such as would send dismay into any enemy's breast—while, when they were partially drilled and supplied with musket or rifle and cartridge-box, they were looked upon as being invincible, and even believed it themselves. But the proof of the pudding is said to be in the eating, and the flavour of the compôte of native allies proved only to be vile. Indeed, in the opinion of our officers many of the blacks seemed to be only of use for the labour of road-making, preparing stations, and accumulating stores up the country, business, all this, which would have been much better carried on by the women, who had already proved themselves invaluable for carrying loads.

Encounter after encounter had taken place with the Ashantis, in which the native allies had done a great amount of

SET THE BRITISH FORCES AT DEFIANCE: *defied the British forces*
COMPÔTE: *a dessert of cooked fruit*

shouting when they stood their ground; but they had more often done this shouting while in full retreat, for they seemed to
consider it a duty to alarm everyone in the rear. Hence it was
decided to do away with our native army, which had proved
itself to be worse than useless; and the police were ordered to
arrest all the men belonging to the Cape Coast contingent as
they came sneaking in through the bush when the fights were
at an end.

Their arms were taken away from them, and orders were giv-
en for them to be marched up under a guard to where the road
had been commenced towards the interior for a more strenu-
ous attack to be made on the enemy. This was considered to
be a move in the right direction, but all wished that the entire
force of the allies had come in to be disarmed, for as long as
they remained under arms they were a trouble and an anxiety. They had to be fed; they expended ammunition largely;
they had to be driven towards the foe, and when they reached
his neighbourhood they proved themselves to be more likely
to shoot their friends than their enemies. In fact, where the
British regiments were strengthened—such was the term—by
these native allies, the latter proved to be an immense anxiety
and cause of weakness to any troops they accompanied. Even
now their measure is not quite taken. They proved to be useless
as scouts; they would not go in front; and they were dangerous
in the rear. They were unreliable even as watchdogs, for they
would run from their own shadow, and they would blaze away
at nothing for half an hour if they heard a night bird flutter in
the bush.

But with all these disadvantages and objections to their presence, the leaders of the expedition could not but feel the difficulty of taking such a step as to disarm them *en masse*. There
was the risk of incurring the wrath of the whole population of

CONTINGENT: *military force*
LARGELY: *in large quantities*
EN MASSE: *"as a group" in French*
INCURRING: *bringing upon themselves*

Cape Coast, as these men, if they could do injury in no other way, might refuse altogether to work or carry loads. There was also the fact that the British had no force which could compel a thousand men to go out and labour on the road. They might have been taken up, of course, under an escort, but no contingent which the little British army could spare could prevent these allies from taking to the bush the first day they went out, and so finding their way down again.

Finding that the men would not come forward to carry loads after the disarmament, it occurred to one of our officers to appeal to the women, as they had proved to be so much better than the men; and this proved to have excellent results, two of the wives of the chiefs going round and haranguing their sisters in very able speeches. They called upon the women to come forward and help the white men by carrying loads up the country. The white men, they said, had come there to protect them from the Ashantis, and the people of Cape Coast ought to help in every way they could. The men, they said, had not done well. They had refused to fight; they had disgraced themselves. Let the women come forward, then, and do their best, and let every one of them go and offer to take a load up the country.

These speeches produced a good deal of talk and excitement among the women, who came to a general agreement that they ought to do as they were asked. Whether they would come forward in any numbers remained to be seen, for, as related by the American humorist, each woman was ready and willing that all her female relations should come forward as carriers, but each was disposed to view her own as an exceptional case. However, after much talk, the assistance of the women did prove valuable, and later, when the Control was much troubled about getting the loads up into the interior for the use of the troops, a brilliant idea occurred to one of the officers of the department. This was, that the services of the children of the place could be utilized, and that by paying half the usual price for the carriage of half the usual load, they might get the troublesome little barrels of provisions taken up the country. The idea was carried out with immense success, for no sooner was it known that boys and girls could get half wages for carrying up light loads, than there was a perfect rush of the juvenile population to the store where the barrels were served out.

Three hundred were sent off the first morning, nearly four hundred the second, and a large number of applicants were told that they must come next day. The glee of the youngsters on being employed was worth watching. They were all accustomed to carry weights, such as great jars of water and baskets of yams, far heavier than those which they had now to take up country, and the fun of the expedition and the satisfaction of earning money proved delightful, while as four hundred boys and girls carried up ten thousand pounds of rice, this addition to the army of carriers was no small help.

The march to Coomassie proved to be a time for carrying out invention. Wants had to be made up for, and in accordance with the proverb that necessity is the mother of invention, our officers appealed pretty largely to that mother.

For instance, during a long halt before making a serious advance, one of the most amusing sights in the town was provided by Captain Rait, of the Royal Artillery. He had a certain number of guns to get to the front, and he very soon discovered that, for purposes of hauling a field-piece through a dense tropical forest, the native black was worse than useless. This discovery, too, was made at a time when there were no Jacks available from the men-of-war to harness themselves on to the limber and run the light pieces up to the front in sailors' cheery fashion.

JUVENILE: *young*

But Captain Rait made his plans, knowing as he did that in camp there were a number of young bullocks which had been sent down from Sierra Leone to the contractor who supplied the meat. "Why," said the gallant officer, "should not these young bullocks be broken in to draw my guns?"

Why, indeed? But here was where the amusing side—amusing to the forces who looked on—came in, for as soon as the attempt was made to yoke or harness the oxen, they began to object.

The heavy dull oxen have never been known to display much understanding, but had they known that the acquirement of the hateful accomplishment in which they were being instructed was saving them from immediate slaughter, they might perchance have become more tractable. The French have a proverb that it is necessary to suffer so as to become beautiful. The oxen were not required to become beautiful, only useful, and, says one of our writers, the useful and the beautiful are one. At any rate, they were called upon to suffer but slightly.

The animals were small, but the weight behind them was not very great—an old-fashioned howitzer weighing, with its cannon and limber, about two hundredweight. The artillery officer acted as driver, and the Hausa gunners ran alongside, leaving the oxen alone when they progressed slowly and steadily, and, when not so disposed, giving them a thrust here and a push there so as to keep the sluggish brutes straight, while others urged the guns along whenever the beasts did not submit readily to the yoke.

So every afternoon for some days the artillery captain drove these peculiar war chariots about the place to the no slight risk of his neck, for the roads were ill-made and intersected by drains, some of which were two feet deep. But the gallant officer faced all this, to the delight of the lookers-on, and he

TRACTABLE: *easily managed*
HOWITZER: *a short-barreled cannon*
HUNDREDWEIGHT: *hundred pounds*

was quite happy and contented, for no accident beyond the occasional breaking of a pole took place. Finally, as a reward for his perseverance Captain Rait had the satisfaction of taking his guns up to the front drawn by these sturdy bullocks, which, though not entirely broken in, were yet sufficiently so to draw their loads in very fair order.

At this time bullocks were being driven regularly up to the front, so as to give the troops a meal of fresh meat twice a week, and the sailors and marines, who were accustomed to the salt junk served on board, got on very well with an occasional change. "But," says Henty, "for white men not so used to salt meat, it would be difficult to imagine a more objectionable food for a tropical climate," and, he continues, once more well launched upon the Commissariat Department, "the preserved meat, which was issued much more frequently than the salt, was no doubt healthier, but men grew very sick of it. Australian meat at the best of times is not an appetizing food, but once or twice a week one can eat it without any great effort. Four or five times a week, however, in a climate where the appetite requires a little humouring, it is really a trial; so that the discovery that bullocks could at any rate live for some time up the country, and that they were able to pick up a subsistence for themselves in the old clearings, was an immense benefit for us all."

Cattle were brought from Sierra Leone, from the Canaries, from Madeira, and even from Lisbon, and in this way an abundant supply was obtained for the use of the troops. "Had they," says Henty, "been obliged to subsist solely upon salt and Australian meat during the march up and back again, I believe that the mortality would have been vastly greater than it really was."

After one of the encounters with the Ashantis, rumour began to reach the British from prisoners and escaped slaves that the enemy had lost a great number of men, and that immediately

SALT JUNK: *salted beef or pork*

the action was over they had begun to retreat. But upon the day after the fight the partly-conquered black army was met by reinforcements seven thousand strong, bringing orders from the king that they were not to retreat, but to attack the English and drive them back. This the retreating army refused to do, declaring that they had done all that was possible and that they could do no more. The newcomers, struck by their wretched appearance, and by their tales of misery and distress, which they now heard for the first time, refused to advance alone, and the whole force fell back together. Several slaves now made their escape, and brought the news that the Ashanti army was crossing the river in canoes and on rafts. But such intelligence could not be relied upon, and Sir Garnet Wolseley, after much inquiry, finding it impossible to obtain trustworthy information, called for volunteers to go on ahead and discover whether the Ashantis had really got across. His troops had plenty of pluck, and two men belonging to one of the West India regiments at once undertook the task, which meant an advance alone some twenty-five miles to the river Prah.

They found how severe had been the enemy's defeat, for all along the whole route of the retreat men were lying dead, while on reaching the banks of the stream it was to find that the survivors of the beaten army and the reinforcements had all crossed.

Elated by their success, the two scouts stopped on the river bank to write their names on a piece of paper and fasten it on a tree to prove that they had been there. This done, in the coolest manner possible they fired their rifles across the stream in the direction of the enemy, as if in contempt for their prowess, and then in the most matter-of-fact way shouldered their pieces and marched back towards their general's camp to bear their news.

"This feat," Henty writes, "appears to me one of the most courageous, if not the most courageous, which was performed during the whole campaign. Nothing could have been more trying to the nerves than that long march through the lonely forest, with the knowledge that at any moment some body of Ashantis who had lingered behind the rest might spring upon them, and that, if not killed at once, they were doomed to a lingering death by torture at Coomassie."

Chapter XXXI

The Battle of Amoaful

A T last, after endless hindrances, the expedition was within measurable distance of coming into direct touch with the Ashantis, and Henty records in dramatic style the great decisive battle of the campaign, when, after five hours and a half of stubborn fighting, the Ashantis were completely discomfited. The Battle of Amoaful will long remain a memory in Ashanti, where it is a superstition to swear by the days which have brought misfortune in their train. And the last day of January in that eventful year, or the word Amoaful, will for centuries be the most solemn of words to the Ashanti people—an oath by which kings will be bound; a legend with which children will be awed. But yet there was no shame in the defeat. The Ashantis fought like the brave men they are, and though worsted they added to their reputation, while nothing but admiration can be felt for the manner in which they came on time and again, notwithstanding the fierce musketry fire which was intended to stop their assaults.

On the day of the battle the marching orders came early. The Naval Brigade and the 23rd Regiment had to come from Kiang Bossu. These united at Insafoo with the 42nd, the Rifle Brigade, and the artillery of Captain Rait, the officer who had succeeded so well in his attempt to utilize oxen for hauling

DISCOMFITED: *defeated*
IN THEIR TRAIN: *along with them*
WORSTED: *beaten*

the guns up country. At Quarman things were well under way at dawn, but it was half-past seven ere the head of the 42nd Regiment entered the village, through which they swung without a halt. Following them came Rait's artillery, a company of the 23rd, and the Naval Brigade, which included the Marines, eighty in number, who distinguished themselves like their comrades. Henty, in reference to the disappointment that was felt in England at the doings by the Marines not being specially commented upon, rightly points out that it would have been difficult to go into details respecting the deeds of this small body, wholly apart from the force with which they were linked. It was enough that they shared in all the glory of the brigade of the "handy men".

Wood's regiment had only three companies and Russell's four, owing to the garrisons which had necessarily to be left *en route*, and these regiments took their position in the rear of the naval men, whom they were to follow in the fight.

When the staff reached Quarman, Henty learned that the difficulties of transport were at last surmounted. Colonel Colley proved an excellent transport officer, and had succeeded in amply provisioning Insafoo. Henty proceeded with the staff in the rear of Russell's regiment, and had not been more than ten minutes on the march ere the brisk rattle of musketry told him that the 42nd were busy at work clearing the village. There was a short pause, and then the firing began again. At this time he was annoyed at the progress being so slow. In front there was much lumber in the way of ammunition and hammocks, which *impedimenta* was in the charge of a large number of bearers—"somewhat scared and wholly stupid men." Still, he managed to get a very good panoramic view of the proceedings, and in the course of his exciting narrative he describes accurately the position of all the leaders of

GARRISONS: *guards*

our troops, from Sir Garnet downwards. He says that the first
shot was fired a few minutes before eight, and it was nearly half
an hour later that the troops came out into the open place
of Agamassie, a village of six or eight houses. The firing was
unceasing, and with bush all round there was heavy work for
the engineers in clearing a way for the baggage. The enemy's
fire came from the front and right and left, and the English
progress was slow.

At the entrance to Agamassie Captain Buckle, of the Royal
Engineers, a brave man and a brilliant officer, was found breath-
ing his last, shot with two slugs just above the heart, while the
doctors were hard at work attending to the wounds of several
men of the 42nd. Not far away Dr. Feagan, of the Naval Brigade, was also busy, having taken up his station under a tree—a
tree which Sir Garnet promoted to be his headquarters.

Here three roads converged, and he was able to receive reports from Colonel M'Leod on the left, Sir Archibald Alison in
the centre, and Colonel Wood on the right. It seems that the
42nd drove the enemy's outposts helter skelter out of the village, and then pushed on for nearly a quarter of a mile, when
they were checked by a tremendous fire. The undergrowth was
dense in the extreme, and the Ashantis contested every inch,
while a great difficulty which our men had to face was the risk
of firing at friends, in consequence of the intricacy of the bush,
which was so bewildering that all idea of the points of the compass was lost. Sir Garnet sent orders to commanding officers to
warn their men against this danger, and to prevent it from hap-
pening the rear of Colonel Wood's column was swung round
so that it advanced more towards the right. "Five minutes with
the Naval Brigade," Henty says, "showed me sufficiently that I
should gain nothing in the way of incidents by remaining there,
for no enemy was actually in sight, while I was running a very

INTRICACY: *tangled nature*

considerable risk of being knocked over. I therefore returned to the headquarters at the village."

It was now ten o'clock; wounded men were coming in fast—42nd Rifles, Naval Brigade, and native allies. On the left the firing had nearly ceased, and a dispatch was received from Colonel M'Leod saying that all was comparatively quiet on his side. Orders were accordingly sent to him to bear to the northeast until he came in contact with the enemy. In so doing he came upon a partial clearing, where a sharp opposition was experienced. The Hausas carried the clearing at a rush, but the enemy, as usual, opened a heavy fire from the edge of the bush. The Hausas were recalled and a fire was opened with the rockets, which soon drove the Ashantis back. The 42nd were meanwhile in the thick of things, and the men were admirably handled by Major M'Pherson; but generalship availed nothing in a swamp where the firing was terrific, so the regiment suffered a temporary check. The enemy could not be seen, but every bush had its white puff of smoke, and the air was full of slugs.

At this juncture Captain Rait's guns proved their efficacy. Assisted by Lieutenant Saunders, the Captain advanced boldly in front of the line and poured round after round of grape into the enemy, with the result that their fire slackened and the 42nd were enabled to continue their advance. Through the camp and up the hill they went; and now the effect of the English fire was to be seen, for the dead Ashantis lay in heaps. Beyond the camp upon the hill the bush was thicker than ever, and here, where it was impossible for the white soldier to skirmish, the Ashantis made a last desperate stand. The narrow lane up which alone the troops could pass was torn as if by hail with the shower of slugs, but a large tree which stood nearly in the centre of the path, and caused it slightly to curve, afforded

EFFICACY: *effectiveness*

some shelter to our men, and they sent back a storm of bullets in return.

The 42nd suffered greatly, and Major M'Pherson had been shot in the leg; but he declined to go to the ambulance, and, helped by a stick, still led his men. Eight other officers were wounded, and the total of 104 killed and wounded out of a force of a little over 450, showed plainly enough how hard fought was the day. However, victory was not far off. The Ashantis found the bush a trifle too hot, and had to take to the open, where the Sniders and the guns proved too much for them. From this point the advance was rapid. Led by Sir A. Alison, the 42nd went with a rush up the narrow path and out into the clearing beyond. There was desultory firing from the houses, but the men drove the enemy out of these, and a single shell down the space (hardly a street) which divided the village burst in a group at the farther end, killing eight and completing the work.

It was midday then, but the Ashantis were not finally beaten, and throughout Henty has high praise for their courage and tenacity, which was evidenced once again in a determined but abortive attempt to retake the village.

Finally, when Sir Garnet gave orders for the general advance, a number of our allies, who had fought admirably while on the defensive, raised their war-cry and, sword in hand, rushed on like so many panthers let loose, while by their side, skirmishing as coolly as if on parade, were the men of the Rifle Brigade. The latter searched every bush with their bullets, and in five minutes from the beginning of the advance the Ashantis were in full retreat.

Such is the story of the Battle of Amoaful, a battle which reflects as much credit on all engaged in it as many affairs in which the number of combatants have been ten times as large.

DESULTORY: *haphazard*
TENACITY: *stubbornness*
ABORTIVE: *unsuccessful*

"Never," says Henty, "was a battle fought admitting less of description. It is impossible, indeed, to give a picturesque account of an encounter in which there was nothing whatever picturesque; in which scarcely a man engaged saw an enemy from the commencement to the end; in which there was no maneuvering, no brilliant charge, no general concentration of troops. The battle consisted simply of five hours of lying down, of creeping through the scrub, of gaining ground foot by foot, and of pouring a ceaseless fire into every bush in front which might conceal an invisible foe."

The scene in Agamassie after the day had been won was full of interest. In the centre of the village Sir Garnet was busy issuing instructions and making sure that his orders were carried out. Fortunately for the wounded, there was but little sunshine, and Henty has a word of praise for the fortitude of the natives, who submitted to the operation of probing and extracting slugs without a murmur. There were in all 250 casualties, but only fifteen or twenty deaths. One poor fellow of the 42nd, unluckily, was separated from his comrades in the bush and was killed, while when found later he was headless.

It was difficult to estimate the number of natives engaged. The total might be anything from fifteen to twenty thousand. No accurate details could be obtained from the enemy, for the Ashantis seem to be unable to count anything higher than thirty. Beyond that the figures are to them too vast for comprehension. They always carry off their killed and wounded unless extremely hard pressed; but after the Battle of Amoaful their dead lay very thickly together, often in groups of five or six. Henty considered, too, that numbers of the wounded could only have crawled away to die. In and about the village eighty bodies were found, and he estimates the Ashanti loss at two thousand, and these the best fighting men. Ammon Quatia, a famous leader, was among the slain, and Aboo, one of the

ADMITTING: *permitting*
FORTITUDE: *mental strength*

six great feudal kings, fell also, likewise the king's chief executioner. The Ashantis were wretchedly armed, and yet for five hours they held out against picked troops who were equipped with the best weapons of precision. The choice of a position, too, was, he considered, admirable.

After the din of the battle the succeeding silence was very strange, but this was soon broken by the rattle of firing to the rear. The Ashantis were still in force along the road, and the first convoys of wounded were forced to return, while Quarman had been attacked—"unpleasant news to a man whose baggage was in that town, and who knew that the garrison was a small one." Fortunately, a few hours later the village in question was relieved.

Amoaful was found to be a dirty town, capable of housing about two thousand people. It was divided into two parts by the high road, some thirty yards wide, and down this road grew three or four shady trees. Under these officers and men sat in groups, the central tree being left to the officers, just as in a French town one café is tacitly reserved for their use. There was nothing to eat, apart from the limited haversack ration, but everyone was in high spirits. Fortunately an immense supply of grain was found, and this came in usefully to the Control. It was served out to the carriers, who much preferred it to rice.

Bequah, only a mile and a quarter from Amoaful, was the capital of a powerful Ashanti king. Here on the following day the enemy were only dislodged after a severe fight, they being in great force; and Henty attributes this victory in part to the moral effect produced by the proceedings at Amoaful. The place was burned down, which action of course proved a damaging blow to the prestige of the king, though so far as permanent damage went, the houses with their palm-leaf roofs could easily be rebuilt.

TACITLY RESERVED: *silently agreed upon as reserved*
HAVERSACK RATION: *ration of food carried in their haversacks*

The many villages that they passed were much like each other, and the programme of the troops in the course of the march onward to Coomassie was marked by a good deal of repetition—bush dangers, sudden fusillades, and then a searching of the scrub in every direction before camp was formed.

Some of the convoys suffered, and in the Quarman attack several officers lost their kits, and were reduced for the remainder of the campaign to the clothes on their backs. This was in consequence of the action of the cowardly carriers, who threw down their loads and ignominiously ran away.

The native troops fought well, and "rushed" several of the villages in good style; still, the advance was slow, the enemy hanging on the flanks. Here and there, though, in the villages there was evidence of panic—war-drums, horns, chiefs' stools and umbrellas being scattered broadcast. Up to the time, however, of a message being received from General Sir Archibald Alison to the effect that all the villages save the last were taken, the firing had been going on without cessation, and Sir Garnet himself received a blow on the helmet from a slug.

A pestilential black swamp surrounded Coomassie, and after this was passed and the town had been entered, the General rode up to the troops, who had formed in line, and called for cheers for the Queen.

There was a great deal to be done, and a beginning was made with disarming all the Ashantis possible. The first night in Coomassie was eventful, for fires broke out in several directions, the result of carriers and others plundering. *Pour encourager les autres*, one man—a policeman, of all people—was hanged at sight. Several others had the lash. The General was much vexed at these fires, as he had asked the king to come in and make peace, stipulating that the town should be spared.

PROGRAMME: *plan of action*
KITS: *changes of clothing*
IGNOMINIOUSLY: *shamefully*
BROADCAST: *widely*
CESSATION: *ceasing*
PESTILENTIAL: *disease-filled*

Coomassie was decidedly picturesque, many of its houses resembling Chinese temples. But the great feature was the "fetish". Everything was fetish. Near the door of each house was a tree, at the foot of which were placed little idols, calabashes, bits of china, bones—an extraordinary medley. Inside there was dust and litter, the result of years of neglect, and the chief apartments were filled with lumber, all kinds of paraphernalia, umbrellas, drums, wooden maces, and whatnot.

Up to the last it was believed by the Ashantis that the fetish would save the day, and the optimism of the king was shown by the state of the royal palace. It was in all respects exactly as he had left it, except that the gold-dust must have been carried off or buried. The royal bed and couch lay in their places, the royal chairs were in their usual raised positions, only oddly enough they had been turned round and over.

In the palace there was a curious jumble of gold masks, gold caps, clocks, china, pillows, guns, etc. It was rather like a saleroom. There were many great alcoved courts, one containing war-drums ornamented either with skulls or thigh-bones. In two or three there was simply a royal chair upon which his majesty used to sit to administer what passed for justice, and several stools were found covered with thick coatings of recently-shed blood. Henty says that a horrible smell of gore pervaded the whole palace. The nauseating odour was everywhere perceptible; and this was not to be wondered at, for twenty yards from one of the fetish trees was a charnel place where thousands had perished. Here were scores of bodies in various stages of putrefaction.

The palace contained fetishes of all kinds, little dolls, and other articles. The king's bedroom was ten feet by eight, and the bed had a ledge on the near side, which the monarch had

POUR ENCOURAGER LES AUTRES: *"to encourage the others" in French*
STIPULATING: *promising*
CALABASHES: *containers made from the calabash gourd*
MACES: *spiked clubs*
GORE: *blood*
CHARNEL PLACE: *place for dead bodies*

to step over when he sought his pillow. Among other weapons found here was an English general's sword, inscribed, "From Queen Victoria to the King of Ashanti," presented to his predecessor.

There is only one term that can be applied to Henty's work in connection with the march to Coomassie, and that is *thorough*, for danger seems not to have been considered for a moment. What the troops had to do, he told himself, that he had to see, and self was never spared.

After the desperate fighting was at an end, and the General's offers to the defeated monarch had been made known, it was anticipated that the king would come in and surrender. But in spite of much waiting and patience on the General's part nothing happened, and all delay and expectation were ultimately brought to an end by a terrific storm. For now, after much thought, it was decided—and Henty applauded the decision— to mark the visit of the punitive troops by the destruction of the place as a warning and an object-lesson in Britain's power to the king and the petty chiefs around. For the moment it was anticipated that to fire the place would be impossible after the saturating by the tremendous rains, as this, it was feared, would prevent the thatch from burning; but the engineers went to work with axe, powder, and palm-leaf torch, with the result that the whole fabric of the place was brought down like a piled-up pack of cards. Palm, bamboo, and thatch, as soon as the flames once got hold and began to leap, rapidly disappeared, and it was soon abundantly clear that before long Coomassie would be a city of the past. The royal residence, which was little more than a cemetery, shared in the general destruction, for it was blown up; and then the men cheered, and every heart grew light, for the task was done.

A CARLIST WAR

CHAPTER XXXII

A CARLIST WAR

HENTY'S return from Ashanti in 1874 is memorable to the writer from its being the commencement of his introduction to a good fellowship which lasted till that event which turns all friendships into a memory.

The meeting was in that famous old street named after the little river of such modest and retiring nature that it was only written down as a ditch, though probably in its beginnings, long before it was lost in Father Thames, it was christened Fleet.

It was just outside the *Standard* office that the acquaintance began with the singular-looking, swarthy, not sun-tanned, but blackened war correspondent freshly arrived from the deadly swamps and black shadows of the West Coast forests.

Scientific writers on the physiology of man and his coloration tell us that the black peoples have been endowed by nature with a curious black pigment[1] lying beneath the skin, and that this is evidently intended as a protection from the too ardent and otherwise injurious rays of the sun. In the case of Henty, his appearance on his first return from the Coomassie campaign was that of one upon whom nature had begun to bestow some of this strange protection. He did not look embrowned, but blackened; so discoloured, in fact, that there was one who laughingly spoke of the discoloration—which lasted for some considerable

[1] Melanin
SWARTHY: *dark-complexioned*
PHYSIOLOGY OF MAN: *workings of the human body*
ARDENT: *intense*
INJURIOUS: *harmful*

time—as making him strongly resemble a chimney-sweep who had been trying hard to wash himself clean for Sunday and had dismally failed.

Henty found time in 1874 to send to the press in book form his account of the West Coast expedition, under the title of *The March to Coomassie*, a work which ran through two editions. But he was not allowed long for the purpose of resuming the natural tint of an Englishman. Fresh work was looming in the almost immediate future, and, as if fate had ordained that he was to have something to do with nearly every warlike episode that recent history records, the summons came that he should start for that hotbed of revolution and insurrection, Spain. Here he was to busy his pen with his accounts of the long-drawn-out, never-seeming-to-end troubles in connection with the succession, and the long duel between Don Alfonso and Don Carlos to decide which should reign as king. Moreover a short-lived Spanish republic was in these days much to the fore. He had come back from Ashanti looking forward to rest and change. The rest was withheld, but the change came in plenty. Peace had been proclaimed in one part of the world, and one war was at an end, but this other war was in full swing, and so almost immediately he received his orders to start for Spain.

Arrived in the Peninsula,[1] he hurried to headquarters, where he was received with the greatest courtesy and furnished with the means of following the army before Bilbao. Here he was soon in his element, penning one of his graphic letters, describing the forces and dealing with the fortifications, batteries, and the strategy of the contending armies. There was no waiting here, no want of exciting matter such as would interest his readers at home, and in the pursuit of information he seems to have kept well to the front, meeting the sad traces of

[1] The Iberian Peninsula, which includes the countries of Spain and Portugal
SUCCESSION: *transfer of the throne*
TO THE FORE: *alive*
GRAPHIC: *vivid, clear*

battle in the shape of stretcher after stretcher being brought in laden with the dead and wounded.

He never seems to have flinched from the duty that was his, and above all, he never lost sympathy with the wounded, even, as in former cases, making a point of exploring the temporary hospitals that were being filled.

He describes soon after his arrival at the front, and just at the close of one of the encounters, how he went out one night in search of information, stopping by the roadside for the space of a couple of hours. The scene was as striking as it was sad. There was but little moonlight, and by the glare of a few camp fires he saw the long line of stretchers go by bearing officers and men to the ambulances. The procession was watched by the startled uninjured soldiers, whose faces showed that they were gazing for the first time on the victims of a civil war.

Those they looked upon were in a way fortunate, for in the long line that passed Henty, or which he passed by, there were many who had found no bearers, and so had crawled along by the aid of some comrade.

Here and there there were ambulances for dressing the wounds of those who required most attention. Many who had been hit in the neck, arms, or feet, had been temporarily bandaged, and he came upon one poor fellow who had been severely wounded in the neck and shoulder, whose dressing had become disarranged as he struggled onward. At length, forced by his suffering, he was resting by the way, moaning piteously, and after Henty had rearranged the dressing with a handkerchief and the sufferer's cravat, the man murmured in Spanish his grateful thanks to the young Englishman who had helped him in his need.

It was truly a time of suffering, for hundreds of wounded had passed the night untended upon the ground, and even the

DISARRANGED: *disordered*
CRAVAT: *scarf*

dead could not be buried, as neither side dared expose themselves to the severe fire that was kept up.

In Henty's earlier letters the sympathy above mentioned affected his descriptions, which were sad in the extreme, in fact those of a man who suffered too. All through the period when he was with the Spanish army, in a quiet unobtrusive way the letters constantly showed how often he was placed in circumstances where there were calls made upon his humanity, and invariably he displayed his readiness to join hands with the members of the Red Cross Society and help the wounded sufferers in their distress.

Experience and his own nature generally found him friends, who from day to day were ready to share with him such provision as was to be had, or to accept a portion of his own scanty military rations. Then setting danger at defiance, he was glad to yield to fatigue and prepare himself for the next day's toil by sleeping anywhere, beneath a shelter if it was to be found, if not, rolled in a waterproof, one of his principal cares always being the protection of his writing-case and pens. Here, however, in spite of his care, he was called upon to suffer the war correspondent's great difficulty. It is comparatively easy for an energetic man, supplied with proper credentials, to gather enough stirring facts in the progress of a war to form an interesting article for his paper, but after hurrying to the nearest shelter where he could write and finish his letter, there would always come the difficulties of dispatch. It was not always easy to find a messenger to bear it to the nearest place where postal communication could be ensured, and afterwards only too often he had the mortification of discovering that the carefully-written communication had miscarried.

The war which Henty was now engaged in describing was not one of great battles with massed brigades against massed

UNOBTRUSIVE: *reserved*
MISCARRIED: *gone astray*

brigades, and troops spread over miles of country, but it was a desultory continuance of what might be spoken of as village warfare. The Carlists fought in a guerrilla-like fashion, and were continually being driven from one position to start up again unexpectedly in another.

There was plenty of artillery brought to bear at times, but more often it was hand-to-hand fighting, kept up with very small results, as far as the main issue was concerned, though defeat and destruction were frequently the fate of either party, while the country itself was the greatest sufferer.

In his many journeyings from place to place in search of information, Henty was constantly brought face to face with the more or less petty horrors and often mischievous ruin caused by civil war—desolated villages, ruined homestead and mansion, and the stagnation of the country's social life by the passing through it of fire and sword. And for what? Too often the answer might be given in the words which our own poet placed in the mouth of Old Kaspar:

> "*I know not why they fought, quoth he*
> *But 'twas a famous victory.*"[1]

The politician alone can tell. What we know is that it seemed to be a never-ending war, one which supplied George Henty with the material which he afterwards made the basis of interesting historical tales. For he was ever to the front, and seems to have led a charmed life, living as he did an existence wherein there was always an impending attack, with the enemy starting up here and there in greater or less force.

One Sunday he was in a town on the banks of a river, when the Carlists suddenly appeared on the other bank and began firing volleys across the water, the bullets coming whistling

---

[1] Based on lines from the poem, "The Battle of Blenheim," by Robert Southey (1774-1843)

STAGNATION: *ceasing*

unpleasantly about the streets. He naïvely says that the inhabitants were getting into a great state of alarm. Naturally! But by midday on Monday the fire ceased, and by the evening it appears that the Carlist commanders received some news that involved retreat, and made them start off guerrilla-like with all their forces through some of the passes leading into the more impregnable valleys. Then came pursuit, till cartridges and grenades began to run short, and a fresh enemy appeared in the shape of a scarcity of provisions. Meanwhile the Carlists distinguished themselves by burning several houses, including a convent and a very fine mansion, which were in no way interfering with their attack. In his description of this petty warfare Henty goes on to say: "From what I gather of the peasantry, the Carlists must have suffered from the shells. Twenty bullock carts with wounded were removed, and a chief is said to have been killed, while on the other side the Republican loss did not exceed a hundred. How pitiful! A sample this of much of the warfare that was carried on, and with so little result!"

In another letter, written from Burgos in June, 1874, he gives a charming description of the beauty of the districts where the Carlists had again and again appeared during their January raids. By this time, though, there was a fresh enemy in the field, namely the weather, and on a certain railway journey he had ample evidence of the havoc wrought by the elements. A lowering sky, he says, and dark clouds which almost touched the roofs of the village churches gave warning of the severest thunderstorm he ever witnessed in that part of Spain. As the train dashed across the plains, the storm burst with such fury that the hailstones actually broke some of the carriage windows, while the clouds were so low that the train seemed to be passing through them. In fact, within human record no storm had done such damage in Old Castile. Finally the train was brought to a standstill in a little station, and the officials made the announcement that the line had been destroyed by the flood. Henty with his colleagues, therefore, had to pass the night as best they could with the rain pouring in torrents and the wind moaning around. Fretting was in vain, and the unhappy station-master could only shrug his shoulders and listen patiently to the upbraidings of the correspondents, who accused him of obstinacy in not sending the train forward. But with the dawn the little party became aware that they had had a very narrow escape. A previous train had become derailed some hours before they came up, and seven poor creatures were lying wounded in the station. The daylight showed them too that, as far as their eyes could see, the country was flooded; fields and crops, walls and roads, were covered with the yellow muddy water. The line was a wreck; the sleepers were held together by the rails, and the embankment had been washed away. Miles and miles of rich country had been destroyed by the fury of the inundation, while the rays of the rising sun cast a lurid glare over the scene. The correspondents had to continue their journey along the line on foot, passing the ruins of the wrecked train which had preceded them, and then onwards to the next quarters of the northern army. Here they learned of the doings of the Carlist generals, and found that four stations had been burned, and that in every peaceful village in this land of vineyards the houses were fortified and held by the soldiery, for the war was being carried on in a more pitiable way than ever. It was the custom for the Carlist bands to sweep down from Navarre in the dead of night, to burn farms or stations, then take up a few rails, or attempt to destroy a bridge, while by daybreak the mischief would be done and the raiders far away.

UPBRAIDINGS: *reproaches*
SLEEPERS: *railroad ties*
INUNDATION: *flooding*

It was an adventurous life for a war correspondent, and one can only repeat how ample was the supply of material for Henty's ready pen. But the end came at last, for in spite of a brave struggle the Carlist star went down in gloom, and Henty returned to England to enjoy a brief rest before taking part in a bright and enjoyable expedition, that of the Prince of Wales—His Majesty, King Edward—to India.

THE ROYAL TOUR IN INDIA

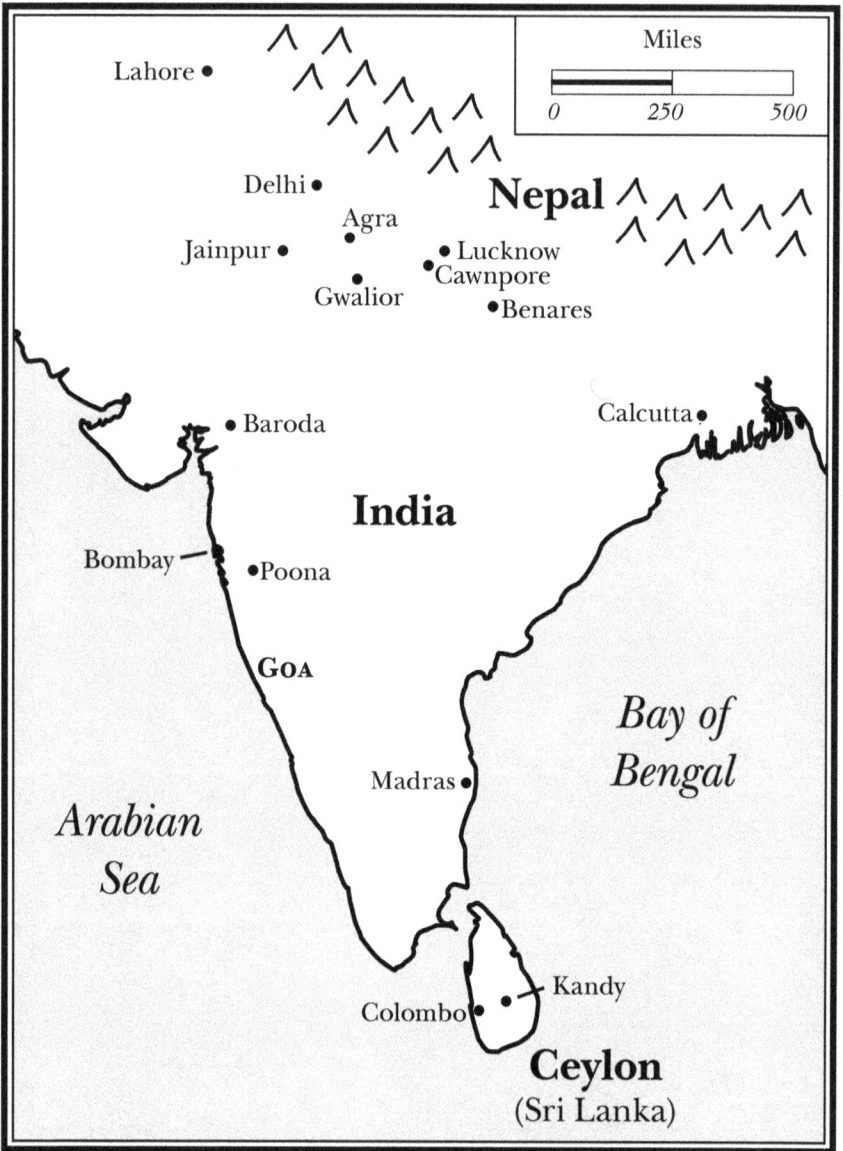

Chapter XXXIII

The Royal Tour in India

THE Royal Tour in India being a matter of supreme importance, it was only right that Henty should be chosen by the journal for which he had done such admirable work to accompany His Majesty, King Edward, then Prince of Wales, and accordingly, in 1875, we find him one of the select corps of artists and correspondents who went on this memorable journey.

It was an agreeable change from the picturesque squalor and misery of civil war to a triumphal spectacular tour through the principal cities of the Indian Empire, in the train of the heir-apparent to the throne. No correspondent's journey can be anything less than arduous. He is always face to face with a heavy call upon his energies; he must be continually on the strain in order that he may feel that he is doing his best for his paper; above all, he must miss nothing that is of importance and worthy of the chronicler's pen. Still, in comparison with Henty's last journey, this was a pleasure trip, with all difficulties smoothed away. He travelled through a country in holiday guise, where day after day the various rajahs and Eastern potentates vied with each other in the splendour of their receptions, in their displays of Eastern magnificence, and in the opulence of their trains. It was all like a long series of Eastern fields

ON THE STRAIN: *exerting himself*
GUISE: *manner*
RAJAHS: *princes*
POTENTATES: *rulers*
VIED: *competed*
OPULENCE: *great wealth*

of the cloth of gold. Notwithstanding that this was the latter half of the nineteenth century, it was like stepping to where medieval pageantry was in full swing, and the brilliant East surpassed itself in dazzling spectacle to do honour to the son of the august lady who on the first of May of the following year was to be proclaimed Empress as well as Queen.[1]

Henty reached Bombay in November. He was present at the receptions at Baroda and Goa, and then went southward to Ceylon. Turning north he went to Madras, and he reached Calcutta at Christmas to be present at the brilliant receptions of the Indian potentates. At the beginning of the following year he saw the unveiling of the statue of the Governor-general, the unfortunate Lord Mayo, who was assassinated by one of the convicts during a visit to the Andaman Islands.

From Calcutta the Prince's train visited the grand old cities of Benares and Lucknow—name of ill omen, shadowed by the horrors of the Mutiny,[2] but now glittering with splendour, the streets crowded with peaceful subjects eager to add to the brilliancy of the scene and to give fitting welcome to the son of the Great White Queen.

Henty visited city after city brilliantly coloured with the pomp of the Orient, before the Prince went northward to Nepal. He was present too at the river-crossing by the great train of elephants in their gorgeous trappings, a scene transferred to canvas by his old fellow club member and companion of the journey, Herbert Johnson, who has also since passed away.

It was in Nepal that Henty was brought face to face with much of the barbaric splendour of Northern India, whose rulers, proud of their independence, have kept up much of the tradition of the past. There are some among us still who can recall the display made by the Nepalese ambassadors in 1850, with their prince, Jung Bahadoor, and it was fitting that our

[1] Queen Victoria   [2] The Sepoy Mutiny (1857)
AUGUST: *majestic*
BARBARIC: *uncivilized*
KUKRI: *curved knives*
PRIMEVAL TRACT OF JUNGLE: *undisturbed or ancient jungle*

Prince should visit an Eastern king who fought bravely and stood firm for England during the horrors of the Mutiny in 1857. The name of the brave little hill men, once our opponents and at war with us, is historic in connection with many a hard fight in which they have done good service for England. They have made their British officers proud to be in command of a Gurkha regiment, and though rifle-armed, they are still wielders of their ancient weapon, the curved, willow-bladed, deadly *kukri*.

It is in Nepal that the primeval tract of jungle, dear to all sportsmen under the name of the Terai, is to be found, and Henty's pen was called upon here to describe the hunting expeditions, with the train of howdah-bearing elephants and beaters in pursuit of tiger and the other savage denizens of the widespread forest. Here the Prince was able to show his prowess with the rifle, and among the presents he received is there not still living one of the little plump elephants he brought back, to become in course of years a huge bearer of juvenile visitors at the Zoo?

At Bombay Henty, of course, had to describe the brilliant illuminations, and he put in a word too for the marvellous coloured fires which flashed from the portholes of the fleet, also for the illuminated fort and esplanade, in all about three-quarters of a mile of general brilliancy and display of loyalty. Reference is made also to the Byculla Club ball and the arrival of the Prince and suite. There was a grand banquet to the soldiers of the Bombay garrison and the sailors of the fleet, and it was a pleasant time for the writer generally, especially after describing the horrors of war.

The display of loyalty to the young Prince was tremendous. Fête succeeded fête, and Henty speaks of a banquet to the juveniles, of receptions galore, and of the Parsee ladies in their wonderful dresses.

HOWDAH-BEARING ELEPHANTS: *elephants carrying howdahs, or covered platforms, upon their backs*
BEATERS: *servants who beat the jungle, driving out the animals to be hunted*
DENIZENS: *inhabitants*
ESPLANADE: *cleared area around the fort*

He, of course, saw the famed Temple of Elephants, but it has been described *ad nauseam*. He has a word in season as to the overpowering force of the sun. After such heat, welcome indeed was the shade of the Cave Temples with their religious figures. Then came the visit to Poona and the approach to the *ghauts*. There were reviews and more fêtes before returning to and leaving Bombay. At the reviews he was struck by the brilliancy of the native troops, especially the Bombay Lancers and Poona Horse. He touched, too, on the trooping of the colours of the Marine Battalion for the last time prior to being presented now with new colours. The Bombay Marine Battalion had been raised a hundred years previously, and enjoyed a fine record.

At Baroda came the visit to the Gaekwar[1] and Sir Madhava Rao. Here the Prince mounted the elephant in waiting, his host having provided a majestic beast, richly caparisoned and gorgeously painted. The howdah was of silver, beautifully decorated with cloth of gold, the gorgeous housings reaching to the ground. It was a resplendent spectacle. The base of the howdah was a platform on which stood attendants to drive off the flies and fan the air. A procession was formed, all the elephants being splendidly caparisoned, and a small escort of dragoons rode in advance.

In the afternoon there was an elephant fight—one of the popular amusements in Baroda—and on the next day a barbaric display of combats between other animals.

The following day came a cheetah hunt, to display the skill of the highly-trained, greyhound-like leopards. Shooting followed during the rest of the stay, including pig-shooting. The Prince took part in the pig-sticking, which he greatly enjoyed.

The expedition returned to Bombay and started at once

---

[1] The title of the ruler of the Indian state of Baroda

AD NAUSEAM: *"to the point of sickness" in Latin; endlessly*
GHAUTS: *mountains*
CAPARISONED: *decorated*
HOUSINGS: *cloth coverings*
RESPLENDENT: *dazzling*

for Ceylon, taking Goa, the picturesque and Lilliputian Portuguese Indian Empire, *en route.*

At Colombo there was a brilliant assemblage of Europeans and native chiefs at the railway station. At Kandy the thoroughfares were thronged with vociferous crowds, while triumphal arches were everywhere, and this in a land where every tropical road seems to pass under a series of nature's beautiful bowers. The Prince left Kandy *en route* for two days' elephant-shooting and for Colombo, and Henty describes the Botanical Gardens and the Temple of Buddha, where the chief headman displayed Buddha's tooth.

Afterwards there took place a grand torchlight procession, with fifty elephants, bands of native music, and natives in the guise of devils performing antics—a novel and successful pageant. The town was illuminated, and beacon fires were lit on neighbouring hills, enhancing the natural picturesque beauties of the place.

It was when returning from an elephant hunt at Colombo that the royal carriage was overturned and smashed, the Prince being thrown underneath, but fortunately escaping unhurt. An exciting feature of the hunt came when the party was pursued through the dense bamboo jungle by a herd of fierce, wild elephants.

At Madras there were grand festivities, with an elaborate Nautch and Hindustani drama. At Calcutta the *maidan* was lined with troops, and, as a sign of peace and prosperity, the National Anthem was sung by ten thousand school-children. Here the renowned Zoological Gardens came in for notice. Everywhere the natives flocked in thousands to see the royal visitor, while the programme at Calcutta also included tent-pegging and another procession of elephants.

DRAGOONS: *cavalry*
PIG-STICKING: *hunting pigs with spears while on horseback; a popular sport*
LILLIPUTIAN: *tiny*
BOWERS: *shaded gardens*
MAIDAN: *a large open area in an Indian town*
TENT-PEGGING: *spearing targets while on horseback; a popular sport*

At Benares there were visits to the temples. The Prince was the Rajah of Benares' guest in a splendid castle on the Ganges, the roof of which afforded a view of the magnificent illuminations. Lucknow supplied more sporting features. At Cawnpore a visit was made to the sad memorial of the cemetery,[1] while at Delhi there was further military display and another grand review. Henty touches on the remarkable appearance of the elephant batteries. The Prince and the brilliant staff rode along the line of eighteen thousand troops. At Lahore they saw the old palace of Jamoo, another brilliant display of fireworks, and a dance of lamas from Ladak.

At other of the great cities of the country there were receptions by the rajahs. The account of the illumination of the Golden Temple reads like an extract from the *Arabian Nights*. At Agra the procession to meet the Prince was gigantic, a most brilliant affair in every way, several hundred elephants bearing gorgeous trappings marching past, while seventeen rajahs were present. Every available man, horse, camel, and elephant were utilized on the occasion of a visit to the Taj Mahal monument, which was illuminated with wondrous effect.

At Gwalior, accompanied by a strong British escort, the Prince was met by the Maharajah Sanda, who accompanied him to the old palace, the route of which was lined by fourteen thousand of the Maharajah's picked troops, who looked uncommonly well, while a sham-fight which was arranged was a noteworthy affair. This, in fact, was one of the grandest receptions of the visit.

From Gwalior the expedition moved on to Jaipur, where the Maharajah gave the Prince the opportunity of shooting his first tiger. The next visit was to the camp at Bunbussa, where the Prince was received by Sir Jung Bahadoor, the ruler of the Nepalese. Here there was a guard of honour of Gurkhas, and it was worthy of remark that the Prince and Sir Jung were in

---

[1] Built to honor those killed during the Cawnpore Massacre (1857)

LAMAS: *Buddhist priests*
MAHARAJA: *King*

plain clothes; but after a brief interval Sir Jung Bahadoor returned, with his suite, all in full dress, blazing with diamonds. A durbar was held, and the Prince paid a return visit. At each durbar there were presentations, and to each member of the Prince's suite the servants brought in trays of presents. Two tigers in cages, many other wild creatures, and a splendid collection of the beautiful pheasant-like birds from the Nepalese mountains, were offered to the royal visitor.

Splendid sport was enjoyed here in the Nepalese dominions, seven tigers being shot, six falling to the Prince's rifle. Upwards of six hundred elephants were employed in beating the jungle, and the sight was of an imposing character. Before leaving, the royal party had a most exciting hunt. The Prince and his suite, accompanied by Sir Jung Bahadoor, went in pursuit of a wild rogue elephant, a splendid animal with huge tusks, which at the end of a long day's chase, and after charging the royal party several times, was eventually captured by means of tame elephants.

Such were some of the scenes and incidents which Henty was called upon to witness and describe, and to a man fresh from the arduous trials of the Coomassie campaign the change must have been both refreshing and delightful.

It is amusing to read a telegram from Aden which gives an account of some of the Prince's presents: "The menagerie is quite comfortable. It contains eighty animals. The elephants walk about the deck"—this, of course, meaning our two little friends that were known so well at the Zoo—"the deer are very tame, and the tigers are domesticated, though they exhibit tendencies to relapse." So says the chronicler sarcastically.

At the conclusion of the Prince's visit, in March, 1876, and shortly after Henty's return, there was more food for his pen, but of a very different character. The Turco-Servian War had broken out, and once more he was the busy war correspondent, though this proved to be the last time that he went to the front.

DURBAR: *official reception*
ROGUE ELEPHANT: *an unnaturally violent elephant*
DOMESTICATED: *tamed*

CHAPTER XXXIV

AMONG THE TURKS

THE year 1876, which was a memorable year in the life of Henty, is familiar to the elders among us in connection with the troubles in the East and the risings in Bulgaria and Servia.[1] Christian England was, politically, ringing with the charges made against Turkey in the matter of the stern suppression of the risings in the former country. "Bulgarian Atrocities" were made a party question, and debate followed debate. All our great parliamentary speakers delivered columns of speeches in the House, denouncing Turkey or speaking in her defence, while special deputations were made to Government by leading members of Parliament, Mr. Gladstone being foremost in the attack.

It fell to the lot of the writer to be in the gallery of the House of Commons upon one of the most important evenings, when he had the opportunity of hearing Mr. Gladstone deliver one of his most fervent and denunciatory speeches—a speech which was replied to by Mr. Disraeli calmly, coldly, and disdainfully. The future Lord Beaconsfield[2] expressed his disbelief in the charges made by the Opposition. He declared that it was not in the nature of the Turks to stoop to such atrocities, that they were too gentlemanly a race of men. They might, when stirred up to anger and in the hot blood of war, slay outright, but they

---

[1] Serbia
[2] Benjamin Disraeli became Lord Beaconsfield in 1876.

ÆGIS: *support*
VOUCHED FOR: *affirmed as true*

would scorn to commit the ruffianly acts of which they were accused.

It was at this time that the Turks were sending their armies into Servia to suppress the rising in that country, in defiance of the protecting ægis of Russia, and Henty, as representative of the *Standard*, was dispatched to the headquarters of the Turkish army to fulfil one of his familiar missions. His letters from the seat of war ring all through with a sturdy conservative belief in the qualities of the Turk as vouched for by the late Lord Beaconsfield; indeed, he is full of high praise for the patience, kindliness, and hospitality of the Turkish soldier. He was well received everywhere by officer and man alike. One and all were ever ready to share with the English representative of the press their shelter, or their last crust of bread and cup of water.

The whole of Asia Minor was at the time in a political volcanic state of eruption, and Prince Milan's[1] name was constantly reaching the Turkish headquarters, while beneath, like a muttering undercurrent of rumour, there was the constant rumble of what was doing among the Russ.

Henty's pen was, of course, as busy as ever, and when he was not reporting some attack or some defence, the creaking of the tumbrel wheels that bore away the wounded from the field, or the rattle and roar of musketry and artillery, he was making his letters attractive with descriptions of the beauty of the country, and of the richness of the orchards whose fruit was to supply the plum brandy of the country. Then, full perhaps of recollections of Moore's poetry descriptive of the attar of the rose, he reverted to the showering petals of the nightingale flower, and drew attention to the copper stills, to be found in almost every cottage or village, used by the peasantry for the distillation of the wondrous penetrating attar of roses. One cannot help thinking, though, that in a country where the inhabitants

---

[1] Milan I of Servia (1854-1901)

RUSS: *Russians*

ATTAR OF THE ROSE: *rose oil; used as perfume*

STILLS: *vessels used for distilling the oil*

DISTILLATION: *concentration by boiling down*

depend upon obtaining their alcohol from the juice of the plum, their brandy may possibly by accident be occasionally obtained from the same copper still.

Be that as it may, the descriptions of the dreamy beauty of such a picturesque and flowery land bring up a feeling of sadness that the nature of both people alike, Christian and Moslem, should tend so strongly towards bloodshed and rapine.

Here, too, in the midst of constant travel and change of quarters, in spite of friendly treatment from the people among whom his lot was cast, the special correspondent was called upon to suffer severely from the intense heat and the consequent thirst, and though he knew it not at the time, it was to find later that he had been laying the foundation for much illhealth and trouble to come.

But Henty was too busy making up, column by column, the long and always interesting letters that by some means or another he sent north and west on their way to the *Standard*, to think much about self. In fact, every note he sent seems to have running through it the spirit of the earnest, hard-working man with a certain duty to fulfil.

There was always something to write about, and when short of material and if in doubt, it seemed as if he played trumps— by this one means that, soldier-like, he fell back upon his old habit of giving a picturesque description of the uniform of the soldiery among whom he was cast. In the case of the Turks the richness of its colour—blue; its newness and well-kept aspect came in for much praise, while at other times he was as graphic and true to nature about the rags to which this uniform was reduced. He always noted, though, that the men's weapons were perfectly serviceable and bright.

In spite of the friendliness with which Henty found himself greeted by the Moslem, Turk, and the Græco-Christian

PLAYED TRUMPS: *went with something that always works*
GRÆCO-CHRISTIAN: *Greek Orthodox*
BULGAR: *people from Bulgaria*
ZAPTIEH: *servant*
BLUFF: *good-natured*

Bulgar alike, he noted that invariably when he and his *zaptieh* approached the Circassians—the dreaded Tcherkesses[1] constituting the Turkish irregular soldiery, who were fierce mercenaries, and undoubtedly answerable for whatever atrocities were perpetrated in Bulgaria—they turned away their heads with a scowl of mingled scorn and hatred.

It was here again that Henty's old training came to his aid, giving him the firmness and determination that impressed those whom he passed, as showing that he was well armed, and that he was ready, if it should prove necessary, to use his weapons. For he states that in spite of their peaceful mission, he and his man had to hold revolver and rifle ready during their advances till they were quite certain that they were approaching Turkish regular soldiers and not Circassians, for if they met the regulars they were always cordially welcomed and received with black coffee and cigarettes.

This reception may possibly be due to the fact that the Turks seem to have a sort of traditionary feeling that a European who is travelling must be a *hakeem*—in plain English, a doctor, in which belief they are somewhat supported by the meaning of the good old word doctor—a learned man.

Now a glance at Henty's portrait seems to stamp him, big-bearded and bluff, with the learned look of one who, being a traveller, must be endowed with the knowledge that would enable him to treat any complaint with skill. As a matter of fact, if called upon for aid in a case of emergency or ordinary ailment, he was quite prepared to open a medical battery upon a sufferer. It is, therefore, in no wise surprising that during his travels in Servia the Turkish gendarmes occasionally applied to him to treat their complaints. Even his own *zaptieh*, who after a few drops of opium was ready to cry, like the man in the old tooth-tincture advertisement, "Ha, ha! Cured in a instant!" was

---

[1] Circassians and Tcherkesses are both names for the same people group living in the Caucasus Mountains of southern Russia.

MERCENARIES: *hired soldiers*
GENDARMES: *military police*
TOOTH-TINCTURE: *a toothache medicine*

always afterwards ready to spread his master's reputation and increase the number of his grateful patients.

Of course there are some who would shrug their shoulders at this and softly murmur, "Quack!" But one fails to see it. In fact, the writer feels disposed to assert that the reputation of *hakeem* was very honestly earned by one who had commenced his profession with a good sound English education, who had served a certain time in the military hospitals of the Crimea and in Italy, who had been a student in sanitary matters, who had worked hard among the sick and wounded, and to whom anything in the shape of a military hospital had an intense attraction. We must remember, too, that he had learned much from the sufferings he was called upon to witness in this later war, where the surgeon and physician were so terribly in the minority, and in a country where, during certain of the horrible attacks and defences, it was no unusual thing for the camp-followers to go round at night, and, to use a horrible, old, and familiar expression, put the enemy's wounded out of their misery.

This knowledge on the part of Henty, and his readiness also and ability to give some slight alleviation of their sufferings and help to the wounded, enabled him to make sure of a friendly welcome, to say nothing of smiles and gratitude, almost wherever he went—except among the Tcherkesses.

ALLEVIATION: *reduction*

CHAPTER XXXV

PHILOSOPHY IN CAMP

No one need wonder that enthusiastic boys and young men who read Henty feel the spirit of emulation rise within them, while their young hearts glow with the desire to imitate him and to become a war correspondent. Well, so it would be grand; but the question has arisen since the last war—Is a war correspondent of Henty's type not a thing of the past? One writes this with the recollection of how a friend met with such discouraging treatment in the Russo-Japanese War that he and his fellows were ready to turn back homeward in disgust. They found that it had become general *versus* editor, and that the general had all the winning cards in his hand, while the troubles which Henty encountered during the Franco-German War, and in which he was worsted, had all become intensified. War correspondents, in brief, were treated as individuals who were to be kept out of danger and hoodwinked as to what was going on; in short, they realized that Othello's occupation, to be Shakespearean, was about gone.[1]

But yea or nay, such a life as Henty's is enough to raise the spirit of emulation among the young, always too prone to see the bright side and not the dull. It is only fair, though, that they should read both sides. Of course, after the weary tramp, the sufferings from heat and cold, hunger and thirst, there was

[1] *Othello, Act 3, Scene 3* by William Shakespeare (1564-1616)

HOODWINKED: *deceived*

something very "jolly", as a boy would say, about the hearty welcome of the camp fire, the odorous cigarette, the fragrant coffee, the song, the story, and the genial looks of man to man in the full enjoyment of a well-earned evening's rest. But then there was that other side: the places he had to stop at, fagged, faint, and hungry after a long day's journey; the bare mud floor, a mat for a bed, the momentary rejoicing at the fact that he had found a sheltering hut, though one innocent of window and with no means of fastening the door. The correspondent is, however, only too glad to throw himself down and yield with a sigh to that terrible overmastering sleep, that letting go of everything, that slackening of the too tight bow-string, that general relaxation—yes, only to sleep—sleep—sleep, and then—ugh!—only to be awakened by the attack, fierce and combined, of every sort of vermin mentioned in natural history, quadrupedal and entomological. Ugh! Horrors, diabolical and disgusting these, calculated to promote a vivid wakefulness such as would make the war correspondent feel keenly that what before had seemed to be impossible had suddenly become possible. With a feeling of despair at such times he would unbuckle his writing-case, tear open ink-holder with a snap, light his lantern, and begin to make notes, or set his teeth hard as he continued to write a portion of a letter already begun—one of those letters so full of picturesque description and vivid account of that last coming-on of the enemy and his gallant defeat, or the enforced retreat, with the horrible slaughter that it entailed—one of those letters, in short, that are so enthralling to read in the morning paper, and tell so well of the ability of the practised writer, but which he, poor fellow, has written from beginning to end in misery and also in supreme doubt as to whether it would ever reach its destination.

But whether it did or not, whatever failure there might be to

ODOROUS: *strong smelling*
FAGGED: *wearied*
QUADRUPEDAL: *four-legged*
ENTOMOLOGICAL: *insect*

face in connection with the postal communication, the letters had to be written. How, when, or where—that is nothing to the reader. There before the writer was the something attempted, and at last the something done, to earn the night's repose, though that repose was too often disturbed or made impossible in the way which one has attempted to depict in connection with the natural history that frequently haunted a Servian hut, in the lovely country where often only man was vile.

Again and again, too, there was the deafening roar of the guns, the Turks especially being great in artillery, and the nauseous, dank, sulphuretted hydrogenous clinging smell of powder in the air, a most familiar odour to the industrious war correspondent who strives hard to do his duty by his paper; and this too often supplemented by that other sickening odour frequently associated with death, horrible when fresh, most horrible when days have gone by and the slain have not been hidden by the busy spade.

The frequent smell of powder in the air to the weary correspondent is often enough safe and antiseptic, though still associated with the horrors of war and connected with death; but with so many risks to be run, one asks in wonder this question, how is it that the war correspondent usually manages to escape unharmed? Fortunate for him it is that he, like so many others who have urgent duties to perform, has no time to think of aught save that which comes in the day's work.

Then there is the food difficulty in a devastated country. That is a matter, of course, which has to be got over; but it is not so easy to surmount the difficulties with servants, and in the Turco-Servian War Henty had a varied experience. He states that he engaged one who professed to be able to cook, but who could not prepare food even in the most primitive way, while another who had undertaken to look after the horses, it

REPOSE: *rest*
SULPHURETTED HYDROGENOUS: *sewer gas like*
ANTISEPTIC: *free from contamination*
ENGAGED: *hired*

would be quite reasonable to declare, had most probably never touched a horse in his life. The consequence was that those most patient of beasts, which were often the very life of a war correspondent, suffered badly, while as to the action of the professed cook—for it is presumed that a man who undertakes to cook properly professes to be that artist, even though he may not be a *chef*—a diet of very bad bread, caviare, and German sausage, though convenient in the extreme in the way of transportation from place to place, begins after a time to pall.

But Henty seems to have taken for his moral aphorism: "Sufficient for the day is the evil thereof."[1] Had it not been so, he could never have passed unscathed through what he did. In fact, his murmurs about the troubles he encountered were few and far between. So patient, indeed, does he show himself to have been, judging from his letters, that one is tempted at times to go so far as to call him a great man. To judge from the calm, easy-going way in which his letters paint him as taking life, he seems often enough to be regarding it and its accidents as a great joke, while one would imagine that if there were one person whom he encountered who deserved to be laughed at, it was himself.

His philosophy is often really great, even if he does not himself deserve the appellation, while his letters read as if he had reached a stage in educating himself wherein the ordinary troubles of life, which we as a rule are accustomed to regard as very serious, were during this campaign shrunk in his eyes to the calibre of the very small. What he does set forth as being a really terrible difficulty is that of obtaining water for an "honest wash".

[1] Matthew 6:34
PALL: *become unpleasant*
APHORISM: *a short true statement*
UNSCATHED: *unharmed*
APPELLATION: *title*

Chapter XXXVI

The Turkish Army

HENTY carefully studied the ways and means of the Turk-ish army, not only the uniform and ornament, but the customs in connection with the various battalions. Though the Ottoman forces are not such as can be held up as examples of military excellence, he extols them as being composed of brave and admirable fighting men who are on the whole abominably paid, whose pittance is shamefully in arrear, but who still go patiently and uncomplainingly on, content with the small mercies they receive, and the kindly treatment of their officers who suffer with them. They march the more cheerfully from the fact that during a campaign every battalion has its own band, while as a rule the bandsmen have gained so much from the West that their performances of popular music are far above contempt.

As a rule here in England ordinary people do not know much of Turkish music. "The Turkish Patrol" and that very old favourite, "The Caliph of Bagdad," seem to belong nearly as much to the West as to the East; but in Servia Henty was made familiar with plenty of good Western operatic music, which was always bright and cheering in dreary times when on march. And while discoursing upon the bands he notes that, just as in English regiments, they take their serious part in the war, their

CALIBRE: *size*
EXTOLS: *praises*
PITTANCE: *small income*

play being of course connected with the production of enliven-
ing strains to lighten the dull hours of a heavy march, their
work being as bearers of the wounded.

National music such as is familiar to the people of the country is abundant and popular, of course; but it was amusing at
one time in camp, when the war was dragging slowly on, to find
that a band which played every evening under the Pasha General's tent finished up with a few bars of "God Save the Queen."

Constantly observant, Henty was always attracted by everything connected with the Turkish hospitals. He was quite fair.
If he saw anything in their management deserving of condemnation he spoke out. On the other hand, if he noticed anything,
however trifling, worthy of praise, it was carefully noted. He records with something like a feeling of pride in his fellow-men,
how an officer, having the power to command, had ordered
that one of the bands should go down to the camp hospital
to play for an hour every day, the Turkish officers declaring to
him that the music raised the spirits and improved the condition of the sick and wounded. He continues with an anecdote
of the *se non è vero, è ben trovato* type, namely, that a poor fellow,
who had lost his arm in one of the first skirmishes, had been so
revived by the music that he had begged permission to join the
ranks again with a limb of wood! Of course it may be true; but
everyone is at liberty to doubt, and one cannot help giving the
Turkish narrators the credit of trying a joke upon their foreign
chronicler.

During this campaign, on the principle that straws sometimes indicate the direction from which the wind blows, Henty
grew more observant of matters connected with the sufferings
of human life. It was as if many of his notes and remarks were
forced upon him by his own feelings, and as though his personal sensations sharpened his observation.

SE NON È VERO, È BEN TROVATO: *"if it isn't true, it should be" in Italian*

Here was he, a man who had passed through the heats and colds of mountainous Africa in the march to Magdala, complaining, justly enough, of course, but in words that indicated how keenly he must have suffered, of the heat and cold of Asia Minor. He says of the one that it is terrible by day, while the other is piercing by night, and both extremes even he, a strong man, found very hard to bear—harder terms these than any which he applied to the heavy stagnant heat of Ashanti.

Then he speaks of the skin tents as being simply unbearable when the sun was up, while the flies were maddening, and he has a thoughtful word for the poor horses, which suffered as much as their riders, being almost devoured by the darkening swarms.

He notes, too, that the Turkish sentinels when on duty were provided with a small umbrella tent to shelter them from the heat of the sun and from the rain; that a Turkish sentinel does not pace up and down when on sentry-go, but stands immovable all the time while he is on duty, and adds dryly that he has plenty of time for observation in the Turkish camp, for the army is dilatory in its movements. Then he turns to make some fresh observation, as there is no fighting going on, upon the appearance of a battalion of Egyptian soldiers which had joined the camp. The men were clothed in white from head to foot, with the exception of the tarboosh, which was, of course, scarlet, and, with his old military instinct aroused, he compares the Egyptian uniform with the Turkish, to the disadvantage of the latter in their blue serge.

He goes on, too, to comment not only upon their dress, but upon their evolutions—unfixing bayonets, grounding arms, etc.—and their activity. The Egyptians were dark brown of skin, but the Turks were no darker than Spaniards, often as fair as Englishmen.

STAGNANT: *still, motionless*
SENTRY-GO: *guard duty*
DILATORY: *slow*
TARBOOSH: *felt hat in the shape of a flat-topped cone*
SERGE: *a heavy fabric*

On another day his attention is attracted by a raid that has been made by the irregulars connected with the army, ending in a skirmish with the Servians, and a return laden with plunder, consisting of goats, cattle, and horses. He ends up with a pithy memorandum that the Bashi-Bazouks receive no pay, so make the surrounding country keep up their supplies.

With regard to the food supplies of the regulars, it seems that every Turk carries a leathern pouch which contains ground coffee and sugar, so that with a little bread and water they can get on pretty well.

As for the Bashi-Bazouks, who depend upon the country, which would probably account for their unpopular character, Henty noted them a good deal. They were a peculiarly mixed lot, apparently raised wherever men could be obtained, many of them being of Herculean proportions. A rough lot, these Bashi-Bazouks, but Henty's eyes must have glistened with eager interest and flashed with the desire of a collector who had a little museum of his own at home, as he examined their weapons. These were the arms of a dozen different nations, some carrying rusty, worthless old pistols, while others had damascened blades of beautiful wavy forging and razor-like keenness, such as could not be bought for money.

Towards the end of his connection with this campaign he constantly recurs to the various skirmishes, many being encounters mostly brought on by Servian patriots—small affairs in which no military skill was brought to bear, and in which the injuries were, for the most part, the result of musket bullets, the wounds by sword and bayonet being few. He goes on to complain bitterly of the Eastern callousness and conduct of man to man, the indifference he witnessed being revolting. And then later, when at last the war became fiercer, his humanity was again stirred and he referred to the hospitals in one of the

PITHY: *brief but significant*
BASHI-BAZOUKS: *Turkish mercenaries who were paid in plunder*
HERCULEAN: *giant*
DAMASCENED: *etched or inlaid*
RECURS: *returns*

towns, which he described as "choke full," so encumbered, in fact, that wounded men had to lie in the streets from day to day, the people passing them by and noticing them no more than if they were logs of timber.

In some of the rooms used there were neither beds nor mattresses, but simply the hard brick floor, for the wounded to lie upon in their blood-saturated clothes, waiting till one of the medical men could find time to attend to them. The doctors were working the while like slaves, extracting bullets or dressing wounds, and then giving the poor fellows a little plum brandy before they were lifted into a bullock-cart, with a truss of hay for a seat, and sent to recover or die elsewhere, while many who could not bear transport had to stay until nature mercifully intervened, and glory and patriotism became the mists of another and a brighter day.

Henty described how he was pulled up on one occasion because a river had to be crossed, and the army had to wait until a bridge then being made was finished. At least half a dozen times did the infantry get under arms and the artillery harness their horses. A more tedious day, he said, he never passed. His tent was packed, he had no place to sit down to write, and his sole amusement was watching the Circassians and Bashi-Bazouks come in laden with plunder.

The selection made by these freebooters had been strange and miscellaneous at first, but as things grew scarce, nothing was considered unworthy of the scoundrels' notice, for they scraped together trifles that would not have fetched a piastre, and they took not the slightest notice of the ridicule of the regular Turkish soldiers around. These laughed scornfully at the plundering habits of the irregulars, and were not above pointing them out to the English looker-on, exclaiming, "No bono Tcherkess—no bono Bashi-Bazouk!" Henty does not scruple to

TRUSS OF HAY: *hay bale*
FREEBOOTERS: *plunderers*
PIASTRE: *a small Turkish coin*
NO BONO: *"no good"*

call these men a disgrace to the Turkish government; but it seems that the army often had to depend upon them for supplies.

And after this fashion the weary war went on. The inexhaustible letters were dispatched, each teeming with interest, till rumours began to reach the writer of overtures being made by the Servians to the Turks for peace; but these were only contradicted and followed by a desperate encounter, or the siege of some little stronghold.

Then more rumours of peace; suggestions in the way of news; a short interregnum; then a recrudescence of the war, with Henty once more afoot, following the movements of the Turkish army or some brigade, to be present at an attack or to watch some threatening Servian movement being driven across one or other of the rivers. All the time the quiet, thoughtful correspondent was supplying his columns of interesting material to his messengers. The long chronicle grew and grew, and no mention was made of weariness, cruel suffering, semi-starvation, want of rest, and the difficulty of obtaining the sinews of war to carry on his fight. For no matter how careful the means taken for transmitting funds, the difficulties of cashing orders, and the troubles incident upon the money passing through foreign hands, which closed upon coin and objected to reopen, were often distressing in the extreme.

Now and then, though, a letter gives a hint about the difficulty of the war correspondent's task—the sort of hint for which one has to read between the lines—and at last, with the year waning and passing into autumn, and while chronicling that difficulties were arising in connection with the army he accompanied, and that Russia, long threatening and working in connection with the politics of Europe, was at last thoroughly taking the field and preparing to give check in the cause of

OVERTURES: *proposals*
INTERREGNUM: *pause*
RECRUDESCENCE: *revival*
SINEWS OF WAR: *strength for the war*
WANING: *drawing to a close*
GIVE CHECK: *act as a restraint*

Christianity against the Moslem, Henty touches on his own situation. Now it was, too, that the time arrived for an announcement of the armistice that was to come into force.

At this period, completely worn out, the correspondent writes: "I leave the camp tomorrow for England, with the conviction that the war is over, as it is hardly possible that the European powers can permit it to recommence.... But even did I think otherwise, I must most reluctantly have given up my post of correspondent with the Turkish army, for the long-continued indisposition brought on by bad food and hard living has at last overpowered me, and the doctors tell me that it is absolutely necessary for me to have rest, good living, and home comforts. I never quitted an army more reluctantly, for never have I been with one where I have received such uniform kindness, and whose men I had so much reason to like. I defy the most anti-Mohammedan fanatic to stop a month with this army without experiencing a complete change of sentiment, for a more liberal set of men than these quiet, willing, patient, and cheerful soldiers does not exist on the face of the earth. I have been with the troops of most nations of Europe, including, of course, our own, under circumstances of hardship and fatigue, and I can say that none of them can compare with the Turkish troops in point of good humour and patient endurance."

Henty struggled on, however, to the last, and we read of him in connection with the campaign in the Dobrudscha. Here his health completely broke down, and for some time he was an invalid.

He never did any further war correspondent's work, but for many years edited the telegrams and letters that came in to the *Standard* from the younger and more active men who had taken up his work. In fact, he went abroad no more, except on one

RECOMMENCE: *begin again*
INDISPOSITION: *sickness*
STOP: *stay*
LIBERAL: *generous*
THE DOBRUDSCHA: *Bulgaria*

trip through the United States to see for himself what mining life was like in Omaha, California, and elsewhere, and also to explore the rich copper country of the shores and islands of Lake Superior. No better man could have been found, from his old experience, for the investigation. But this was to him more of a holiday.

Chapter XXXVII

A Busy Convalescence

NATURE had given George Henty plenty of latitude, but now he was compelled to accept her warnings that he must take no more liberties with his health. He was so broken down by hard work and the rough experiences through which he had passed that he had become quite an invalid, with the stern task plainly before him of doing everything possible to restore his health.

As the old epitaph says, "Affliction sore long time he bore;" but physicians were not in vain, for Henty was a man of strong common sense, who knew well the value of self-denial. His ailments, too, were not of his own seeking, for no man knew better than he the value of moderation and attention to hygiene.

He followed out what he knew was due to a man who wished to lead a healthy life, and he supplemented his medical men's advice by devoting himself more than ever to his favourite pursuit of yachting. He spent almost every hour he could spare on board his little craft, keeping her within easy reach of town and taking a few hours here, a day there, and when work did not enchain him, making his little vacation a week, with the result that he was rapidly restored to health. It is doubtless due to the health-giving, strength-producing breezes that blow around the British shore that he retained the vigour of a

CONVALESCENCE: *period of recovery*
LATITUDE: *freedom*
EPITAPH: *an inscription in memory of someone*
HYGIENE: *healthy practices*

carefully-preserved manhood to the very last, so that when his summons came it found him upon his yacht.

If a candid recorder of George Henty's career is bound to set down all and criticize adversely, he might reasonably say that this man's one great excess was his indulgence in ink. This fault, however, was not a very black one, for, so to speak, he softened it by using ink of a pleasant violet hue! But, to be matter-of-fact, writing when at home and at rest in his study seems to have been a perfect stimulant, and, combined as it was with his open-air pursuit, a complete recreation, and in no sense a work of toil.

Many men are great readers. Henty, in one acceptation of the term, was a great writer, who, with the assistance for a score of years of his swift-penned amanuensis, Mr. Griffith, sat down daily, not to write, but to call upon his wonderful imagination. This he supplemented by what he had seen, and when necessary by the study of history, and literally passed hours of what to him must have been intense enjoyment. Picture after picture of the past at these times floated before his brain as he set his young characters to work performing the manly tasks his brain suggested, otherwise there would never have been the reality, the variety, and above all the long series of entertaining and instructive works which have so largely aided the schoolmaster in Great Britain in the education of our youth.

During the period of Henty's convalescence he was never idle, though the year 1876 marks the completion of his long career as a war correspondent. Others took up his old duties abroad, but his pen and his knowledge were still of so much value to the journal with which he was connected, that it became his duty, as already indicated, to receive all the telegraphic messages sent in by the *Standard's* correspondents in time of war. He carefully read and studied the crabbed and

CANDID: *honest*
ACCEPTATION: *usual meaning*
CRABBED: *difficult to read*

G. A. Henty at 45

condensed messages that had come over the wire, as well as the communications of Reuter and other agencies from different parts of the world, and rewrote them in the vulgar tongue so that they might be comprehensible to the British public. This placed him, as it were, still at the head of war correspondence, so that when war broke out he was, so to speak, always at the front. Even though his post was his editorial chair in his journal's office, the wires kept him in touch with everything that was taking place at all points of the compass.

So it happened that in this restless age his work should be pretty constant, and the exigencies of this form of historical chronicle kept him tied very tightly to his journalistic duties, the late arrival or expected arrival of fresh telegraphic news forcing him to stay till almost the time of the great newspaper's going to press in the extremely early hours of the day; and this lasted right down through the troublous times and agitation in England during the Boer War.

VULGAR TONGUE: *common language*
EXIGENCIES: *urgency*

CHAPTER XXXVIII

CONCERNING WAR CORRESPONDENTS

THERE is a sadness attached to the task of describing Henty's capabilities as a war correspondent, from the fact that so many of his colleagues and brothers of the pen who knew him well and went to the front have passed away. Some who shared the lot of the brave officers and men, ran the same risks, and died the same deaths. Cameron was shot soon after being at a farewell dinner at his club, where he sat next to the writer of these lines; Pearce, though he lived through the horrors and starvation of the siege of Ladysmith[1]—to see by the strange working of fate his own son ride up in the train of Lord Dundonald with the gallant relief party, as one of the volunteers—came back a mere shadow of his former self and died soon after, weakened by the privations connected with his duties; Archibald Forbes, possibly the hardest worker and most energetic of all, shortened his life in the cause of duty; and the same may be said of Henry Stanley; while of those who might have supplied many recollections or anecdotes, and who knew Henty well, death has claimed a long roll of brothers of the pen and correspondents, including Charles Williams, Godfrey Turner, Walter Wood, and Robert Brown.

One good old friend, active as ever, William Senior, now editor of *The Field*, gives a genial tribute to Henty's memory from

---

[1] This siege took place from November, 1899, to February, 1900, during the Second Boer War in South Africa.

PRIVATIONS: *lack of necessities*

personal knowledge when he says, that as a special correspondent his readiness to help, and the practical manner in which he set about his work, combined with the thoroughness with which he took care of every small detail, were at once an encouragement and a stimulus to his colleagues.

Fortunately one has at command Henty's own description of what he considers a special correspondent should be. To begin with, he says that he should be a man capable of supporting hardships and fatigues; that he should possess a certain amount of pluck, a good seat in the saddle such as would enable him to manage any mount whose services he could command; and lastly, that he should have the manners of a gentleman and the knack of getting on well with all sorts and conditions of men. This is a good deal to expect from one man, but without being eulogistic it may rightly be said that Henty possessed all these qualifications.

To a certain extent he was gifted with these qualities by nature, and where he felt himself to be wanting in any one point, his energy urged him to strengthen that weakness and strain every nerve until he had mastered the failing.

Accident has had much to do with the making of war correspondents, as in his own case; but Dr. Russell and Wood of the *Morning Post* had both been connected with the press before being sent to the Crimea. Sometimes, however, military men with a ready gift of writing have offered their services to report on the wars in which their regiments were engaged, as in the case of Captains Hozier and Brackenbury, who made excellent correspondents and still continued in the army. Archibald Forbes, when quite a young man, served in a cavalry regiment, and after leaving the army did a little reporting before going out with a sort of roving commission to the Franco-German War. Thence he sent divers reports to a London newspaper,

MOUNT: *horse*
WITHOUT BEING EULOGISTIC: *without praising too highly*
COMMISSION: *assignment*
DIVERS: *various*

with the unpleasant result of being recalled, and this, too, at a time when he was primed with news of the most important nature. So special was his information, and of such extreme value, that, without writing a line, as he told the writer, he hurried over to England with all the speed possible, presented himself at the *Times* office, and asked to see the editor. In most newspaper offices, when the application is made by a perfect stranger, this is a privilege that the busy head of an important paper is rather loath to grant, and a messenger was sent out to Forbes asking his business. Forbes's reply was that he had come straight from the front with most important news, and he was told, after sending in that message, that if he would write an article containing what he had to communicate, the editor would consider his manuscript, and, if it were approved, use and pay for it. Forbes told me in his sharp military way that he was not going to write and be treated like that, knowing how important was his information; and he said, "I went out from the *Times* office, walked into Fleet Street, and stood at the edge of the pavement halfway between, hesitating as to whether I should go to the *Telegraph* office, or down Bouverie Street to the *Daily News*."

His hesitation did not last long. He went down the latter street and asked to see the manager. He was shown in at once to the office of my old friend, the late Sir John Robinson (Mr. Robinson in those days), who listened to what he had to say, and like the keen man of business that he was, he grasped the value of Forbes's information, and told him to go into a room which he pointed out and write a column. This he did, and it was put into type as fast as it was written. Soon after it was done he asked to see the manager again, and being shown in once more, Sir John Robinson said, "Have you got any more?" "Yes," said Forbes; "plenty." "Then go and write another column."

PRIMED: *supplied*
LOATH: *unwilling*
ACERBITY: *severe temper*
DUDGEON: *offended anger*
MUNITIONS: *equipment*

This was written in turn, and after it was done Forbes, still rather indignant about his previous ill-successes with the press, and not being blessed with Henty's way of dealing with all sorts and conditions of men, took offence at some words spoken by Sir John, which roused his acerbity and resulted in his being highly offended and leaving the manager's room in dudgeon. The *Daily News* "chief" was taken by surprise at the way in which the hot-blooded Scot had quitted him, and, hurrying down the stairs out into Bouverie Street, he overtook the angry ex-dragoon in Fleet Street. Having thus captured him and brought him back to his own room, he explained to him laughingly that he wanted him to go on writing until he had exhausted his information, and then he was to go off back immediately to the front as the representative of the *Daily News*, with full munitions, and to send over at his discretion all information that he could collect concerning the war.

This was a strange commencement of the important career of one who in the opinion of journalists began at once to make a brilliant name for himself, for this, Forbes's first literary coup, placed him at one stride in the same rank as William Howard Russell of the *Times*, the well-known author of *My Diary in India*. The opinion of the journalistic world was directly endorsed by the British public, who proved it by sending up the circulation of the *Daily News* to a wonderful extent throughout the war; and this lasted until the day when, passing by the *Daily News* publishing office in Fleet Street, the writer saw posted up Forbes's terse telegrams announcing to an astonished world the utter defeat of the French. The rest is familiar history.

Henty states that a good seat upon a horse is one of the valuable qualifications for a war correspondent, for it may come to pass that when at great risk and effort the gleaner of intelligence has obtained his requisite information by following the

COUP: *success*
ENDORSED: *approved*
TERSE: *brief*
GLEANER: *gatherer*
REQUISITE: *required*

vicissitudes of the campaign wheresoever the battle rages, he may find himself perhaps thirty or forty miles away from the nearest telegraph station. There is nothing to be done in such a case but for the correspondent to write his valuable dispatch as crisply and as carefully as possible, and then ride away at full speed so as to get the message at the earliest moment upon the wires. This task accomplished, he must, after a brief rest, mount once more and return to the front.

Later, it was in this way that, during the Zulu War,[1] Forbes was the first to send home an account of the Battle of Ulundi, bearing with him, so trusted was he, some of the general's dispatches as well as his own report. Where, however, the telegraphic facilities are not within reach, it is necessary for the correspondent to entrust the report he has written to the official post-bag, for he dare not absent himself long from the front, not knowing what events of importance may happen while he is away.

In the Franco-German War another correspondent, Beattie Kingston—polished gentleman, scholar, and able musician, who had been representing the *Daily Telegraph* in Vienna and elsewhere—was acting as correspondent with the German army; and of other war correspondents it remains to mention the familiar names of Bennett Burleigh and E. F. Knight, the latter of whom distinguished himself by writing the brilliant little account of *The Cruise of the "Falcon"*, which reads as graphically as if it had come from the pen of Defoe.[2] After Knight had taken up the risky duties of reporting wars, and had been sent to the Pamir[3] to report our little frontier engagement with the restless mountain tribes, he did something more than go to the front, for in one of the engagements he was with a little column whose officers were all shot down, and with the splendid energy and pluck of the fighting penman he dashed into the fighting

[1] The Zulu War was fought in 1879 in South Africa.
[2] Daniel Defoe (1660-1731), author of *Robinson Crusoe*

VICISSITUDES: *changing situations*
PAMIR: *a region in central Asia*

line, took the place of the fallen leader, and led the men to success.

This struggle—not his own special fight, for he is too simple and modest a man to play the part of Plautus's braggart captain[1]—he recorded in his work, *Where Three Empires Meet.* Later, when journalism claimed him again to be the war correspondent and he went out to the Boer War, news came to the little club of which he is one of the most popular members, that he was with the advancing line of the 42nd Highlanders at Magersfontein[2] and had been shot down. He lay with the rest of the unfortunates of that saddening day, trusting for first aid to one of the sergeants of the regiment who knelt down to bandage his shattered arm, panting with excitement to be off the while.

Another sufferer this in the great cause of gathering the freshest news, for E. F. Knight paid dearly for his well-earned fame. He was sent down with another wounded man picked out from about forty hopeless cases, "just to give me a chance," and though he suffered the complete loss of an arm, he finally recovered, thanks to Sir Frederick Treves. After this he studied and practised the art of writing quickly and clearly with his left hand, and from the Far East sent graphic reports of the Russo-Japanese War. That is the kind of stuff of which George Henty's friends and companions were made.

---

[1] A comic character from *Miles Gloriosus,* a play by Roman playwright Plautus (c. 254-184 B.C.)

[2] A battle fought in December, 1899, during the Second Boer War in South Africa

CHAPTER XXXIX

HENTY AND HIS BOOKS

FOR the benefit of his many boy readers with whom Henty's stories were most popular, a writer on the staff of *Chums*[1] paid Henty a visit one day. He described him as a tall man, massive in build, with a fine head and a commanding presence, the lower part of his face adorned with a great flowing beard, and though his hair was almost white, the dark beard was only slightly flecked with silver threads. He had the appearance of a man who had knocked about the world and rubbed shoulders with strange bed-fellows, and looked as though he would be a capital companion and just the sort of person with whom one would like to share the solitude of a desert island. There is no doubt that the writer said this in the full belief that Henty would have been an ideal comrade—a brave man, amiable, happy in temper, straightforward, and ready at a pinch to dare danger to the very death.

The visit paid to him was, primarily, to ask him how he wrote his books. "How does a man write his books?" is a question that calls for a little thought before answering. One man will write them mentally from end to end before putting pen to paper; another will jot down sketchy notes which, after months of thought and labour, represent so many scraps that have to be picked out, set in something like order, and then fitted

[1] A British boys' newspaper

G. A. Henty at Work

into shape as if they were pieces of a dissected puzzle; and only then, after much work, do they take form as a comprehensive whole. Again, another will spend years over the construction of a book, sparing no pains, in the full knowledge that he will never be able to write another; and after all it may prove to be not worth the reading, or, if worth the trouble, it may be utterly wanting in that indescribable element which enchains the reader at once and keeps his attention riveted to the very end. Yes, that indescribable something which is given to so few by nature—the few who, somehow, find themselves writing as no man to their knowledge ever wrote before; and so say their readers. For there is a peculiarity in some men's thoughts when placed on paper in print—a something which attracts, through the soul that is in it, people of all ranks and classes—the highly-cultivated classical scholar, the student of other men's works, the great criminal or civil judge whose life has been spent in examining the ways, thoughts, and acts of every form of human nature, the best as well as the vilest and worst.

And yet this book which affords such intense delight to its reader, often by its pathos, less often by its mirth—for, strangely enough, one finds that the gift of being humorous is extremely rare—will give as much pleasure to the half-educated child as it does to the man whom poor old Captain Cuttle,[1] Dickens's simple-hearted child-like creation, described as "chockful of science". Now, how is this? I, the writer of these lines, have been a reader for seventy years, and I must frankly confess that I don't know, and my honest belief is that I never shall. But this I do know, that I found all this attraction ready for my reading thirst in a story entitled *Rip Van Winkle*, in the pages of an old, old magazine called the *Queen Bee*. This story somehow painted a picture in my young brain of the Catskill Mountains

---

[1] A character from *Dombey and Sons* by Charles Dickens (1812-1870)

RIVETED: *held firmly*
PATHOS: *emotion*

and the Dutchmen playing ninepins, while the roll of the balls resounded and re-echoed like thunder, and the voice that rang out, crying, "Rip Van Winkle! Rip Van Winkle!" sounds, at any time when I think upon it, loud and clear. There is the picture still, like a dream of the photography that I was to live to see in all its present beauty, only clear and bright and better still; for there are the colours of nature which some of us yet may see photographed in the continuation of these wondrous days in which science has given us so much.

There is no saying how a man contrives to write a book; but this is the question that George Henty's visitor asked, as he sat near a table where closely-written sheets lay in a heap, apparently just as they had been laid together by the writer. There was a half laugh, followed by the rather disconcerting reply: "I do not write any of my books myself. I get a man to do them for me—an amanuensis, of course; it all comes out of my head, but he does all the actual writing. I never see any of my work until it comes to me from the printers in the shape of proof sheets. My amanuensis sits at the table, and I sit near him, or lie on the sofa, and dictate the stories which I publish."

So said Henty to his visitor, and he might have added, "and smoke the while," for nature must have needed something in the way of sedative for the brain so constantly upon the strain.

Then questions were asked by the eager inquirer as to how long this writing went on for so great an output, as a manufacturer would call it, to result. In the words that followed the real secret was explained—and it lay in the quiet, steady, regular application which is seen in the man who is discovered one day, trowel in hand, by a small pile of bricks which he goes on laying in position; he gives each a tap or two and a scrape, and in course of time, lo and behold! as the old writers say, there stands a magnificent house.

"What do I call a good day's work?" said Henty. "Well, say my man comes at half-past nine in the morning and stays for four hours, till half-past one; we can get through a good deal of work in that space of time. Then perhaps he comes round in the evening for a couple of hours; so in the course of a day I finish a chapter, that is, about six thousand, five hundred words. I call that a good day's work."

And so would anyone. Six thousand five hundred words of consistent description and conversation, all forming a portion of an interesting tale which will hold a boy's attention—often a man's! Think of it! At half-past nine that morning there was nothing; when work was knocked off in the evening there was a chapter that would someday be read with satisfaction—a something made out of nothing save a few flying thoughts. With George Henty that was how a story was written.

Such books as these would average in length from a hundred and thirty to a hundred and fifty thousand words; that is to say, about the length of the old three-volume novel, a class of work at which Henty also tried his hand. One of his first novels, *A Search for a Secret*, was published by Tinsley Brothers in 1867, and from time to time another was turned out which achieved a fair amount of success; indeed, almost up to the end of his life Henty wrote an occasional novel when a good plot occurred to him and when he felt in the mood. But quite early in his career he was invited by an old club friend, the late Thomas Archer, to contribute a story suitable for the reading of boys to a series of juvenile works that Messrs. Blackie & Son were about to produce, and which Mr. Archer was to see through the press.

This was the commencement of a long series of boys' books— a long way on towards a hundred—which achieved universal success, and for the task of writing which their author, in his avocation of war correspondent and descriptive writer, had in a manner passed his life priming himself.

In his choice of subjects, almost from the first, he drew on his old experience, and in one of his earliest essays he, the son of a coal-mine proprietor, naturally enough began upon a story dealing with the perils and dangers (not of the sea where the stormy winds do blow) encountered by the stern-visaged grimy men who gain their daily bread by descending with their lives in their hands into the bowels of the earth. He tells a tale here of the men who, with Davy lamp[1] in hand, go right down among the coal seams, to where the atmospheric pressure is light and the insidious gas can be heard hissing out of the strata. He describes how, weary and tempted by the longing for a pipe, some weak-minded comrade may contrive by the help of a nail to pick the lock of his carefully-secured safety lamp, so as to expose the flame for a pipe to be lit. Then comes the ignition of the gas in one scathing burning blast, the herald of death to the offender and to those nearest the explosion, while for those who are farther away, and who are warned by the thunderous roar, there is the race for life as they tear for the pit's mouth, to be too often overtaken by the deadly choke-damp, whose poisonous strangling fumes follow the firing of the gas. Others, imprisoned by the falling rock and coal, after fighting hard to escape, have to sit and wait and pray that the help which they know will be trying to reach them as soon as comrades can descend, may not come too late.

This, *Facing Death*, was Henty's first story for boys. But a soldier by training, he soon turned to the military element. It speedily dawned upon him that there is nothing a boy likes better than a good description of a fight—with fisticuffs not objected to against some school tyrant—and here, in his

---

[1] A small lantern, invented by Sir Humphry Davy (1778-1829), using a metal screen to shield the flame from explosive mine gasses

PRIMING: *preparing*

STERN-VISAGED: *stern-faced*

INSIDIOUS: *stealthy, treacherous*

SCATHING: *scorching*

descriptions, the writer was thoroughly at home. He knew how his heroes should behave, and in such encounters there was the vraisemblance that added power to his narrative. Then, too, as war correspondent who had seen fighting in the Crimea, in Italy with Garibaldi during the War of Independence, with Lord Napier in Abyssinia, in the Franco-German War and during the Commune, in Russia, in the West Coast forests on the way to Coomassie, in Spain during the Carlist Insurrection, and in the Turco-Servian War, his mind was stored with material and with picturesque backgrounds for stories to come.

Here was a stupendous collection of embryo "copy" for boys' books on fighting full of reality from beginning to end. From his wide experience he knew and described how fighting should be, and was carried on. When he felt a desire for change, he struck farther back, and enlisted as the years went by various heroes of history whose names have been immortalized. At one time he would be weaving a story about the prowess of our men in India with Clive, at another time following Wellington through the Peninsular War. He was, in imagination, with Roberts at Kandahar, with Kitchener at Khartoum, and with Buller in Natal. He often made a plunge into naval history and dealt with our naval heroes. Unconsciously, too, all this while he was building up a greater success for his boys' books by enlisting on their behalf the suffrages of that great and powerful body of buyers of presents who had the selection of their gifts. By this body is meant our boys' instructors, who, in conning the publishers' lists, would come upon some famous name for the hero of the story and exclaim: "Ha! history; that's safe." In this way Henty linked himself with the great body of teachers who joined with him hand in hand; hence it was that the book-writer who kept up for so many years his wonderful supply of

CHOKE-DAMP: *carbon dioxide*
FISTICUFFS: *fist fighting*
VRAISEMBLANCE: *truthfulness*
EMBRYO "COPY": *the beginning of material*
SUFFRAGES: *votes*
CONNING: *studying*

two, three, and often four boys' books a year, full of solid inter-est and striking natural adventure, taught more lasting history to boys than all the schoolmasters of his generation.

Naturally the works that dealt with his own experience were the simple honest truth; but the same may be said of those in which he had to deal with the past, and therefore had to strengthen and supplement his knowledge by the study of the best works he could get hold of preparatory to writing fiction dealing with some particular epoch. For, following upon the choice of his subject, say the battles of some war through which he carried his heroes, he confessed that he got together a pile of books from one of the big libraries and stored his mind with material for the purpose of the story he was about to weave; so that his fiction was very near akin to fact, though possibly it was highly coloured. No boy dislikes colour, and Henty's read-ers did not object to a little blood. His boys were fighting boys, and very manly, full, as he termed it, of pluck; and though he dressed them up and carried them through peril and adven-ture galore, it was all good honest excitement, even if here and there a little too bright in hue. As to that, he had the example of the famous romanticist of the north, the great Sir Walter,[1] who said that in equipping a character in one of his romances he liked to give him a cocked hat and a walking-stick to add to his appearance.

There was nothing namby-pamby in Henty's writings, for his adolescent characters were not so much boys as men, saving in this, that he kept them to boy life, and never made his works sickly by the introduction of what an effeminate writer would term the tender passion. "No," he said, "I never touch on love interest. Once I ventured to make a boy of twelve kiss a little girl of eleven, and I received a very indignant letter from a dis-senting minister."

[1] Sir Walter Scott
ROMANTICIST: *a writer in the Romantic style, a style of art and writing popular in the 1800's*
NAMBY-PAMBY: *weak*
EFFEMINATE: *weak or girlish*

Men who write books build up for themselves plenty of critics besides the authorized judges to whom their works are sent out by the publishers, and unfortunately the self-constituted censors do not possess the broad knowledge of the genuine critic.

But for outspoken, downright, honest but self-satisfied criticism, no one equals the "cocky" schoolboy who has entered upon the phase when he begins to feel that he can write, and has begun to get over the natural repugnance to express himself in correspondence. Early in life your natural boy only writes as much as he feels bound to set down with pen, ink, and paper. These effusions one may call duty-letters home. The next letters are those relating to his wants; they come more freely, and of course often savour of pocket-money. It is later, when he has taken to reading, and has arrived at the stage when his spelling is more regular, his grammar fairly correct, and his words flow more freely from his pen, that he becomes opinionated, and informs those to whom he writes what he thinks.

Sometimes an author is favoured by these young gentlemen, and more than one communicated with Henty and informed him that he had read his last book, which was, of course, satisfactory; but the criticisms and the points fallen foul of would have been unpleasant only for the fact that they formed food for mirth.

One day, during a chat concerning the success of a well-known magazine that was current some five-and-twenty or thirty years ago, which he edited, Henty laughingly complained to the writer about the way in which boys of this type troubled him with their opinions. One of them—it was in the early days when this corrupt word was beginning to be utilized in boy life as something very forcible and expressive—wrote and asked him why he put such "rot" in his paper. One fancies one can recall at the present moment the grim, half-amused, half-angry

DISSENTING MINISTER: *a minister not part of the Church of England*
CENSORS: *people who looks for objectionable content*
REPUGNANCE: *opposition*
EFFUSIONS: *outpourings*
SAVOUR: *contain suggestions*

expression of the editor's face as he related the anecdote. But it is only fair to say that such young gentlemen are the exceptions, and when a boy does praise, he can do it with a warmth that makes his favourite author's cheeks glow with pride, for he feels that the criticism is very honest and true.

And boys can write very very pleasant letters, such as set one thinking that one would like to know the writers. Some of their letters show very plainly what the young correspondents have thought as they read, though they often enough cause much amusement by their *naïveté*, especially those which come suddenly from the most out-of-the-way places. These are some of the great rewards which come to a writer, and make up for many a long day of drudgery in the cause of duty on days when nature is preaching idleness to a worker, and is calling to him with her myriad voices to leave the pen and desk and come and commune with her while there is time; on days—those rare days—when she is all smiles, and full of suggestions of those bright days of the past, which seem to have become rarer as one has been growing old.

Henty had a little selection of correspondents' letters sent from out-of-the-way places. One was from an American boy, written with all the quaint *naïveté* and ignorance of one who was on his travels to see what the world was really like. He writes from Italy, after "doing" England with his father:

> HOTEL EUROPA, VENEZIA,
> *March 22nd, 1889.*
>
> DEAR MR. HENTY,
>
> I am an American boy, ten years old, travelling in Europe. I read some of your books at home, and enjoyed them so much that, as soon as I arrived in London, I wanted to go to Mr. Blackie's, hoping to see you and all your books. So when I had been to Westminster Abbey

and the Tower, my father took me there; but I could not see you, and the books were shut up. But the gentleman was very kind to me, and brought some of them out, and I went home laden. I think *The Lion of St. Mark* is splendid. I am reading it here, and am sure Matteo lived in this house. I have been to the very place in the Piazetta where Matteo and Francis had their first conversation.

Yours respectfully,

Nothing could be more amusing than the boy's mingling of shrewdness and innocence respecting the author's connection with his publisher. There is something in it suggestive of the days of Newbery and Dodsley,[1] with an idea evidently in the boy's mind that publishers kept authors in stock. But it is the letter of a clever boy notwithstanding, blessed with a father aiming at increasing his boy's store of knowledge in the wisest way extant.

Such letters come abundantly to a boys' author; but Henty thought far more highly of those which he received from girls, for where there is a girl in the same family the brothers' books are generally common stock, and are carefully read, appreciated, and judged. The author declares that girls write more intelligently and evince greater judgment in their criticisms, while those who write, especially American girls, make a point of requesting an answer, and do not shrink from asking for the author's autograph to add to the collection being made.

At the same time, unconscious of the estimation in which the sister is held by her correspondent, the boy does not fail to write in a half-contemptuous spirit like this: "Dear Mr. ——, I have read your story, which I and my brother think splendid. Emmie has read it too, and she says it's delightful; but then, she's only a girl."

[1] English authors and booksellers during the 1700's

EVINCE: *clearly show*

Apropos of the boy seeker for an author's autograph, there are many of these acquisitive young gentlemen who make applications by post and do not get one, even on days when the author is in his most amiable frame of mind. Possibly this is due to the fact that they are perfectly unconscious of being propagators of a custom which has grown into a heavy tax. Others, more wise in their young generation, make a point of enclosing a carefully-directed and stamped envelope, which places the person addressed in the position of a creditor, whose conscience immediately smites him with the suggestion that it would be churlish and rude not to reply. And somehow almost invariably those young gentlemen obtain the addition to their collection that they have sought.

Boys' writers most probably do not have more worries than other people, but they have to submit to one nuisance from the selfish and thoughtless which does go very much against the grain. Fancy being a man who feels himself in duty bound to fulfil an engagement to write some four, five, or six thousand words of a story pretty well every day. Is it not extremely probable that when that long tale of words is written he will lay the pen down with a feeling of weariness, almost of loathing and disgust. Imagine his feelings, then, when he finds in his correspondence a letter from some absolute stranger, enclosing a long manuscript which he has written "especially for boys," with the request that "as the recipient is so clever and knows so well exactly what a boy likes, he will be good enough to read it at once and give his opinion upon its merits?" Now, human nature is human nature, and as a weary writer has a great deal of that sad human nature in his composition, and is prone to be irritable, surely it is not surprising that for a few minutes he falls into a fretful state, and mentally asks this would-be scribe why he does not send his MS. to an editor or other practised

ACQUISITIVE: *eager to acquire*
BY POST: *by mail*
PROPAGATORS: *spreaders*
CHURLISH: *ill bred*
MS.: *manuscript*

judge of people's works for his opinion about the unknown one's literary production?

Henty uttered his wail to one of his visitors who recorded an interview, and then confessed to being as weak and amiable as many others of his craft, for he says: "I do generally read them, and have helped several men to get publishers; but, of course, the great majority of the stories are hopelessly unfit for boys. One does not like to write back and say that the work is confounded rubbish, although I suppose it would be the most merciful thing to do, as it would prevent the writer from wasting his time. I let them down as lightly as I can."

There is a well-known old proverb, for which we have to thank one of the old Roman writers, who spread their Latin and their works through the civilized world, that a poet is born, not made, and it applies equally to the story-teller or writer of narrative. Henty was a story-teller from quite early days; for, following up his boyish attempts, the days came when, as a married man, with his children gathering round his fireside, it became a custom for them to come and say the familiar good-night, with the appeal to father to tell them a story. At first the stories were brief of the briefest, and doubtless versions of the old popular nursery tales. These, however, soon began to give way to invention, and these again would be followed by flights of fancy as the young author's wings grew stronger, till, from being so brief that they only sufficed for one evening, his stories expanded and gradually merged into those which were cut short with, "There, it's growing too late now. I must finish tomorrow night." Doubtless invention in the furnishing of these little narratives, composed expressly for the juvenile audience, soon had to give way to study, and their author began to seek his inspiration from some incident in history. Gradually, too, as he realized the interest taken in his narratives by his own

BRIEF OF THE BRIEFEST: *very short*

children, they began to be more thoughtfully designed, and grew longer, while the idea strengthened that they might prove as attractive to other children as to his own, until by a natural sequence the story-constructing took up more thought, grew more businesslike, and developed, as it were, into a profession.

It is easy, too, to imagine that as some of these stories—which were told for the benefit of his two boys, and the two little girls who were carried off by consumption on the verge of womanhood—ran to a length of four or five nights, they gave their originator the power to compose with fluency and ease. For throughout his life Henty practised storytelling as opposed to story-writing. It is not everyone who finds dictation easy, but for twenty years he dictated all his fiction to his secretary and amanuensis, Mr. Griffiths, even down to the very last tale which he finished, prior to his being stricken down by paralysis.

In writing his books Henty was wonderfully practical. He thoroughly enjoyed a quiet evening and a dinner with friends at his club, but, speaking from old experience, he never allowed this to interfere with the work he had on hand. More than once the writer has said to him, "What! going already?" ("already" being almost directly after dinner). "Yes," he would reply; "I shall perhaps have some telegrams to write up next door" ("next door" being the *Standard* office). On other occasions it would be, "Yes; going home. My man will be waiting when I get there" ("my man" representing his amanuensis, ready for him in his study at Lavender Hill). And in response to the remark, "Rather late to begin when you get home," "Oh yes, but I daresay I shall get a couple of thousand words done;" and that meant from Henty that the work would be done, for he was a man who meant work, and did it. This would happen usually when he was extra busy preparing some book for the press. He had a quiet, determined way of making hay when the sun

CONSUMPTION: *tuberculosis*

shone, for the *Standard* made great calls upon his time, requiring him to write matters of fact, and at such times fiction had to be laid aside. His long absences from home in times of war interfered greatly with his peaceful avocations, but he treated all these journeys as so many copy-collecting trips. They provided him with material which he would afterwards cleverly utilize, as can be gathered from passage after passage in his many works.

For details of the many stories for the young written by Henty, one is disposed to refer the reader to the publisher's list; but to follow upon what has been said respecting the correspondence that reaches a writer from his young readers, a letter that has come to hand, written by a Canadian boy some years ago, is very amusing in its admiration of his favourite author. It indicates such an amount of steady reading, it evinces so much ingenuity, and (if it should ever reach the young writer's eyes and he will take the criticism in the good part in which it is meant) displays so much need for improvement, that one gives it in full as an amusing list of the author's works from the boy's point of view.

The little lad calls it "a story". Well, it is an original story of stories, and, as intimated, emanates from Canada. It is here given in a confidence which suppresses names, and thus cloaks the literary mistakes of the past:

G. A. HENTY, ESQ.
DEAR SIR,
Hoping you will excuse me for troubling you, but I would like you to read the little story I have made (while staying home from school with the measles). I have read and enjoyed a great many of your books. Following is the story made out of the names of some of the books you have written:

MAKING HAY WHEN THE SUN SHONE: *doing his work when he had the opportunity*
INTIMATED: *hinted at*
EMANATES FROM: *had its source in*
CLOAKS: *conceals*

"Jack Archer", while travelling "Through Russian Snows", met "Captain Bayley's Heir", who had been "Through the Sikh War" as "One of the 28th" and was "True to the Old Flag", was swimming "In Greek Waters", being pursued by "The Tiger of Mysore", which had come "Through the Fray" "By Sheer Pluck". All of a sudden along came a man who was "The Bravest of the Brave" while "With Wolfe in Canada" and "With Clive in India"; he also showed valour "At Agincourt", which was "Won by the Sword" "By England's Aid", headed by "A Knight of the White Cross", who was with "Wulf the Saxon" and "Beric the Briton" in fighting "The Dragon and the Raven", which were "For the Temple", met "The Cat of Bubastes", followed by "The Young Carthaginian", who was "Condemned as a Nihilist" for killing "The Lion of the North" and "The Lion of St. Mark", which were owned by "The Young Colonist" and "Maori and Settler", who said they were "With Buller in Natal", and had come to arrest him as "A Jacobite Exile", with their colours "Orange and Green", in the name of "Bonnie Prince Charlie". It happened when on "St. Bartholomew's Eve" along came "St. George for England" "By Right of Conquest". "In Freedom's Cause" he was "Held Fast for England" "In the Reign of Terror". "Under Drake's Flag" he made "The Dash for Khartoum", which "With Lee in Virginia" "For Name and Fame" he fought and won "By Pike and Dyke", assisted by "Redskin and Cowboy". All this happened "When London Burned".

Trusting you will let me know if you receive this, and how you like the story, Yours very truly,

———————

Doubtless, as was often his custom, George Henty, who was proud of as well as amused by, the above letter, replied to the young writer. One would be glad to know.

In addition to the three-volume story, *A Search for a Secret*, mentioned earlier, Henty produced several more, so that he may claim to be one of those who saw out the old days which preceded the six-shilling novel. He concluded his series of novels with another secret—*Colonel Thorndykes'*—but this, like those which had preceded it, only achieved what the super-fine *littérateur* terms a *succès d'estime*, which is not the success beloved of the publisher, who has a bad habit of judging an author's merits by reference to his ledger and counting the number of copies sold. Henty's novels were well contrived and thought out, and full of interesting matter, but not one of them seemed to contain that unknown quality which nobody appears as yet to have been able to analyse, but which causes the British public to go reading mad over something which hits the fancy of the time. As a novelist he was unsuccessful; not that it mattered, for he soon laid the foundation of what was to prove an enduring fame, one which set an enormous clientele of young readers looking forward year by year for his next book or books—one, two, three, or even four per annum—until he had erected a literary column familiar in the bright young memories of thousands upon thousands of readers to whom the names of his works are well known.

In the long list of his other writings, *A Story of the Carlist Troubles*, another volume more modern and up-to-date, relating to the Sudan when Kitchener was in command, and a romance telling of a search for the treasure of the Peruvian kings, were among his last productions, while editions after editions of his earlier works kept on appearing, and were eagerly read. These new issues of his earlier books of course appealed to a much wider public than before, since the writer's popularity had gone on increasing with every fresh story from his pen.

SUPER-FINE: *refined*
LITTÉRATEUR: *"writer" in French*
SUCCÈS D'ESTIME: *"critical success" in French; a success with critics*
ANNUM: *year*

As is often the case with a young and enthusiastic writer, Henty in his early days made more than one attempt to publish his productions at his own cost, only to learn the severe lesson that these business transactions are matters of trade, and do not often prosper in the hands of an author.

One of his hardest fights was over the *Union Jack*,[1] which he edited for some years. It was a boys' journal, which ought to have succeeded, and over which he worked very hard both as author and editor; but somehow, in spite of the names of the able men whom he enlisted as his literary lieutenants, the sun of prosperity did not shine upon it brightly, and after a last effort, in which he took in new blood, he gave it up in disgust. He must have thought, after the fashion of others before him, that the success of periodicals is a matter of accident. It would be difficult indeed to come to any other conclusion when one sees the way in which clever and scholarly productions, fostered by the best literary ability, struggle into life and hold on to a precarious existence for a few brief weeks or months, and then die from lack of appreciation, while others that are perfect marvels of all that a magazine should not be, rush up into popularity and become, as it were, gold-mines to their proprietors.

So far as Henty was concerned, however, there is the consolation that whatever disappointments he may have had over his early productions, they formed a portion of the literary concrete upon which he raised a structure that made his name familiar to every young reader of his time.

---

[1] A boys' weekly magazine

TOOK IN NEW BLOOD: *hired new writers*

Chapter XL

An Appreciation

MUCH has been said about the writing of a boys' book and the changes that have taken place during the present generation or two. It may be taken into consideration that to go back to, say, 1830, there were hardly any books for a boy to read. We had *Evenings at Home* and *Robinson Crusoe*, of course, and there were some cheaply-issued stories by Pierce Egan the younger. A very attractive volume, too, was a tremendously thumbed and dog's-eared *Boy's Country Book*, by William Howitt. Marryat's and Cooper's works, with a few of Scott's, however, found plenty of favour with boys, who soon afterwards began to read Dickens, a writer who caught on with them at once. Soon after this Kingston and Ballantyne had the field almost to themselves, while the publishers were shy about publishing exclusively for boys; even to this day the trade, as it is termed, class books written especially for boys as juvenile literature. The term is correct, of course, for our recollections of Latin teach us that juvenile relates to youth; but to a boy the very term seems to suggest a toy-book, untearable, perhaps, with gaudy coloured pictures, and this begets in him a feeling of scorn. He does not want juvenile literature. His aim is to become a man and read what men do and have done. Hence the great success of George Henty's works. They are essentially manly, and he used to say that he wanted his boys to be bold, straightforward, and

THUMBED AND DOG'S-EARED: *well-worn*
BEGETS: *produces*

ready to play a young man's part, not to be milksops. He had a horror of a lad who displayed any weak emotion and shrank from shedding blood, or winced at any encounter. The result is shown again and again in his pages, and though some of his readers may object to the deeds of his heroes, no one could look down upon their vigour and determination. The fact is, he painted his own boyhood in all—the boy—the young man as he wished him to be, and the man.

There was a reality and power about Henty's work which caused many of his characters to be remembered long after the book had been laid aside, though, of course, it was not really characterization which was his forte, but rather the depicting of historical incidents and brave deeds on the frontiers of the empire. He did a great work for the boy reader in throwing open for him the big doorway of history. There was scarcely a book from his pen, and especially is this the case with the later ones, which did not serve to impress some important period of fighting or diplomatic action upon the mind of the reader. Knowledge thus gained is generally the most useful, for it is imbibed with avidity. Henty came out of long years of exciting work as a chronicler of things seen on the battlefields of the world, and he had the gift of ready portrayal, allied to a retentive and observant mind. Amidst the purple slopes and white walls of Italy he seemed as much at home as on the Venetian lagoons or in the forests of Germany. The entire panorama of the world was his sphere of action, and old-world romance suggestive of forgotten stairways and ancient palaces was, so to speak, a department in which he excelled. He could write as few men could of that mediæval tramp of crusading hosts, of glinting armour, of all that stirring pageantry of the old, old days which sometimes in the heat of interest makes our own time seem trivial and of poor account; and yet, although he possessed this key to romance, maybe he was really at his best

MILKSOPS: *wimps*
FORTE: *strength*
IMBIBED: *drunk in, absorbed*
LAGOONS: *waters*

in dealing with the thin red line of modern times. Still, among his older books, *The Cornet of Horse* stands out as pre-eminently strong and dramatic, and the account of a remarkable adventure during the campaign in the Netherlands,[1] when the commander, who was afterwards cited as "Marlbrouck" to naughty French children, defeated the French at Oudenarde and Malplaquet, is outlined clearly in the memory; so does the miller near Lille who befriended the young Englishman. The writing was strong, the colour vivid, and the reader had a bird's-eye view of what was passing at that time when Good Queen Anne was on the throne, and, as a bard put it, sometimes counsel took and sometimes tea, while in France the Grand Monarque[2] ruled as few kings have ever ruled before or since. It was a book that made boys think, giving them a wonderful impression of the time, making John Churchill a real live general, and showing why we went to war with France in defence of the stolid Dutch. Then a story of quite another type is probably still a first favourite, namely, *The Young Franc Tireurs*, which deals with the Franco-German War in a style to be expected from one who was there. How real is the talk between some German soldiers after the capture of Napoleon the Third!

The merit of these stories is their directness. No nervous under-view, no imagining of things which are not there, but the easy, straightforward writing of a manly Englishman who took things as they were, who disdained the building of structures on flimsy might-have-beens, but liked a solid foundation of fact. His campaigning stories brought the stress of war right home. He imparted a real touch to these with maps and charts. He had been close into so many firing lines that these tales had the ring of absolute truth, while he knew the soldier by heart and could depict him to life without any sham heroics or exaggeration. War's grim traffic had indeed few mysteries for the pleasant, frank Englishman who could talk

[1] Part of the War of Spanish Succession (1701-1714)
[2] Louis XIV (1638-1715)
THIN RED LINE: *British troops*
PRE-EMINENTLY: *supremely*

of the graver issues of life with distinction and advantage to the listener.

Far less known than his boys' books are his novels. Yet there is ingenuity and interest in such stories as *The Curse of Carnes Hold*, while through one and all of his works there is to be found a spirit of bold endeavour and a deep insight into the apparent puzzles of life. It was inevitable that a war correspondent who had had a front seat for years in the great arena of the world's happenings should know better than most men how events would shape themselves, and what occurrences might be looked for in the largest sphere of politics. Perhaps this acquaintance with the greater issues of life gave him more sympathy. He knew men, knew their failings, their ambitions. You met him in some springtime in the Strand with its unceasing rumble of traffic and its colour, and the glimpse of green at the end of a street leading to the Embankment Gardens, and you heard that he was just back from "over there," a long way beyond town and the Silver Streak,[1] maybe from Ashanti or Abyssinia. He had the warrior's look—the look of one who knows too much ever to be trivial—and the stirring days of European war were all familiar to him. Perhaps this is what gives even his books which deal with the long ago a vital interest. Fashions change; humanity scarcely at all. On the battlefield men are much the same as when Alexander swept southward with his legions to India, or when the great wars of the Middle Ages threatened to obliterate the arts. So it is that his historical books have a deep significance. Pick up one of these, and you are taken back into the dim old past, and realize why men fought, though the reasons for the warfare are now as cold as the watch fires of then. Here we have the grandeur of the chronicler's task. His to revive any latent ardour in a nation or an individual by drawing aside the curtain on what men did, and how they acted nobly for God and the king, for truth and the right, in the bygone

---

[1] The English Channel

OBLITERATE: *completely destroy*
EDICT: *proclamation*

days. Not in vain these wars, though the map of Europe has changed; and the historical writer who re-creates the best out of the stirring times that have lapsed, who shows in dramatic style why this gage of battle was thrown down, why that edict went out from Versailles, and what really was the inwardness of the long campaigns, which at a casual glance seem only to bewilder the mind, has a task which in importance is second to none. The young generation which has read his books and had its imagination fired will contain, of course, only a small percentage of soldiers, but the sense of grit and the dogged indomitable spirit to be derived from such works will stand in good stead to all, whether the battle be faced in the humdrum of daily life or actually with the forces of the king. Henty's was a grand influence for good in times of easy belittlement and cheap disparaging criticism of many of those elemental virtues which are nevertheless supreme in the making of a nation. He showed in rugged, graphic style what had been done—on tented field, in grim old mediæval castle. He recalled deeds which are a lesson for all time, and in his brilliant martial scenes there is the echo of the clash of arms. It does not require a poet to give value and significance to such a retrospect, though in this re-creation of past scenes, of the going and coming, the tramp of armies, the riding in of couriers to unfamiliar cities, there necessarily is much poetry as well as brave and heart-stirring effect, for in the panorama conjured up there is the whole sum of life, its doubt, its passion, and its tears.

As for his soldiers, they are excellent. The soldier is the soldier all the ages through—full of strange oaths, and with a particular view of things. In this connection it may be permissible to refer to the cosmopolitan side of Henty, to his intimate acquaintance with the byways of Europe, and to the undeniable grip he possessed of the European way of looking at matters— a way which is far more excitable than ours. He could talk of

DOGGED: *persistent*
ELEMENTAL: *simple*
RETROSPECT: *look at the past*
COSMOPOLITAN: *citizen of the world*

the days before the '70 War[1] which brought the Teuton into Alsace and made of fragmentary Germany a consolidated state; of the times when Bismarck was, comparatively speaking, a young man, and when men were more given to sonorous phrase-making than is the case at present. He had the "behind the scenes" attitude, and with reason, for a war correspondent, like a diplomatist, is the one who is there. He had met the leading men, the statesmen, the Herzog[2] of the Fatherland,[3] the Gospodar[4] of Holy Russia, and the hysterical agitator of Paris who seized the moment of his country's downfall venomously to compass further ruin, and in a lighter vein he had, too, all that rare anecdotal interest of the man who has met the bold Bulgar in Sofia and knows him *au fond,* and who has fraternized with the Serb in the questionable security of Belgrade.

Small wonder, indeed, that Henty, who knew of what the world was capable and what men could accomplish, held in light esteem the narrow but loud-talking cult which condemns patriotism, scoffs at civic merit, and would reduce society to an unsatisfactory incoherent brew. He was one of those whose influence makes for the greatness of England, an England which will fight, if duty really calls, at one of those crises in a nation's life which show which is the true worth and which the base.

His stories reflect the man, and their great and enduring success among boys, who are perhaps the most difficult of all to satisfy, must be looked for in part in the great seriousness with which he went to work. There was no difficulty about his style, which was as smooth-running as the Thames, and no parade, while he pleased his readers especially by a simple, unaffected touch of confidence and certainly attractive suggestion of doing his utmost to satisfy the legion who looked to him for literary

---

[1] The Franco-German War (1870-1871)   [2] Duke
[3] Germany   [4] Prince

SONOROUS: *rich, impressive-sounding*
COMPASS: *plot*
AU FOND: *"thoroughly" in French*
BASE: *worthless*

fare. With such a character, typical of many, as Signor Polani in *The Lion of St. Mark*, he showed his really great skill in portraiture; and though season by season his books were reviewed as boys' books, there was much that necessarily escaped the notice of the critic, much that was as deeply imaginative and inwardly significant as passages in genre stories which received a larger measure of the critic's attention. It could not have come as any particular disappointment to Henty when he found that his *métier* was writing boys' books rather than novels. We are told that there are many people who can write novels, and maybe with certain qualifications this is true, but there are comparatively few who can write for, and please, the exacting boy. The latter severe, if not absolutely erudite, critic may not be able to define precisely what he wants, but he knows enough to be certain that Henty could and did supply the requisite article. He knew, like a great artist, what to leave out, which knowledge is the prime factor in the making of the greatest works. It was the intuitive perception of where the youthful imagination required to come into play. It was grateful, gracious work this, of supplying boys with literature which held them engrossed and helped them to think, and think well. Youth has its troubles, its little ennuis, its griefs, the same as the rest of the world, and despite disparity in years these phases are not to be considered in miniature, for the imagination is larger and more elastic in early days, and trouble assumes a very extended front. The boy who is plagued by a dead tongue, or the perversity of circumstance, or any other worriment of the flying day, as likely as not picks up his favourite author to help him to forget the suggestion of the presence of black care.

The name of Henty became one to refer to in another sort of literature—the smart afternoon paper with its flippant

GENRE STORIES: *styles of stories*
MÉTIER: *greatest strength*
ERUDITE: *learned*
ENNUIS: *boredoms*
DISPARITY: *difference*
BLACK CARE: *troubles*

dialogues referred to him jocularly as the panacea for boys.
It was all correct enough. The boys worshipped him; and for
years he went on working, pushing as it were into untouched
galleries in his mining after fresh subjects—and the simile may
be allowed, as even Carlyle speaks of the pursuit of literature
as subterranean labour. He never lost a point. No work was too
arduous, no preparation too exacting; and as regards many
of his books, a vast amount of "prep," as students dub their
preliminary labours, was entailed. He would have accuracy if
history had to be dealt with, and through all the years during
which he was delving for new treasures in the lumber rooms
or cellars of the past, he kept up his custom of carefully studying each phase or epoch before he commenced his romance
or made ready his mould. He imbibed many tomes to make
one.

It is a great mistake to place any reliance on the glib statements concerning the length of time that a book takes to write.
Henty gave an interviewer certain facts, but it must have been
with an inward smile, since all such figures are misleading,
though not intentionally so. One man will take five months to
write a book, another two, and so on, for there is practically no
limit one way or the other; but the lay observer who hears such
statements as these generally makes a gross misuse of them,
and in his calculations as to how many books a man may write
a year, absolutely forgets that in writing time is not a very accurate vehicle for arriving at an estimate.

The author lays down his pen and goes to his club to dine,
but he takes his work with him; it is keeping him close company
in the train, and a new situation, or the germ of an additional
complication, is woven into the scenery as he is being borne
townwards. He cannot escape. Nothing is more pertinacious
than an unfinished character; while in the cab as likely as not
one of his creations is sitting by him, insisting on his being

JOCULARLY: *jokingly*
PANACEA: *cure-all*
PERTINACIOUS: *stubborn*
SATELLITE: *supporting character*

allowed a little more elbow-room, or a minor satellite peers at him through the judas in the roof. That is to say, there are no early hours, so-called, for writers, no getting away from work and comfortably shutting up the shop. It is not in the nature of things that this should be so. The writer has never done, and practically every thousand words composed by Henty was the result of long and careful prior work and thought.

As regards many of his stories, he admitted starting them on the "go-as-you-please" system; that is to say, events and characters were allowed to shape themselves in their own way; but then it must be remembered that Henty had a good store to work upon, and that he had, moreover, accustomed himself, through many years of press work, to quickness of thought and the swift maturing of the line of reasoning, since in writing for newspapers the man who hesitates is lost, for the master printer takes no denial.

In popularity he may be reckoned to have passed W. H. G. Kingston and R. M. Ballantyne, while he was, as it were, quite level with Captain Mayne Reid and Jules Verne; the last-named writer's skeleton frameworks rather than romances had deservedly an enormous vogue, partly because of their tremendous scope, and also on account of the fillip they gave to the imagination of the young reader. With such a man as Henty it seems like begging the question to speak of "atmosphere;" but by whatever name that intangible quality is designated, certain it is that Henty possessed himself of it before he started work. Francis Hammond in his gondola in old-world Venice, or Mademoiselle de Pignerol in the days of the Grand Monarque, are all part and parcel of their respective times, and it is this ring of truth which makes his stories prevail. The neurotic was as far from Henty as are the poles asunder; but in giving to boyhood something more substantial to dream about than "the gay castles of the clouds that pass,"[1] in the story of

---

[1] Lines from the poem, *The Castle of Indolence,* by James Thomson

JUDAS: *peep hole*

VOGUE: *popularity*

NEUROTIC: *emotionally unstable person*

the azure main, of England's greatness, and the whole stirring, many-coloured panorama of ancient days and battles fought on the other side of uncounted sunsets, it is reasonable to imagine that at times he lived and perhaps almost lost himself in the old world which he re-created. The man who knew the byways of history as he did would be graceless and inconsistent if he did not feel the grandeur of all those things, seen for a flying moment down the winding turret stairway as the curtain is drawn aside. It is as good to regard his masterly treatment of historic themes as it is painful to witness the wretched spectacle of feeble handling of subjects vast as these. Life, as Macbeth said, is but a walking shadow; but there is a good deal of reality in it too, and there was nothing visionary about the people Henty created: they were genial, good-humoured, time-serving, sluggish, magnificent, or Boeotian, as circumstance and occasion warranted, while in delineating a soldier of our time his hand was unerring. His sketch of the linesman or the trooper was as true as that of the medieval Spaniard in his shabby cloak, the plump landlady of the inn, the bragging mountebank in questionable buskins, the adventurer ready to sell his sword to the highest bidder, or any other of the sometimes brilliant, sometimes lack-lustre company with whom he had to deal on that broad white route of historical romance which it was given to him to traverse that others might appreciate these things. It is not only a question of boys, for many an old stager whose life now is his club, likes these breezy, healthy stories, and enjoys meeting once more the grave signors who managed the political world in the bygone, and saluting yet once again the kings whose weaknesses and whose grandeur filled a world that has vanished. And his treatment of these legends, or facts, as the case may be, is full of charm, just as his writing is simple and sincere and instinct with the insight of a mind which had that greatest of all gifts—the gift of keeping young.

AZURE MAIN: *blue sea*
VISIONARY: *imaginary*
BOEOTIAN: *ignorant*
IN QUESTIONABLE BUSKINS: *playing a part*

A Corner of G. A. Henty's Library

CHAPTER XLI

PERSONAL NOTES

HENTY'S study was an ideal room for a writer, with all kinds of suggestive objects around, such as would be useful to a man who wrote about war's alarms; for he did not go upon any of his adventurous journeys without keeping in mind the walls of the study, which was practically a museum. It must be quite five-and-twenty years since, after dining with him one evening, Henty took the writer into his den to show and describe (from out of the cloud emitted by a favourite brier-root pipe which he used steadily) the various weapons hanging from the walls, some of which were very beautiful, in spite of the purpose for which they had been formed. One memorable, clumsy-looking, straight, two-edged sword seemed to be about as unsuitable for causing destruction and death as it could have been made. It was Indian, of considerable length, and peculiar in this way. The armourer who made it had so contrived that the hilt was fused, as it were, into a gauntlet for the protection of the knuckles of the man who wielded it, and the handle was exactly the reverse of that joined to an ordinary sword, for the warrior who grasped it would have to take hold at right angles to the course of the blade, in fact, precisely as a gardener would take hold of a spade. To us this seems a curious clumsy fashion, but it is one which we find repeated in many of the Indian knives or daggers, and to some extent in the Malay creese, which, roughly speaking, bears round towards right angles like the butt of a horse pistol.

On commenting upon the peculiarity of the great Indian sword, and the impossibility of a man using it to thrust, or make an adequate cut, Henty rose from his seat and gave the writer an exemplification of how such a weapon would be used by a native foot-soldier in a mêlée. Single-handed, he would rush into a crowd with outstretched arm stiffened by the steel gauntlet-like hilt, and would clear a space all round him by the murderous sweep of the blade which he wielded, turning himself into a sort of human windmill. In fact, in the hands of a strong man it was about the most horrible, butcher-like weapon ever invented for the destruction of human life. By comparison, as the great blade was replaced with its fellows, a far preferable death would have been inflicted by a gracefully-curved, razor-edged, exquisitely forged and grained Damascus blade. This had probably been the pride of some Mahratta chief, some keen, dark, aquiline-nosed soldier whose hands must have been as delicate as a woman's, for the hilt of this, as well as those of its fellows upon the wall, seemed toy-like in the grip of such a man as Henty.

He possessed quite a museum of such objects as these, and his armoury of trophies went on growing till his death, when he was the possessor of an endless number of choice little treasures. These were considerably added to by his son, Captain C. G. Henty, in the shape of weapons collected during the late Boer War (where he distinguished himself in command of the detachment of volunteers of the London Irish Rifles), and by another son during the latter's adventurous life in the Wild West.

A treasure of Henty's own collecting was a beautiful suit of Northern Indian armour, exquisitely damascened and inlaid

CREESE: *a dagger with a wavy blade*
EXEMPLIFICATION: *illustration*
MÊLÉE: *hand-to-hand fight*
MAHRATTA: *a native of central India*
AQUILINE-NOSED: *eagle-nosed*

with gold, the skullcap-like spiked helmet being provided with sliding face-guard and hood of chain mail, while the almost gauze-like steel shirt, with sleeves, breast, and arm-plates of beautiful workmanship, were all perfect. From Abyssinia came a silver shield, massive and brilliantly polished, and trophy after trophy had been garnered in other countries, including weapons from China and Japan. About one and all of these treasures, from the most costly weapons to the spears, arrows, and shields of savage warfare, the owner could discourse eloquently and well, for concerning each he had some history or anecdote to tell.

He was much liked in the little social company he affected, and here his discourse and ways seemed to show how warmly he felt towards his companions; while of his thorough sincerity he unobtrusively gave them most ample proof.

In such coteries of literary and artistic men, workers for the ordinary income as well as for the praise of the world, there are, of course, some who prosper far beyond their highest hopes, and, sad to say, more who, in spite of every effort, only gain disappointment, with its concomitants—poverty and despair. It was in such cases as these that, with evident care that his action should not hurt the feelings of a friend, Henty's hand, so to speak, glided unseen towards his pocket, to plunge in pretty deeply, and return far better filled than those of his fellows who had taken similar action. And this was not from the possession of wealth, but from true fellow-feeling and generosity of heart.

He numbered fewer friends, perhaps, than others who were his colleagues and fellow-workers, but those whom he classed as intimates were of the more sterling metal, stamped with the brand of solidity, and the most lasting in their wear; while they on their side, possibly from their being the choice of one who,

COTERIES: *groups*
CONCOMITANTS: *accompaniments*
INTIMATES: *close personal friends*
MORE STERLING METAL: *most excellent quality*

after the long gatherings of experience, was no mean judge of human nature, were no doubt as staunch as he. Certainly they enjoyed the satisfaction of being numbered among his friends.

Washington Irving, in his *Knickerbocker Papers*, when describing the sages among the old Dutch settlers in the Hudson region, refers to the way in which they were looked up to for their wisdom and for the character they obtained and kept by much smoking and preserving silence, in addition to never being found out. This comes to mind when thinking over Henty's quiet, stolid way in after-dinner communion at his clubs. He always looked calm, grave, and thoughtful, but, unlike the old Dutch settlers recorded by that charming American writer, he did think; he thought deeply, but spoke little. When he did open his lips though, he was outspoken, plain, straightforward, and to the point.

As a rule he left speaking to those who were gifted, or cursed, with fluency. Debating was a horror to be avoided and denounced; but all the same it was no unusual thing for him to be chosen to preside at a social dinner, or to take the chair at a committee meeting, and when this happened he always distinguished himself.

A fellow-member of one of his clubs supplies the writer with a characteristic anecdote, which carries with it an impression of the downright, straightforward character and outspoken nature of Henty in his utter detestation of sharp practice in every form. The incident occurred during the after-dinner conversation, throughout which the subject of this memoir sat like a modern literary Jupiter in the midst of the clouds of smoke which he had largely helped to evolve. Out of this smoke he could be seen glowering at one of the speakers. This man was a stranger to him, and he had listened to him in silence, quite unaware that he was a city journalist connected with one of the

STAUNCH: *steadfast*
SAGES: *wise men*
TAKE THE CHAIR: *serve as chairman*
DETESTATION: *hatred*
SHARP PRACTICE: *deceit*

financial papers. The speaker had been making a great and verbose use of his knowledge of his own particular subject, and for a long time Henty had sat and frowned at him. No better term could possibly be found for describing my old friend's aspect at the time. It suggested a revival of Samuel Johnson[1] visiting his old haunts, and those who knew Henty became silent listeners too, in the full expectation that he would be moved to show his displeasure, and would make some remark upon the revelations about the peculiar ways of transacting business occasionally carried out in the neighbourhood of Throgmorton Street.

But Jupiter was still silent, and the fluent speaker prattled on about bulls and bears, about the great *coups* that were made, and about the immense profits of some and the heavy losses and ruin of the weak and foolish who, in the fierce race for wealth, were tempted in their folly into city gambling.

Matters went on, and Henty grew more heated. The smoke of his brier pipe rolled out in increased volume; his eyes grew more fierce; but no interruption came, and as he still remained silent, a feeling of disappointment began to grow among those who knew him best. He was only waiting, however, until the financial discourse died out, not for want of material, since, unfortunately, that is always too plentiful, but more probably on account of weariness on the speaker's part. Then, to the great satisfaction of Henty's listeners, he growled out: "Well, have you done? Now I will tell you what I think about financial newspapers and their conductors—they are a set of confounded thieves."

It is recorded of him that he was upon one occasion called upon to preside at a meeting in which someone was suspected of having been a defaulter in a case in which full confidence had been placed. It was a serious matter, one which had been

---

[1] Samuel Johnson (1709-1784) was an influential English writer, literary critic and moralist.

VERBOSE: *wordy*

BULLS AND BEARS: *the movements of the stock market*

CONDUCTORS: *directors*

fully discussed, and at last it fell to Henty's lot to give something like the casting vote. He had been seated very silently, full of severe earnestness, till with stern, solemn dignity he stood up to speak, his words shaping themselves for some time like those of a prosecuting counsel, till at last he finished by being almost denunciatory in tone, as with grim irony he exclaimed: "And then he told us that lie! Now, why should he have told us such a lie as that, when he knew very well that he must be found out? If he wanted to tell a lie," he continued, his voice growing more cutting in his bitter sarcasm, "why did he not choose one that we had not a chance of finding out?"

G. A. Henty at 60

CHAPTER XLII

CLUB LIFE

HENTY was a man who always enjoyed mixing with his fellows, and being constantly associated with members of the fourth estate, it was quite natural that he should join certain clubs. It followed therefore that, as years rolled by in a long life, he had a pretty good list in the way of membership to his name.

He was, of course, a member of various yachting clubs; but coming to literary gatherings, he early became a member of the world-known Savage,[1] which he joined in its old days, and his was a familiar, quiet, thoughtful face at the weekly dinners, while he was a welcome and trusted chairman at the gatherings of the committee. Later, without giving up his membership, he joined, consequent upon some little tiff, the select band of the oldest members, who formed what, if they had been members of St. Stephen's, would have been called the Cave of Adullam.[2] Here, however, the little branch or lodge was dubbed the Wigwam, whose cognizance, still printed on the circulars which announce the chairman and the date of the next dinner, is a clever sketch of a Red Indian's wigwam. This was drawn by a clever artist member, who has passed away almost as these lines are being written—namely, Wallis Mackay. The skin lodge is looped back to display a group of occupants in full war-paint, feathers, and blanket, seated smoking. These represent in

[1] A social club for gentlemen formed in London in 1857
[2] The cave where David hid from King Saul in I Samuel 22:1-5
FOURTH ESTATE: *journalists*
TIFF: *quarrel*
COGNIZANCE: *badge*

admirable likeness a few familiar members, numbering, among others, Tegetmeier the naturalist, Henry Lee of Brighton Aquarium and of octopus celebrity, and Ravenstein the geographer, while, glass in eye, raising himself like a look-out from the smoke aperture at the top, there are the unmistakable features of the late J. L. Toole. To name one more, there is the subject of this memoir. It is a playful little skit, with a grim caricature in the distance shaped like a skeleton, suspended from a blasted tree, as if suggestive of the fate of an intruder, while plainly written upon one of the folds of the skin tent is "No admission except on business."

For many years also Henty's was a face heartily welcomed as a friend and fellow clubman at the quiet little social tavern club known as the Whitefriars, a club at which in its early days politics was tabooed. But as years passed on times altered, and political and social debate became the rule, much to Henty's annoyance. His idea of a club was that it should be a gathering-place where a few old friends, freed for the time being from quill-driving and thinking out books, leading articles, and other brain-worrying tasks, should meet for a social chat, and where there should be no delivering of speeches, no debates. So soon, therefore, as this debating and speech-delivering became the custom, Henty began to talk to those with whom he was most intimate of withdrawing his name from the club. Such a proceeding, it was pointed out to him, would be depriving his oldest friends of his company. He seemed to see the force of this, and matters went on, and a proposal he had made to a few friends that they should follow the example of the dwellers in the Wigwam and meet together in peace, seemed to have died out. Nevertheless Henty was a man of very strong political feeling, and possessed all the firm attributes of a thoroughly stanch Conservative gentleman, one might say Tory, of the

APERTURE: *opening or hole*
CARICATURE: *exaggerated picture*
TABOOED: *prohibited*
QUILL-DRIVING: *writing*
TRUCULENT: *aggressive*

past. If he had taken a motto, his would have been that of the old *John Bull* newspaper: "God, the Sovereign, and the People." Throughout his life, though gentle and kindly by nature, he was, when roused by what he looked upon as injustice or cowardice, a fierce and truculent Briton, ready to defy the whole world.

On the whole, though, perhaps from its propinquity to the newspaper world, Henty was most frequently seen at that centre of which the late Andrew Halliday wrote that the qualification for admission was to be "a working-man in literature or art, and a good fellow." Of course the rendezvous meant is the Savage Club—that place "apart from the chilling splendour of the modern club"—the club over which so many disputes have taken place amongst its members as to its title, as to whether it borrows it from poor, improvident Richard Savage, or from its supposed Bohemian savagery. Be that as it may, it is certainly the spot where the bow of everyday warfare is unstrung and set aside.

It has long been the custom here to invite to dine at the social Saturday evening gathering pretty well everyone who has become famous, and whose name is upon the public lips, and these invitations have been accepted by warrior and statesman, by our greatest artists and travellers, whether they have sought to discover the Boreal mysteries or to cross the Torrid Zone. Even those who have become great rulers have not disdained to accept "Savage" hospitality, and upon such nights some popular or distinguished member of the club is called upon to take the chair. Now it so happens that there is extant a copy of the menu of a dinner, drawn by one of the cleverest members, which depicts in quaint, characteristic, and light-hearted fashion the imaginary proceedings and post-prandial entertainment connected with the aforesaid unstrung bow. In the case in question Lord Kitchener was the guest, fresh from

IMPROVIDENT: *thoughtless*
BOHEMIAN: *unconventional*
BOREAL: *northern*
TORRID ZONE: *the tropics*
POST-PRANDIAL: *after dinner*

his victories in the Sudan, and no better chairman could have been chosen than the popular war correspondent, George Henty, whose portrait and that of the famous general occupy the centre of the dinner card represented here.

It would be difficult to over-estimate the interest of such a typical meeting at the club, one which had naturally drawn together a crowded gathering of men who had more or less deeply cut their names upon the column of popularity, if not of fame.

The names of the general and war correspondent attracted to that dinner a distinguished company; the singer possessed of sweet tenor voice or deepest bass; the musician who excelled as pianist or who could bring forth the sweetest tones from the strings; the flautist; the skilful prestidigitator who puzzled the gathering with the latest Egyptian card trick, but who will amuse no more; the clever actor ready to give expression to some recitation, serious or laughable; the delineator of quaint phases of life; the artist whose works have provoked thought and admiration in the picture galleries; the scientist with the secrets of his laboratory gradually developing into life-saving and labour-economizing reforms; to say nothing of the keen-visaged diplomatist whose range covers the mysteries of the chancelleries of Europe and cabinets where whispers are sacred and policies are shaped; and the writer to whom the wide world is but the sunning ground of cogitation.

At the club's improvised concerts and entertainments all are ready to amuse or be amused; even the learned judge and the argumentative counsel who takes his brief from some clever lawyer, now his companion for the evening, meet the eye of physician or surgeon upon common ground.

Later, the deeply-engaged actor, when his part is at an end, comes in straight from the boards, bringing with him the

---

FLAUTIST: *flute player*
PRESTIDIGITATOR: *someone who performs slight of hand tricks*
DELINEATOR: *portrayer*
CHANCELLERIES: *embassies*
CABINETS: *governing councils*
SUNNING GROUND: *resting place*

buoyancy and imaginativeness of the strange fantastic realm where he is so popular—a realm so different from all others, although merely divided from the commonplace world by a row of lights.

Here all are friends, gathered by the attractions of music, song, and repartee. Men who have striven greatly all their lives and have gained much, and maybe lost something too, are here in good fellowship. Irksome trammels for the time are cast aside, permitting one and all to partake of what seems to be like a whiff of ozone or a breath from the pine-scented Surrey hills, after the contracted arena of the struggle for life.

On the particular occasion referred to above, supported as he was by those who had shared his past and been his companions and the witnesses of many a deadly battle, Henty was thoroughly at home; and it was a happy choice of a chairman which brought him to preside on that November evening when Kitchener was the special guest.

It was only a few short months after Kitchener's crowning victory at Omdurman, which had finally crushed the Dervish power and set Slatin and his fellow captives free, and established law and order at Khartoum and through the immense territories which separate that city from Cairo. It was, therefore, a bright idea that inspired Oliver Paque, to give him his *nom de plume*, in his merry caricature to depict the gallant general as a *beau sabreur* leading a charge at full gallop and riding in to the feast. He is seen, as the illustration shows, leaping triumphantly through a circus paper hoop supported by a swarthy Sudanese, and the tatters of the paper ingeniously form the map of Africa. Right through Africa he leaps, as it were, into the fire of cheers and applause that greet him—into the smoke of the "Savage" pipe of peace, started by the chairman.

COGITATION: *reflective thought*
BRIEF: *information regarding a legal case*
BOARDS: *stage*
REPARTEE: *witty conversation*
IRKSOME TRAMMELS: *troublesome restraints*
NOM DE PLUME: *pen name*

THRILLING TALES OF HISTORY & ADVENTURE

GEORGE DEAR, YOU MUST GO TO BED & READ THAT TOMORROW

...TY-FIRST

...IVERSARY

...INNER

...: SAT.Y 26.TH

...1898

A DASH FOR KHARTOUM

TRUE TO THE OLD FLAG

THROUGH FRAY

BY RIGHT OF CONQUEST

HELD FAST FOR ENGLAND

BY ENGLAND'S AID

...ENU

...HITSTABLE NATIVES

...CHABLIS

...OUPS

...TURTLE

...SICILIENNE

...ERRY SHRRY

...FISH

SUPREME OF SOLE MARQUERY
FRIED SMELTS AU CITRON
HOCK

ENTREES
LARKS FARCIE EN COCOTTE
SWEETBREADS PIQUE RENAISSANCE
CHAMPAGNE - LOUIS ROEDERER 1893
MAX SUTAINE 1889

A LOT TO DO

PUNCH A LA ROMAINE

SWEETS
COSMOPOLITAN PUDDING
TIMBALES A LA RUSSE
MACEDOINE JELLY
ICE PUDDING

ROAST
PHEASANT BARDE SUR CROUSTADE
COMPOTE

LIQUEURS
CHEESE — CELERY
DESSERT

GEO:
A-HENTY
in the Chair

REMOVES
SADDLE OF MUTTON & RED CURRANT JELLY
BRUSSELS SROUTS DUCHESSE POTATOES
YORK HAM AU MADEIRA
SPINACH AU JUS

I WILL NOW SHOW YOU
THE CELEBRATED EGYPTIAN
CARD TRICK

BRO SAVAGES

...IV. WE'LL CONQUEOR

...OR WE'LL DIE.

WELCOME
TO THE
SAVAGE CLUB
HON. SEC.

SOUDAN PUNCH

PORT . CLARET . CAFE NOIR

But that memorable night is not so far back in the Hinterland that one has any need to strain the memory assiduously for the leading details of historic incidents sketched in upon the menu card. The tattered indication of a map recalls Major Marchand and his march across desert and through forest and swamp to Fashoda. There are pleasant suggestions, too, in the tribute paid to the chairman by the artist's pencil, which playfully deals with the fame the chairman had reaped by his books. Boys are shown eagerly reading his thrilling tales of history and adventure, a young mother is depicted admonishing a lad who is engrossed in some stirring work, while the list of titles—*A Dash for Khartoum, True to the Old Flag, Through the Fray, By Right of Conquest, Held Fast for England*—is alone a tribute to the sturdy chairman, for though titles only they illustrate the feelings of a patriotic man.

The pen-painter of the merry scene, indeed, notwithstanding the grotesqueness of the work, has contrived to suggest by many a happy touch little peculiarities in the individualities of his subjects. Thus he gives a wonderful likeness of such a familiar member as Dan Godfrey, the well-known band-master of the Guards, who is shown leading the concert in heroic bearskin what time Handel's march of "The Conquering Hero" is blown by one of the most popular humorists of the club. The name of another member—Slaughter—seems by the irony of fate to be singularly apposite at a war correspondent's banquet, while the drum and cymbals and the tom-tom tell their own tale as beaten by members whose faces are familiar to those behind the scenes. Everything, in short, tended to make this dinner a great success.

Sometimes when taking the chair, however, at one of these club dinners, Henty would fancy that the attendance was not so good as it might have been, and attributing it to a want of

HINTERLAND: *remote past*
ASSIDUOUSLY: *diligently*
GROTESQUENESS: *unusual appearance*
APPOSITE: *suitable*

popularity, he would turn to the writer and whisper with almost a sigh, "Another frost!" This quaint bit of dramatic slang is, of course, popularly used in the theatrical world when the British public displays a tendency not to throng the seats, and there is a grim array of empty benches to crush all the spirit out of the actors in some clever piece. It was quite a mistake, though, to use it in connection with Henty's dinners, for he was always surrounded by plenty of warm-hearted friends whose presence and sunshiny aspect were sufficient to set the wintry chill of unsociability at defiance.

THRONG: *crowd*

CHAPTER XLIII

HIS GREAT HOBBY

PROBABLY Henty never so much enjoyed release from his
workshop study as when he could get on board his yacht,
the *Egret*. He was especially fond of this boat, which was really a
most comfortable vessel, not built upon racing lines, but somewhat reminding one of the small cruising schooners which
were fashionable at Cowes in the sixties and early seventies.[1]

He had an honest, plain-spoken skipper and crew, who knew
their business thoroughly, and they evidently looked upon the
owner as more of a friend than a captain. One of his favourite
cruising-grounds was the estuary of the Thames. The yacht
would sometimes lie off Leigh, and sometimes up the Medway.
The locality is not one which many other yachtsmen would
choose, for there are shoals and tidal eccentricities that require
a watchful eye. Owner and skipper, however, knew every inch of
that broad waterway.

Henty's cabin lay aft, and was well lighted from the deck. It
was thoroughly roomy, and by an ingenious contrivance the
luxury of a bath could at any time be indulged in, through
merely lifting a panel from the floor.

To see Henty at his most peaceful stage was to watch him lying back high upon the pillows on the deck of his yacht reading
some favourite author. This would generally be an old friend,

[1] 1860's and early 1870's
ESTUARY: *mouth*
SHOALS: *sandbars*
TIDAL ECCENTRICITIES: *unusual tides*
GALLEY: *ship's kitchen*

G. A. Henty's Yacht "The Egret"

for like many another, he was fond of renewing his acquaintance with writers who had attracted him in the years gone by.

The galley was in charge of a good substantial sea cook, who could turn out a plain meal that was sufficient for any reasonable man's wants, though it need not be explained in detail that in the appointments of the state rooms and main cabin table there was no affectation of luxury. The yacht would be always well provisioned with joints that not only admitted, but invited a cut-and-come-again principle.

Of course, everybody who knew Henty could, all his life through, testify to his perfect abstemiousness. In fact, one has known many instances in which the serious warning spoken by Henty to young colleagues, who were with him on journalistic expeditions, saved them from much mischief. He would deliver his little lecture on a weakness which he had noticed, and

APPOINTMENTS: *furnishings*
AFFECTATION: *pretense*
JOINTS: *cuts of meat*
CUT-AND-COME-AGAIN: *second helpings*
ABSTEMIOUSNESS: *self-control*

invariably finish with, "Pardon me for being so free, old chap, but if you take my advice you will watch it."

Except when he went across the North Sea, the yachting cruises were of fairly long weekend duration, but sooner or later the yacht would be passing in review whatever naval operations were on the way at Sheerness,[1] while a favourite mooring for the night was up towards Chatham[2] at a spot where there was a wood on the northern bank.

Henty always seemed to the manner born when on board his yacht, and an early cup of coffee, in pyjamas on deck, sometimes not a great while after sunrise, was invariably indulged in. This was followed, of course, by the faithful pipe, which, indeed, was in constant action from morning to night.

He was a man who used to attribute his good health and spirits as much to his yacht as to anything in the world, and more than once his friends, in commenting upon his love for the sea, have declared that no better representative of the old sea kings of England could have been seen afloat than George Alfred Henty. No one really saw him at his best who did not see him in rough weather, bare-headed, with the wind whistling through his grey hair, and the foam torn from the waves bedewing his big beard and making his suntanned, bronzed visage glisten, as he stood at the wheel, firm of aspect, gazing defiantly before him in a kind of rapture, and thoroughly enjoying life the while he ploughed the waves. If any endorsement of this were needed by the reader who never met the subject face to face, let him turn to the photograph showing Henty reading the proofs of his last book aboard his yacht. The portrait was taken not long before his death, and gives a far better idea to the reader of the big, bluff, sturdy war correspondent than would pages of writing.

For he was born to be a sailor, and the wonder is that he did not develop into being the captain of some great liner, instead

---

[1] The site of a naval dockyard
[2] A town on the southeastern coast of England
TO THE MANNER BORN: *born for it*
BEDEWING: *covering with dew*
PLOUGHED: *sailed through*

of a wielder of the pen. One striking phase in his character that was developed in his yachting pursuits was that, though he thoroughly enjoyed inviting and having the company of some old friend on board, to whom he was the most genial and hospitable of hosts, he was yet perfectly happy when alone with his crew. At such times he would carry out various manœuvres, and quite contentedly occupy himself with his own thoughts.

One man will make friend and companion of a faithful dog; another is never more content than when he is with his horse. To Henty, from quite early in life, his yacht took the place of some living sentient being—his yacht and its movement, whether driven forward under the pressure of a light breeze, or throbbing beneath his feet as it bounded and leaped from wave to wave in a gale. For he was no smooth-water sailor, but had grown into a hardened and masterly mariner, who thoroughly understood the varied caprices of the deep.

He would generally manage to be afloat somewhere about Easter, for a few days each week, cruising, as has been said, about the mouth of the Thames, and once in a way he would shoot across to Heligoland[1] for the Emperor's Cup race. He seldom studied much about the weather so long as he could be well afloat; though at times he would encounter a furious gale out in the open sea, and get what he himself termed a thorough good knocking about.

He related to a friend that upon one occasion he passed through a fearful gale, with the force of the wind so great that he and his crew ran two hundred and sixty knots in twenty-seven hours, putting in at Harwich without shipping a bucket of water in the run home.

One of Henty's greatest regrets when the weather was fairly fine was that his literary avocations prevented him from being oftener afloat. This was especially the case at times when there

---

[1] An island off the German coast

SENTIENT: *feeling*
CAPRICES: *changing impulses*
SHIPPING A BUCKET OF WATER: *taking in any water over the side*

was war or rumour of war, for then he would be on duty at the *Standard* waiting for the brief telegrams that came in at all hours from Reuter's and elsewhere. These were brought to him, as before mentioned, to be expanded from their key-like brevity into plain straightforward reading for the printers to set up.

As already stated, in this favourite pursuit of yachting Henty heartily enjoyed the companionship of friends who liked the sea, but at the same time if men of similar tastes did not present themselves, he was well content to be alone. A thoroughly social man, he had his own strong ideas upon companionship. He set limits to such a means of enjoyment, and he could speak out very strongly against excursion trips in which he was asked to take part. "I like to see things," he said. "I like to go into the country on a little trip to see some object of interest, or to pay a visit to some historic town, but I don't like these excursion trips, and I won't go!" Alluding to the parties of "trippers" so numerous in summer weather, who make our railway stations unpleasant for those who wish to travel, he denounced them in the most forcible way. "I like to go," he said, "with a few fellows in a friendly way. What I object to is going in a mob." In plain English, it touched Henty's pride to visit some excursionist haunt where he felt that his party would be classed as beanfeasters, or what is known as the members of a wayzgoose, and he resented the whole position as unworthy of the dignity of a literary man.

Henty's love of yachting began early in life, when he was holding a commission in the army and stationed at Kingstown, where he owned a ten-tonner called *The Pet*. It was his first craft, and very nearly proved to be his last, for upon one occasion he had been out sailing with his little crew for some distance, and had the misfortune to be caught in a heavy gale,

BREVITY: *shortness*
BEAN-FEASTERS: *people celebrating a beanfeast, or company dinner*
WAYZGOOSE: *a group outing made by the employees of a printer or newspaper*

which gave him and his men a very severe lesson in seamanship. There was a tremendous sea, and before they were able to make the harbour, and anchor, their position was so perilous that a huge crowd collected, in momentary expectation of seeing the yacht go down, for it was impossible for her crew to land.

To make matters worse, and to add to the excitement, the officer's young wife was one of those who joined the crowd, and she kept appealing in her agony of mind to the sea-going men around to save her husband's life. Finally a boat was manned by a sturdy party, and with great difficulty the little crew were brought ashore in safety. This was early in the sixties, and after that, enthusiastic yachtsman though he was, his avocations and absence from England put a stop to his sea-going till about 1887, when, opportunity serving, he bought an old life-boat and converted her into a yacht. The buoyancy of her build attracted him, and for some years this little thirteen-ton vessel, the *Kittiwake* as he called her (and well did she deserve her name),[1] afforded him a long series of pleasant runs.

But previous to owning the *Kittiwake* Henty became possessed of a small half-decked canoe, which afforded him an opportunity of bringing to bear that inventive genius which at different periods of his career had induced him to try his hand at various contrivances, any one of which might have brought him fame and fortune such as came to a fellow-member of his club in connection with a torpedo that was taken over by the British government. At one time he constructed a spar torpedo. This was during the American Civil War, and upon its completion he offered it to the United States authorities. Another of his ideas, also of a warlike character, was an invention the necessity of which he had probably seen practically demonstrated. This was a contrivance for the practice of long-range firing where

---

[1] The kittiwake is a type of seabird.

SPAR TORPEDO: *a torpedo held on the end of a spar (pole); designed to be rammed into an enemy ship*

opportunity did not serve, that is to say, in a limited space of ground. By means of Henty's arrangement, practice up to a thousand or twelve hundred yards range could be indulged in, though only eighty to a hundred yards were available. When finished, he offered the result to our own War Office, but, strange to relate, this outcome of long and careful thought was allowed to join the limbo of thousands of other inventions, good, bad, and indifferent, for it was not accepted. He laid no more of his ideas before boards for consideration, but after this devoted himself to his half-decked canoe, which was tinkered and altered about in a pursuit which always afforded him intense gratification. It filled a gap while he was waiting, and toiling hard, to place himself in a position in which he could, without pinching, purchase for himself an *Egret*—a yacht which he could enter for an Emperor's Cup. Journalists who marry, and have sons to push forward in the world, and who also have to meet ordinary expenses, have not much money to waste, even if they are successful war correspondents. Henty's yachting desires, therefore, for a long time were not wholly gratified, and he had to occupy himself with the pen, which industriously built up the long series of books that made his name so well known to the rising generation.

Nevertheless his yachting moved by degrees, and he gave full vent to his inventive powers with this little half-decked canoe. First, after much study, he lengthened her, to find most probably that she was now what a sailor would call "crank". To meet this difficulty, he took a lesson from the naïve and clever notions of the canoe-sailers of the South Seas, and fitted on outriggers with gratings on the outrigger spars. His boat was then a great success when used for sailing about the mouth of the Thames, for the scheme answered admirably, and he was very proud of offering a sail therein to a friend or brother

LIMBO: *forgotten place*
PINCHING: *causing financial distress*
CRANK: *unstable*
OUTRIGGERS: *floats*
SPARS: *poles*

journalist or editor. Still not content with his conversion, and doubtless incited thereto by the leeway his little craft made, he added to it what is known amongst boating men as a centre-board—a very unusual addition this to a canoe—namely, a deep keel, which acted after the fashion of the leeboards of a Thames barge.

His ambition growing, he next bought the *Dream*, a thirty-two ton yawl. But Henty was no dreamer, and he changed her name to the *Meerschaum*, not after his pipe, but because of his love of sending her careening over and through the sea foam.

The *Meerschaum* only satisfied his desires, though, for about three years, when he purchased a vessel better worthy of his attention as an enthusiastic yachtsman, in the shape of the before-mentioned *Egret*, an eighty-three ton schooner. This boat he sailed with a skilful crew for years, indulging now and then in a handicap in the Corinthian or the Thames Yacht Club, of both of which, as well as of the Medway Club, he was a member.

He had various cups to show as the reward of his prowess. One of these, a handsome trophy, of which he was very proud, he would display to his friends with sparkling eyes, though the modest nature of the man stepped in at once as he hastened to say, "That was won by my men of the *Egret* at Cowes. They had the money prize, and out of it purchased this cup for me"—a little fact this which clearly showed the friendly feeling existing between skipper and crew. The ambition to win what would be looked upon as a greater prize was shown more than once in his crossing the North Sea to enter the lists for the German Emperor's Cup. On one occasion so brave a fight was made that the *Egret* would have proved the winner had not fate been against her; she was ready to battle with the sea no matter how rough, but was helpless when the wind failed, and this was what happened, to her owner's intense disappointment.

LEEWAY: *sideways drifting*
LEEBOARDS: *boards on the sides of a ship, used to prevent sideways drifting*
YAWL: *a two-masted sailing ship*
ENTER THE LISTS: *enter the contest*

Apropos of prize cups, the sideboard in Henty's museum-like study had a pretty good display of silver trophies, many of which were the prizes won during the time when he was a member of the London Rowing Club, where his broad, deep chest, heavy muscles, long reach, and powers of endurance made him a formidable competitor. And it was in this club, oddly enough, that he first made the acquaintance of Mr. J. P. Griffith, who, being a very rapid scribe, became the amanuensis and writer to whom he dictated every one of the books which, calf bound, all *en suite*, made such an imposing show on the shelves of one large bookcase.

In the summer of 1897, the Diamond Jubilee year,[1] it fell to Henty's lot to describe for the *Standard* the passing of the procession along the Piccadilly portion of the route, while a fellow correspondent for the *Standard*, Mr. Bloundelle Burton, described the Queen's journey along the Strand. This gentleman in the same year was acting as correspondent on board one of our battleships at the Naval Review off Portsmouth, and Henty, taking advantage of his position as a yacht owner, stationed the *Egret* off the Isle of Wight, and there in hospitable fashion kept "open house" for his friends.

He took a very keen and wholly natural pride in this graceful yacht, the *Egret*, perhaps because in acquiring her he pretty well reached the height of his ambition. He liked to talk about her prowess in sailing, which he modestly veiled by setting it down to the skill of his men. But his pride in the *Egret* when she walked the waters like a thing of life, shone out of his eyes, and he did what he could to make her fame lasting by having her photographed. The accompanying admirable representation, which was taken for him by Messrs. Kirk & Son, of Cowes, shows the little yacht running free before a brisk breeze off the coast of the Isle of Wight.

[1] The fiftieth year of Queen Victoria's reign

CALF BOUND: *bound in calfskin leather*
EN SUITE: *in a set*

G. A. Henty Reading the Proofs of His Last Book

CHAPTER XLIV

A FINAL WORD

IN all probability the portrait of George Alfred Henty, which shows him on his yacht, was the last that was taken prior to his death. It is certainly Henty as we know him, and it shows him in his most natural aspect, for it was taken when he was not merely in the full enjoyment of his favourite pastime, but combining it with his work. It represents him unexpectant, grave, and intent, reading over and making corrections in the proof-sheets of one of his last books. Being a genuine snap-shot, nothing possibly could have been more happy, and it certainly deserves to be termed a perfectly natural untouched likeness. The taking of this photograph came about almost by accident. Just before his last cruise, Henty wished to have some alterations made in the sails of the *Egret*. A local sail-maker—a Mr. Ainger—came on board to carry out the task, and he chanced to have brought his camera. Seizing an opportune moment, he took the portrait, with the accompanying excellent result, and in sending it to the writer Captain C. G. Henty adds these words, "It seems to me singularly characteristic"—a comment that everyone who is well acquainted with the subject must feel bound to endorse.

Captain Henty goes on to state: "For some years before his death my father suffered from gouty diabetes. In the autumn

GOUTY DIABETES: *gout brought on by diabetes*

of 1902 he complained of feeling very unwell, and, although he had laid up the *Egret*, he got her into commission again. After a short cruise, however, he returned, and finally brought the schooner to an anchor in Weymouth Harbour, and from there he never moved again.

"On Saturday morning, the first of November, he was stricken with paralysis, but after a few days he showed signs of recovering the vigorous health which he had enjoyed almost throughout his life. His great powers of recuperation stood him in good stead, and he steadily improved to such an extent that hopes were entertained of his being brought up to town. Exactly a fortnight, though, after the first seizure he was attacked by bronchitis, and on Sunday morning, the sixteenth of the month, he passed quietly away."

He was laid to rest in Brompton Cemetery, in the same grave as his first wife and his two daughters.

Heading a long article descriptive of his career, the *Standard*, the journal with which he had been intimately connected since the year 1865, says in reference to his passing: "We regret to announce the death of Mr. G. A. Henty, which occurred yesterday on his yacht at Weymouth. He had been in weak health for some time, but almost to the last he retained his capacity for work."

Finis

ABOUT THE AUTHOR

The following was excerpted from a series of essays entitled,
Peeps into the Past, by Frank Jay in October 1920

Perhaps a brief notice of Mr. George Manville Fenn "Uncle George" may not be out of place. He was born in London on January 3, 1831, and was the son of well-to-do parents. His early years were passed in comparative luxury, but whilst he was still a boy his family suffered reverses, and he was thrown upon his own resources somewhat. He was always fond of reading, and had a great love for books, and he taught himself a good deal before entering the training colleges on connection with the National Society. He afterwards became a schoolmaster in Lincolnshire, and a private tutor. One of his first literary attempts was a humorous sketch which appeared in *Chambers' Journal.* This attracted the attention of the Editor, Mr. James Payn (who, it will be found, contributed some serials to *Young Folks*), and afterwards several of Mr. Fenn's stories appeared in *Chambers' Journal.*

He also contributed to *All the Year Round,* under the Editorship of Mr. Charles Dickens, one of his best being a short graphic paper. *In Jeopardy* was its name, and from this he was invited to contribute to other magazines, and he soon began a long series of sketches in humble life, which appeared under the heading of *Readings by Starlight* in *The Star,* of which Mr. Justice McCarthy was at that time Editor.

In 1866 he wrote for *Cassell's Magazine.* His best known works are *Ship Ahoy, A Little World*, and *Bent, not Broken*, and, as is well-known, he wrote many short stories for boys. He also wrote some plays, including *The Barrister,* produced in 1888, and *The Balloon,* produced in 1889.

ABOUT THE AUTHOR

Altogether Mr. Fenn was the author of close upon one hundred novels of all kinds, many of which have become classics and famous, and are still in great demand at the Libraries. He was a most prolific author, and his official records in the Catalogues of the British Museum reach the great number of 234, in which he beats Mr. Robert Michael Ballantyne, who has 169, and Mr. George Alfred Henty, who has 212, but not Mr. William Henry Giles Kingston, who tops the list of authors of boys' stories with 315 records. Mr. Fenn was a writer of fiction for over fifty years. He died at his well-known residence, Syon Lodge, Isleworth (a fine old-fashioned house) on August 27, 1909, leaving a splendid library of over 25,000 well-chosen volumes, and an estate which was sworn for probate at £11,778.* Unlike many of the old Fleet Street Bohemian writers of fiction who passed away in obscurity and oblivion penniless and nameless, Mr. Fenn left his family a respectable fortune and revered name. Apart from his literary achievements, Mr. Fenn was an expert gardener, as those who know Syon Lodge, a well-known landmark, can testify.

* *over $35,000,000 in today's dollars*

ADDITIONAL TITLES REPUBLISHED BY
SALEM RIDGE PRESS

THE EMMA LESLIE CHURCH HISTORY SERIES

Glaucia the Greek Slave: A Tale of Athens in the First Century
ATHENS IN 59 - 64 A.D.

After the death of her father, Glaucia is sold to a wealthy Roman family to pay his debts. Meanwhile, her brother, Laon, struggles to find her and to earn enough money to buy her freedom. But what is the mystery that surrounds their mother's disappearance years earlier and will they ever be able to read the message in the parchments she left for them?

The Captives: Or, Escape from the Druid Council
ROMAN ENGLAND IN 66 - 67 A.D.

Guntra, the chief of her tribe of Britons, must make a desperate deal with the Druid priests, while Jugurtha, her son, longs to drive the hated Romans from the land. When he encounters the Christian Centurion, Marcinius, Jugurtha mocks the idea of a God of love, but there comes a day when he is in need of love and kindness for himself and his beloved little sister.

Out of the Mouth of the Lion: Or, The Church in the Catacombs
ASIA MINOR IN 163 - 166 A.D.

When Flaminius takes his wife to the Colosseum to see Christians thrown to the lions, he has no idea the effect it will have on her. As he and his family travel to the seven cities of Asia Minor mentioned in Revelation, his attitude toward the despised Christians begins to change, but does he dare forsake the gods of Rome and embrace the Lord Jesus Christ?

Sowing Beside All Waters: A Tale of the World in the Church
THE ROMAN EMPIRE IN 313 - 363 A.D.

There is newfound freedom from persecution for Christians under the emperor, Constantine, but newfound troubles as well. Errors and pagan ways are creeping into the Church, while many of the most devoted Christians are withdrawing from the world into the desert as hermits and nuns. Can the Church handle the new freedom, and remain faithful?

From Bondage to Freedom: A Tale of the Times of Mohammed
ROME AND ARABIA IN 594 - 632 A.D.

At a Syrian market two Christian women are sold as slaves. One of the slaves ends up in Rome where Bishop Gregory is teaching his new doctrine of "purgatory". The other slave travels with her new master, Mohammed, back to Arabia. In Rome and Arabia, the two women and countless others fall into the bondage of man-made religions—will they learn at last to find true freedom in the Lord Jesus Christ alone?

www.SalemRidgePress.com

The Martyr's Victory: A Story of Danish England
DANISH ENGLAND IN 879 - 883 A.D.

Knowing full well they may die in the attempt, a small band of monks sets out to convert the savage Danes who have laid waste to the surrounding countryside year after year. Then the monks discover a young Christian woman who has escaped being sacrificed to the Danish gods—can she help reach those who had enslaved her and tried to kill her?

Gytha's Message: A Tale of Saxon England
SAXON ENGLAND IN 1053 - 1066 A.D.

Having discovered God's love for her, Gytha, a young slave, longs to escape the violence and cruelty of the world and devote herself to learning more about this God of love. Instead she lives in a Saxon household that despises the name of Christ. Can Gytha learn to trust that God often has greater work for us to do *in* the world than *out* of it?

Leofwine the Monk: Or, The Curse of the Ericsons
MEDIEVAL EUROPE AND THE MIDDLE EAST IN 1052 - 1066 A.D.

Leofwine, unlike his wild, younger brother, finds no pleasure in terrorizing the countryside and longs to enter a monastery. His search for inner peace takes him to France and Rome and finally to Jerusalem, but in his travels, he uncovers a plot against his beloved country. Will he be able to help save England? And will he ever find true rest for his troubled soul?

Elfreda the Saxon: Or, The Orphan of Jerusalem, A Sequel to Leofwine
MEDIEVAL EUROPE AND THE MIDDLE EAST IN 1189 - 1215 A.D.

When Jerusalem is captured by the Muslims, Elfreda, a young orphan, is sent back to England, but her aunt and uncle fear she may have brought the family curse with her. Elfreda's cousin, Guy, promises her that he will win such honor as a crusader that the curse will be removed but as severe trials befall the family, Elfreda despairs of the curse ever being lifted.

Dearer Than Life: A Tale of the Times of Wycliffe
ENGLAND IN 1366 - 1384 A.D.

Sir Hugh Middleton is shocked to learn that a monastery has laid claim to one of his fields. He refuses to yield his property, and further offends the monastery by sending his son, Stephen, to study under Dr. John Wycliffe. Stephen and his brother and sisters help Wycliffe spread the truth, but what will it cost them in the dangerous day in which they live?

Before the Dawn: A Story of Wycliffe and Huss
ENGLAND AND BOHEMIA IN 1382 - 1453 A.D.

Dame Ursula welcomes the visits of a kindly blacksmith to her crippled grandson, Conrad, but soon becomes suspicious that the blacksmith and his friend, Ned Trueman, are followers of John Wycliffe and his evil "heresy". Will Conrad accept these dangerous new ideas of Wycliffe and Huss? And will he ever find out what happened to his father?

Faithful But Not Famous: A Tale of the French Reformation
FRANCE IN 1510 - 1522 A.D.

Young Claude Leclerc travels to Paris to begin his training for the priesthood, but he is not sure *what* he believes about God. His questions lead Dr. Lefevre to set aside his study of the saints and study the Scriptures. As Dr. Lefevre grasps the wonderful truth of salvation by grace, he wants to share it with Claude, but Claude has mysteriously disappeared.

THE EMMA LESLIE JUNIOR CHURCH HISTORY SERIES

Hilda the Briton: Or, The Golden Age, The Story of a Roman Slave Girl
ANCIENT ROME IN 63 A.D.

When their tribe in Britain is conquered by the Romans, Bran and his young sister, Hilda, are taken to Rome and sold as slaves. One day, an elderly slave takes Hilda to hear a prisoner named Paul and she learns of a God who made the heavens and the earth and who loves slaves. What will it cost Hilda and Bran if they decide to follow this new God?

The Magic Runes: A Tale of the Times of Charlemagne
FRANCE AND SAXONY IN 782 - 785 A.D.

Young Adalinda is startled to come upon a Saxon family in the forest where she lives with her father. The family is in desperate need but the husband, Godrith, is suspicious of Adalinda's offers of help, especially when he learns that she is a Christian. Will Adalinda and her father be able to show Godrith a different picture of Christianity?

For Merrie England: A Tale of the Weavers of Norfolk
ENGLAND IN 1357 - 1360 A.D.

A Flemish weaver travels around the countryside in England, seeking apprentices to learn his trade. Along the way he meets a prosperous wool merchant with two sons—big, strong, sixteen-year-old Roger and small, crippled, thirteen-year-old Tom. When Roger suddenly disappears one evening, the weaver sees his opportunity to help Tom.

Soldier Fritz and the Enemies He Fought: A Story of the Reformation
GERMANY IN 1525 - 1526 A.D.

Young Fritz wants to follow in the footsteps of Martin Luther and be a soldier for the Lord, so he chooses a Bible from the peddler's pack as his birthday gift. When his father, the Count, goes off to war, however, Fritz and his mother and little sister are forced to flee into the forest to escape being thrown in prison for their new faith.

Through Stress and Strain: A Story of the Huguenot Persecution
FRANCE IN 1666 - 1685 A.D.

These are difficult times when Jules Marot comes to visit his brother's family and brings bad news about their young son, Jacques. Huguenot schools and churches are being torn down and these faithful Christians are forbidden to gather for services. Can the whole Marot family, including their sons, Jacques and François, learn to trust God more than ever before?

OTHER HISTORICAL FICTION

The Sign Above the Door
by William W. Canfield

Young Prince Martiesen has been forced by Pharaoh to further increase the burden of the Hebrews, however Martiesen is in love with the beautiful Hebrew maiden, Elisheba. As the nation despairs, the other nobles turn to Martiesen for leadership, but before he can decide what to do, Elisheba is kidnapped by the evil Peshala and terrifying darkness falls over the land. An exciting tale woven around the events of the Exodus from the Egyptian perspective!

Marie's Home
by Caroline Austin; Illustrations by Gordon Browne R.I.

Eleven-year-old Marie Hamilton and her family travel to France at the invitation of Louis XVI, just before the start of the French Revolution. Marie and her family are rescued from grave danger by a strange twist of events, but Marie's story of courage, self-sacrifice and true nobility is not yet over! Honor, duty, compassion and forgiveness are all portrayed in this uplifting story.

The American Twins of the Revolution
by Lucy Fitch Perkins; With illustrations by the Author

Twins Sally and Roger are asked by their father, General Priestly, to help hide a shipment of gold which will be used to pay the American soldiers. Unfortunately, British spies have also learned about the gold and will stop at nothing to prevent it from reaching General Washington. Based on a true story, this is a thrilling episode from our nation's history!

The White Seneca
by William W. Canfield; Illustrations by G.A. Harker

Captured by the Senecas, fifteen-year-old Henry Cochrane grows to love the Indian ways, but when he is captured by an enemy tribe, he must make a desperate attempt to escape from them and rescue fellow captive, Constance Leonard. But what will happen to the young woman if they do reach safety? And will he ever be able to return to his own people?

At Seneca Castle
by William W. Canfield; Illustrations by G.A. Harker

In this sequel to *The White Seneca*, Henry Cochrane, now eighteen, faces many perils as he serves as a scout for the Continental Army. General Washington is determined to do whatever it takes to stop the constant Indian attacks on the settlers and yet Henry is torn between his love for the Senecas and his loyalty to his own people. And what has happened to the beautiful Constance Leonard whom he had been forced to leave in captivity a year earlier?

ADVENTURE

Yussuf the Guide
by George Manville Fenn; Illustrations by John Schönberg

Young Lawrence, an invalid, convinces his guardians, Burne the Lawyer and Preston the Professor, to take him along on an archaeological expedition to Turkey. Yussuf their guide proves his worth time and time again as they face dangers from a murderous ship captain, poisonous snakes, sheer precipices, bands of robbers and more. Memorable characters, humor and adventure abound in this exciting story!

www.SalemRidgePress.com

ESPECIALLY FOR YOUNGER READERS

Down the Snow Stairs: Or, From Goodnight to Goodmorning
by Alice Corkran; Sixty black and white illustrations by Gordon Browne R.I.

An imaginative allegory about the sorrows that disobedience brings and the blessings that obedience brings. Traveling in a dream to Naughty Children Land, eight-year-old Kitty seeks to return to the Path of Obedience while there is still time. A delightful read-aloud for the whole family!

Mary Jane – Her Book
by Clara Ingram Judson; Illustrations by Francis White

This story recounts the happy, wholesome adventures of five-year-old Mary Jane and her family as she helps her mother around the house, goes on a picnic with the big girls, plants a garden with her father, learns to sew and more!

Mary Jane – Her Visit
by Clara Ingram Judson; Illustrations by Francis White

In this sequel to *Mary Jane – Her Book,* Mary Jane travels to her great-grandparents' farm in the country where she hunts for eggs, picks berries, finds baby rabbits, goes to the circus and more!

Young Robin Hood
by George Manville Fenn; Illustrations by Victor Venner

In the days of Robin Hood, a young boy named Robin is journeying through Sherwood Forest when suddenly the company is surrounded by men in green. Deserted in the commotion by an unfaithful servant, Robin finds himself alone in the forest. After a miserable night, Robin is found by Little John. Robin is treated kindly by Robin Hood, Maid Marian and the Merry Men, but how long must he wait for his father, the Sheriff of Nottingham, to come to take him home?

www.ingramcontent.com/pod-product-compliance
Lightning Source LLC
Chambersburg PA
CBHW032032080426
42733CB00006B/63